QUESTIONING SLAVERY

By teasing apart the history of slavery into its major components, and by examining those themes that recent historians have brought to the fore, this book makes sense of what has become a confused and confusing historical debate.

Each chapter offers a guide to the most recent scholarship. The themes chosen – race, gender, resistance, domination and control – are those that currently engage the attention of the most inno vative scholars in a range of disciplines. The comparative analysis on slavery throughout the English-speaking Americas gives new perspectives on the phenomenon.

Written in a clear and lively style, *Questioning Slavery* is an up-to-date guide to slavery, to black historical experience and to on-going historical debates.

James Walvin is Professor of History at the University of York. He is a leading authority on the history of slavery and has published extensively. His latest books include *Slaves and Slavery: The British Colonial Experience* (1992) and *Black Ivory: A History of British Slavery* (1992).

QUESTIONING
SLAVERY

James Walvin

London and New York

First published 1996
by Routledge
11 New Fetter Lane, London EC4P 4EE

Simultaneously published in the USA and Canada
by Routledge
29 West 35th Street, New York, NY 10001

© 1996 James Walvin

Typeset in Palatino by Routledge
Printed and bound in Great Britain by
Biddles Ltd, Guildford and King's Lynn

British Library Cataloguing in Publication Data
A catalogue record for this book is available from the British Library

Library of Congress Cataloguing in Publication Data
Walvin, James.
Questioning slavery / James Walvin.
p. cm.
Includes bibliographical references and index.
1. Slavery—Great Britain—Colonies—History. 2. Slave-trade—
Great Britain—History. I. Title.
HT1165.W346 1996
306.3'62'0942—dc20
96–14794
CIP

ISBN 0–415–15356–5 (hbk)
ISBN 0–415–15357–3 (pbk)

CONTENTS

PREFACE

For the best part of three centuries the development and well-being of the English-speaking world (on both sides of the Atlantic) was inextricably linked to the rise and progress of black slavery. Research since World War II (but especially over the past generation) has confirmed the centrality of slavery in the development of the Atlantic system.[1] Yet it was not always so clearly or demonstrably the case. In the past twenty-five years, scholars of slavery have not only transformed our understanding of the minutiae of slavery itself, but have confirmed that the importance of slavery transcended the narrower confines of its own particular specialism. When I first began to work on slavery in the British West Indies in 1967, the corpus of relevant secondary literature was relatively thin. Now – in the mid-1990s – it is virtually impossible to keep abreast of current scholarship. The academic study of slavery has, in effect, shifted from the margins of scholarly interest (even of respectability) to become the focus of innovative and imaginative work at the very core of modern historical scholarship. It is not, however, always easy to make sense of that abundant scholarship, or to see the current directions in slave studies. Indeed, the *genre* of 'slave studies' is itself undergoing massive changes, spawning in its turn new subspecies of scholarly interests, most notably 'Diaspora Studies'.[2] But if any simple conclusion has emerged from recent findings on slavery it is that slavery in the Americas was quite different from other forms of slavery (then or earlier). In addition, it is now clear that, for all their superficial similarities, there were enormous differences between the various American slave societies.

What this book seeks to do is, in effect, to pick a path through the scholarly thickets. It is concerned with those forms of slavery

vii

which developed in the English-speaking Americas (in the Caribbean and North America) but, inevitably, I have in places been greatly influenced by ideas and findings from other regions. It would, for example, be perverse to ignore the excellent work recently published on Brazil.[3] Equally I cannot discount the influence of having read dozens of articles on various forms of slavery submitted to the journal I co-edit.[4] That said, the focus of this book is simple enough: the English-speaking settlements of the Americas.

It is important to explain, from the start, what this book does *not* try to do. It is not a comprehensive history of slavery. For students interested in recent narrative accounts of slavery in the English-speaking world, three books spring to mind.[5] Readers keen to locate slavery in its broader setting should address the remarkable work of Orlando Patterson.[6] Similarly, anyone keen to study the intellectual problems of slavery should turn to the monumental writings of David Brion Davis.[7] This book's aim, on the other hand, is altogether simpler.

In trying to make sense of a generation's scholarship, I have adopted a thematic approach. This inevitably involves a degree of artificial ordering and arrangement of the material. To slice up the confusions of the past (and the scholarly confusions of the present) into neatly packaged themes is, of course, to create artificial structures. The study of slavery is at once more confusing, more adversarial and disputative – indeed, more in doubt – than this book might sometimes suggest. Beneath the (sometimes) rather bland generalizations there occasionally bubbles an intellectual conflict. I have tried to approach the topic by asking questions of slavery in the hope that those questions will prompt replies. Each chapter tries to confront one of the main questions or problems which have attracted scholarly attention over the past twenty-five years or so. This is not, however, a historiographical book, but it has been shaped by my own reading of and engagement with the writings of other historians.

There is a tendency to imagine that slavery is necessarily black. Curiously, the massive scholarly output in recent years has served to compound the impression that slavery is best represented (and certainly best known) by the slave systems of the Americas. Of course, no serious historian would openly make such claims and would point, instead, to the ubiquity of slave cultures in greatly different periods and regions. But it is un-

viii

doubtedly true that the bulk of recent slave scholarship has been concerned with black slavery.[8] Moreover, the transformation of slave history into popular cultural format has also lent strength to the feeling that because slavery was black it was necessarily racial. As we shall see, this is not the case. It is also true that without slavery – without those Africans shipped into the Americas – the course of modern racial thinking would have been utterly different. We will then need to return to the complex question of slavery and race, not simply in its historical setting, but in the links forged between history and modern racism.

Naturally enough, what follows is very much my book. Most of the time it may reflect a broad consensus of opinion among contemporary slave historians. But I do not expect everyone to agree with all the questions I ask – or with the emergent answers. To that extent, the book is offered as part summary of, part contribution to, the continuing debate about the history of slavery in the English-speaking world.

ACKNOWLEDGEMENTS

One colleague in particular, Alan Forrest, deserves special mention for helping me with this book, for he has frequently gone out of his way to enable me to pursue the interests which have found their way into this study. Many of the ideas which follow were first aired in my teaching at the University of York. There, my students have, by turns, been critical and informative. Parts of the book were discusssed in seminars and lectures at York, at Flinders University, Australia, at the University of Toronto, the Victorian Studies Association of Ontario, the University of Edinburgh and at meetings of the Association of Caribbean Historians in Jamaica and Puerto Rico. Above all else, however, it was in the Library Company of Philadelphia and the Historical Society of Pennsylvania that the book took its final shape. There, I was fortunate enough to hold a Barra Fellowship and was greatly helped by a group of wonderfully attentive librarians. I hope others do not take it amiss if I single out Phil Lapsansky for praise and thanks. He steered me towards sources and books I did not know about and generally acted as my mentor and guide – often above the call of duty. In Philadelphia, Rod McDonald was a patient host who made me feel at home. Once again Gad Heuman took time out from his own work to discuss my work. I am most grateful to the publisher's anonymous reviewer whose helpful remarks greatly improved this text. In this book, more than in others, I am very conscious of how much I am indebted to other historians working in the field.

JW, York

1

FORGING THE LINK
Europe, Africa and the Americas

The European invasion of the Americas, tentative and hesitant initially, had dramatic consequences for three continents: first, and most obvious, for the Americas and its various civilizations and native peoples; second, for Europe which soon developed a voracious appetite for the land, products and staples of the Americas; and third, for Africa which, in time, came to provide the workforce which broke open key areas of the Americas to profitable cultivation. Looking back, the association between black slavery and the Americas seems so natural, so much a part of the historical and economic development of the region, that the two seemed obvious partners. Quite the contrary, it was no such thing; but by, say, the mid-eighteenth century, when the European appetite for African slaves seemed insatiable, Africa seemed the natural place to recruit labour for the Americas.

When the Europeans launched their first invasion of the Americas, in the wake of Columbus, they encountered various local peoples and indigenous civilizations throughout the region: nomadic and agricultural Indian societies were scattered across the hemisphere. Three major civilizations – Mayan, Aztec and Incan – had control of, or access to, products which were much prized by the invading Europeans. One by one, their civilizations fell: many were put to the sword by ruthless invaders, more were weakened by disease and sickness transmitted unknowingly by the Europeans. It is, even now, hard to grasp what happened to the Indian peoples of the Americas. They died in their hundreds of thousands, first in the Caribbean, then in Central America and Peru, later in North and South America. In Mexico, the population is thought to have fallen by 95 per cent in seventy-five years; in Peru the population of 9,000,000 fell to 600,000 in a century.

1

Time and again, the story was repeated wherever Europeans (and Africans) made contact with local people.[1]

The early contacts provided a grim foretaste of what was to come. In Hispaniola, one of the first European settlements, the local population collapsed from 4,000,000 to 100,000 by 1508. Cuba followed the same route. Indian peoples everywhere bemoaned their fate, capturing the stunned horror which overtook them in haunting words. Before the white men, said one Indian from the Yucatan,

> There was then no sickness; they had no aching bones; they had then no high fevers: they had then no smallpox . . . At that time, the course of humanity was orderly. The foreigners made it otherwise when they arrived here.[2]

They fell, not to the gun or the sword (though there was plenty of violent killing), but to hidden and unknown microbes; to influenza, typhus, measles, chickenpox, diphtheria, scarlet fever, typhoid, whooping cough, bubonic plague. But worst of all was smallpox, which spread from the Caribbean in 1518 throughout the hemisphere, sometimes advancing ahead of the white man. It killed whole communities, leaving survivors stunned, disfigured and utterly demoralized. Some scholars have calculated that up to 90,000,000 people died.[3] A German missionary wrote, in 1619, that Indians 'die so easily that the bare look and smell of a Spaniard causes them to give up the ghost'.[4]

Nor was it just the Spaniards. The French and Portuguese took smallpox to Brazil, the English to Florida and New England, the French to the Indian tribes of Canada. By 1600 some twenty epidemics had surged through the native peoples of the Americas – leaving a mere ten per cent of the population surviving. And more was to come. To use the words of an Inca lament, night fell on the Indian peoples. Of course Europeans (and Africans) also suffered. But never on the same scale.

What was abundantly clear, from the early days of settlement, was that Indian peoples *en masse* would never be likely to help their conquerors in their new ventures of settlement and economic development. Some, of course, worked side by side with the invaders in shaping the initial settlements in towns and rural areas. But the decline of the Indian populations and the demoralization (and flight) of survivors ensured that there were rarely enough indigenous people to help Europeans with their local

2

schemes. Nor were there enough European settlers available for the back-breaking work of pioneering, frontier life. But there were other forms of labour, already in use in other parts of the world, which were to provide the missing pieces in the European equation. They had, in the Americas, other important assets – land, natural resources and potential – in an abundance which even they could scarcely imagine. They also had access to European capital and technical and managerial know-how. What they also needed, however, was labour to unlock the potential of the region.

The answer to their labour problems had already been suggested in the earlier experience of plantation management, in the Mediterranean and Atlantic islands. Europeans first developed plantations for sugar cane cultivation in the eastern Mediterranean at the time of the Crusades. Slowly, these early sugar plantations moved westward, from Palestine to Cyprus – though always on a small scale – on to southern Spain and North Africa. European maritime expansion took settlement – and the plantation – on to the Atlantic islands of the Azores, Madeira, the Canaries and the Cape Verde islands, later still to Fernando Po and São Tomé. These islands were, in effect, stepping-stones between the old societies and economics of the Mediterranean and the New World of colonial settlement on the far side of the Atlantic. The most crucial spot was São Tomé, close to Africa, ideally suited to sugar cane production and close to supplies of African labour in the Kingdoms of Kongo and Benin.[5]

Though small-scale compared to the later history of plantations, the basic elements of plantation production were in place: colonial lands, settled by marauding and mercantile Europeans, alien labour, and European finance and expertise. It seemed natural enough to try these arrangements in the New World after 1492. Cane cultivation was tried unsuccessfully in the Caribbean in 1493, again in 1503, and more successfully (with labour from the Canaries) in 1517. But wherever cane was planted in the early sixteenth century – in Spanish settlements in Jamaica, Puerto Rico and coastal Mexico – the problem remained that of labour. The Portuguese had more luck.

In the mid-1540s, they transplanted sugar from Madeira to Brazil. Within twenty years, Brazilian production matched the tonnage from Madeira, and by 1580, Brazil produced 5000 tons. Fifty years later the output reached 20,000 tons.[6] The Portuguese were able to make this dramatic progress thanks to their trading connections in West Africa. European explorations in West Africa had revealed complex trading systems which involved the movement of a host of goods and products within Africa. Among those items of trade were slaves, normally prisoners of war sold and bartered as trade and removed from their native region. Some were shifted north, across the Sahara, for sale to North Africa. The total number was very small, however; no more perhaps than 5000 a year.[7] Whatever the scale, when Europeans made their early maritime contacts with West Africa, they found slave systems in place which they could turn to their own advantage. Initially, however, West Africa offered other more lucrative prospects, most spectacularly gold. The thriving African gold industry used slave labour. Thus, both in the embryonic gold trade between Europeans and Africans, and in the development of the offshore São Tomé sugar industry, the Portuguese quickly involved themselves in trading in African slaves. When sugar plantations began to thrive in Brazil in the mid-sixteenth century, it seemed natural (easy, an extension of existing systems and, thanks to convenient currents and trade winds, navigationally direct) to ship slaves from West Africa to Brazil.

Early experiments in sugar cultivation in Brazil had used Amerindian slaves. But the Indians tended to die out in the face of diseases from Europe and Africa. Nor was the problem solved by simply bringing more Indians from the interior to the coast, for they too had no resistance to alien diseases. Slowly, but perceptibly, imported Africans began to fill their place. They, too, died in large numbers; but unlike the local Indians the Africans could be replaced by fresh imports from West Africa. Moreover, the Atlantic crossing to Brazil was relatively quick; the faster the crossing, the lower the on-board mortality rates. African slaves imported to Brazil were thus relatively cheap. So was Brazilian sugar. The abundance of suitable land offered economies of scale which enabled the Brazilian sugar industry to overtake quickly the volumes and costs of sugar from the Atlantic islands. Brazil soon attracted European capital, and the human/economic mould took shape. European money and skills, American land and African labour – together, on the plantation, they produced a commodity which Europeans consumed in ever-growing volumes. Here, then, was a form of tropical production and colonial investment which seemed to yield prosperity and well-being in

4

all directions: to the Brazilian settlers, to the European capitalists, to European mercantile interests and European consumers. But where was the profit, the well-being, for the local Indians and imported Africans? The example of Brazil – and of Brazilian sugar – was to dazzle Europeans in other parts of the Americas. And, from the first, European settlers appreciated the benefits of African imported labour.

Over a period of fifty years, there was a marked shift from using Indian to African labour in Brazilian sugar. As sugar yielded profits to the Portuguese planters, they invested their money in Africans and material improvements. In the 1550s and 1560s there were virtually no slaves in the sugar mills of northeast Brazil. Twenty years later, they formed a striking minority. But between 1600 and 1620, Africans began to dominate the labour force: these were years of relative international calm, good sugar prices in Europe and consequent expansion throughout the Brazilian sugar industry.

The Portuguese had long used Africans as slaves, at home and on their Atlantic islands. They knew their skills and benefits but, above all, were impressed by their experience of sugar work in Madeira and São Tomé. It seemed natural enough for their contemporaries in Brazil – closer in sailing times than the maps suggest – to think of Africans as *the* natural workers for their northeastern sugar industry. Skilled sugar workers were among the first Africans working on plantations. But, as the Atlantic slave trade grew in the last decades of the sixteenth century, as more Africans arrived direct from Africa, growing numbers were to be found in the fields. More than that, it was perfectly clear that planters quickly came to value Africans much more highly than local Indians. Wherever we look in the Americas, planters paid Indians much less than what they paid for slaves. The formula was simple: Africans were a better investment than Indians. In the words of one commentator in Carolina in 1740 (but in a quote that rings true for other regions and times), 'with them [Indians] one cannot accomplish as much as with Negroes'.[8]

This was clearly true in Brazil where prices of/wages for the two groups were always different. The African labourer was worth more, however we compute their relative value. More than that, recent calculations suggest that Africans produced more than the Indians (whose productivity was notoriously low).

The simple truth remained that, although it seemed that Portuguese planters paid more initially for their African slaves, they got a better return on their investment. Though Indians were valuable as a source of very cheap local labour in the early days of settlement and in the drift to sugar in Brazil, they were soon revealed to be much less valuable when the industry slipped into higher gear. In all this, the international market played its own crucial role. The development of the Atlantic slave trade needed outside economic agencies. Fortunately for planters, financial and maritime organizations were in place to support and make possible the movement of African slaves across the Atlantic. Compared to the mature Atlantic system of the eighteenth century, it looks simple, even rudimentary, though in outline it was recognizably similar. The Atlantic slave economy was conceived and nurtured by European capitalist interests, able and willing to marshal finance, expertise (and labour), and to move it relatively quickly from one part of the world to another. In the process Africans were quickly transmuted into the human commodity which was to shape the Atlantic economy for the best part of three centuries.

The Portuguese had pioneered the first major Atlantic slave trade systems, moving Africans to Europe, the Atlantic islands and then the Americas. Their effective monopoly had seen 40,000 Africans moved across the Atlantic. But when the Dutch conquered northern Brazil in 1630, they were in a position to put a colony and the maritime strength to take over from the Portuguese. The Dutch had some experience of the industry, for their ships and refineries (in Holland) had already tapped into the Portuguese sugar trade. Conquest consolidated that trade. The Dutch quickly moved into the old Portuguese empire around the world, acquiring all the economic benefits that flowed from that far-flung system of colonies and trading stations. In the Atlantic, they secured major entrées to West Africa, in northern Brazil and a string of West Indian islands. Most of these possessions were run by the two major Dutch trading companies: in the Atlantic, control fell to the West India Company whose prime aim was to squeeze out competitors, on both sides of the Atlantic, and to create, as far as possible, a Dutch monopoly.

With their own colony in Brazil after 1630, the Dutch company took a much keener interest in its African trading posts and in the

6

necessary trade of supplying Africans to the sugar industry in Brazil. Whatever doubts the Dutch may have had about the morality of buying and selling Africans, those doubts simply did not surface in the early papers of the West India Company: scruples were swept aside by the power of economic self-interest.[9] Dutch traders to Africa had put down their first tentative roots in 1612, though the initial interest was in gold. Now, the Brazilian need for labour shifted their African concerns from natural products to human commodities. Gradually, the Dutch displaced the slave-trading Portuguese on the African coast by force of arms and through commercial deals with Africans. By 1641, the Dutch had completely usurped the Portuguese, removing them from their forts and trading posts. It was now their turn to contend with the piratical raids of other (northern) Europeans, themselves anxious to secure a share in the lucrative trade in black humanity.[10] Thus, from the first, events in the New World were the key to what happened in Africa. But such a formula is, of course, far too simple. Though the labour demands of the Americas – in this case Brazil – prompted the search for African slaves, it was all made possible by that more broadly based economic change which saw the rapid emergence of powerful mercantile states in northern Europe, their wealth enhanced by trading links to the wider world.

The Dutch grip on Brazil was tenuous, and had been made possible by internal Iberian conflicts. Portuguese planters eventually rose against the Dutch, who lost control of Brazil by 1654. Not surprisingly, the Dutch importation of slaves had been small-scale, and riddled with uncertainty. In the era of Dutch control over northern Brazil, some 26,000 slaves were imported. Though dwarfed by the numbers that followed, the Dutch trade established the Dutch as the main players in the Atlantic slave trade. Moreover, the loss of Brazil was not catastrophic for the Dutch because, at the point they lost control of Brazil, tempting commercial prospects revealed themselves further north, in the Caribbean. Though it was a longer, and therefore more costly, venture to ship Africans to the West Indies rather than to Brazil, the islands offered prospects which seemed boundless. Thwarted in Brazil, Dutch merchants turned their attention to Barbados.

The European settlement of the Caribbean was part of a much broader migration of people to the Americas, which saw the proliferation of European colonies planted throughout the hemisphere. Such colonies offered a relief from social pressures at home, freedom on the far side of the Atlantic for persecuted minorities, and a beachhead, in the Americas, for further attacks on the fabled wealth unlocked particularly by the Spaniards. Early settlers had little intention of using imported labour – except their own. Europeans used their own labour in winning over the land to useful and profitable cultivation. However, the regions settled by the British, for example, were remarkably different one from another – from Massachusetts to Barbados – and some regions developed quite differently from their original intentions. Geography, climate and the emergence of particular, successful crops – all these and more were the determinants of the human and economic transformation of the British (and French) settlements.

In Barbados, pioneer settlers broke open the land to small-scale cultivation, using indentured labour from Britain. But Brazil already provided powerful evidence that Africans were much more useful. For a start, they seemed more durable: more resistant to the ailments which afflicted and killed so many European settlers. In fact, they had different immunities and, though they too died in horrifying numbers, Africans seemed to be a better long-term economic bet. Even when they died prematurely, they could be readily replaced; quickly, cheaply and with little fuss. The same improved vessels which carried the bigger cargoes of sugar back to Europe, could carry larger cargoes of Africans across the Atlantic. Thus the haphazard, almost accidental, trickle of slaves to Brazil became something quite different. In the process, morality was simply relegated or ignored; cast aside by a burgeoning demand which disregarded any human sensibilities in pursuit of profit.

Barbadian settlers borrowed money from Dutch financiers, reinvesting their early profits in further agricultural expansion. Initially they grew tobacco, lured by the profits already being made in London. In its early days of settlement, Barbados was described as a colony 'wholly built on smoke'.[11] But as profits in London fell, and as British politicians began to favour Virginians, Barbados lost faith in tobacco. There was a consequent switch to cotton, later to indigo, but these too led to disappointment. But in all these experiments, Barbadian planters used white indentured 'servants'. Indeed, a majority of whites settling in the island in the 1630s and 1640s were in this category, contracted to labour

8

for up to seven years in return for their passage and keep. From the first, however, planters complained of never being able to get enough labour. Once in the island, these servants were bartered and auctioned, swapped and inherited, much like other inanimate personal objects. They were also tied to their workplace, unable to move without written permission. They had certain rights, however, and their employers took trouble to distinguish them from black slaves.[12]

Africans took their place alongside the early white settlers in Barbados (free and indentured). Black settlers were in a small minority – perhaps 800 in the 1630s. Slavery for imported Africans was not formally sanctioned until 1636, but from the first the English settlers 'categorised the Negroes and Indians who worked for them as heathen brutes and very quickly treated them as chattels'.[13] From the beginning, blacks were slaves for life – and bequeathed their bondage to their offspring. The blacks' fate (their role, treatment and status) was to change utterly with the coming of sugar.

Brazil produced 80 per cent of the cane sugar for Europe up to the 1640s; but war, and the defeat of the Dutch, switched attention (most notably of Dutch investors) to other prospective regions. Barbados was ideal. The Dutch could provide money, technical experience (and machinery), and the maritime capacity for importing Africans and exporting produce. By 1650, Barbados was thought to be the richest place in the Americas.[14]

The adventurous and the imaginative – the lucky – made fortunes from the expansive industry. Gradually, the original smallholdings gave way to larger plantations; by 1651 they exported 3750 tons of sugar. Eighteen years later it had risen to 9525 tons. All appropriate land was devoured in the rush to produce sugar, and the sugar planters established for themselves a reputation which lived on long after the heyday of sugar: that of wealthy men whose lifestyle was enviably lavish, and whose homes were adorned with the most precious artefacts money could buy.[15] They formed a tight political class, able to advance their interests at home and in London. And they built their fortunes on the backs of their African slaves.

As demand for labour increased, the cost of indentured white servants rose (in the 1640s and 1650s). But, at the same time, the cost of African slaves fell. Naturally enough, planters turned to Africa, not Britain, for its growing labour force. Between 1640

9

and 1700, some 134,500 Africans were shipped to Barbados. But the number of whites began to fall, from 23,000 in 1655 to 17,528 in 1712.[16] The face of the island began to change. By 1670 there were 900 plantations, and perhaps as many as 400 windmills (for grinding the sugar cane). And all were worked by African slaves. The success of Barbados – itself made possible by the earlier Dutch experience in Brazil – was contagious. When, in 1655, the British took Jamaica from the Spaniards, the example of Barbados was naturally uppermost in the minds of the early settlers. For a start, large numbers of the British army of conquest in Jamaica were from Barbados; they knew that sugar was the obvious way to quick prosperity. There was land in abundance in Jamaica, lavishly distributed to the men of the conquering army. They also needed labour, and few doubted that that meant slaves. Africans were poured into Jamaica, just as they had been a few years earlier into Barbados. Between 1640 and 1700, about 85,100 were shipped into Jamaica. Altogether, more than 250,000 Africans were landed in the British islands by 1700.[17] The rise in importation matched the growth in sugar production: the more Africans arrived, the more sugar was exported. In time, however, not all slaves worked in sugar. Africans and their local-born descendants took up a range of occupations in the maturing economies of the West Indies. And, as the economies developed, their crops diversified. But until the end of slavery in the Caribbean, it was sugar, above all else, which was the engine behind the islands' development. In its turn, sugar was made possible by Africans.

A similar story was repeated in other parts of the Americas. But, as in the Caribbean, the intrusion of black slavery was by no means inevitable or, at the time, predictable. In North America, European invaders were displacing indigenous Indians by settlement and by consequent agricultural changes.[18] From the first, it was clear that working the land was the only really viable form of settlement. And that created a demand for labour which the pioneers could not satisfy. Food cultivation, especially tobacco in the Chesapeake region and rice in South Carolina, demanded more and more hands. Local Indians were tried and – in common with much of the Americas – were found wanting. Indians were used as slaves throughout the colonies, but always in small numbers and always to poor economic effect. The men disclaimed agricultural labour (dismissing it as women's work). But the real

10

problem of managing Indian slaves was illness and disease, as they died out in enormous numbers, and survivors were generally enfeebled and demoralized. Time and again, they proved themselves inadequate for European needs. Much more reliable were indentured Europeans – mainly from Ireland and Scotland – many of whom were already proving their worth in the Caribbean. Criminals, prisoners, volunteers, political refugees, all (and more) swelled the ranks of indentured labourers crossing the Atlantic.[19] Most found their way into agriculture (the majority were young men), notably in the tobacco fields of the Chesapeake. Between 1630 and 1680, about 75,000 Britons migrated to the region and somewhere between a half and three-quarters were indentured servants.[20] Among those who survived, few remained on the land when their period of service expired: they migrated elsewhere or sought other work. By the 1680s, it proved ever-more difficult to acquire new indentured servants. Even poor Irish *women* proved reluctant.[21] Planters needed other sources.

The obvious answer was the African slave. Obvious, because Africans were already there, in small numbers, working alongside free and unfree white people. Obvious, too, in that Africans had, for years, been imported throughout the Americas, notably into Brazil. In 1660 there were perhaps no more than 1700 blacks in the whole Chesapeake region, which had increased to 4000 in 1680 (the new arrivals coming mainly from the West Indies). By 1695, a further 3000 black people joined their ranks. In the last five years of the century another 3000 Africans were purchased for labour in the burgeoning tobacco industry. As late as 1690, blacks formed only 15 per cent of Virginia's population. But the numbers increased as tobacco expanded, though the local plantations rarely matched the size of their sugar counterparts in the Caribbean: slaves imported into Maryland and Virginia between 1700 and 1740 numbered 54,000.[22] The end result was not merely the augmenting of the local labour force, but the opening up of a chasm between black and white. Previously, the small bands of blacks had worked side by side with whites. Now, black slaves formed the bulk of the unfree population. Indentured white labour declined in importance, in proportion to the rise of local black slavery. Chesapeake planters, for so long insistent that the best field hands were indentured whites, became ever keener – later enthusiastic – for black slaves.

11

The cause of their changed loyalties lay, not so much in the respective labour of the two groups, but in the price they cost the planters. White servants became more costly and slaves relatively cheaper. It was, however, more complicated than that. The *supply* of white labour became more and more difficult. Europeans were unhappy, thanks to the stories which filtered back across the Atlantic, at the prospects of taking up an indenture. African slaves, of course, had no such option or choice. Gradually there emerged a different kind of tobacco plantation – quite unlike the initial farms – where white families employed outside white overseers to supervise the slaves who undertook most of the field work. A class and caste system emerged which characterized the region throughout the eighteenth century, where all hinged on a subservient black labouring class, separated from their white superiors in almost every respect: in the nature of their work, and in the way they were treated (face to face and by the law).[23] Slaves were forced into that separate sphere which was to contain them, for all practical purposes, until the coming of freedom in the mid-nineteenth century.

The human face of the region began to change. In 1680 only 7 per cent of Virginia's population was black; by 1750 it had risen to 44 per cent. In the words of the local planter, William Byrd II in 1736, 'They import so many Negros hither, that I fear this Colony will some time or other be confirmed by the name of New Guinea.'[24]

Supplies of Africans were guaranteed by the emergence of British naval superiority from the late seventeenth century. Gradually the British became *the* Atlantic slave traders. The Dutch, the major pioneers in the Atlantic slave trade, were pushed aside first by military defeat and later by British maritime success. The ships of the Royal African Company (founded in 1672) began to supply the labour which Europe could not supply. The power of the British Navy was part cause, part function of emergent British power. In the Atlantic (but also in other parts of the world) it was the crucial determinant in the course and pattern of settlement and trade. Britain had begun to rule the waves – with all the economic benefits that flowed from such domination. The Africans themselves had also started to change. In the early years, Africans in North America had poor survival prospects and little chance of a healthy life. By the early eighteenth century, however, many more were surviving to become

12

healthy adults and were producing children of their own. Thus the planters who bought slaves also bought their future offspring. This was a formula which planters in many of the West Indian islands (where conditions were much harsher and the disease environment more dangerous) did not enjoy. In this, however, even the West Indians realized the utility of encouraging healthy, settled and fertile slave families. But this appreciation of slave life was rooted in practical utility, not sentiment.

Slaves transformed another region of North America in the last years of the seventeenth century. The 'lower South' of South Carolina and Georgia was settled fifty years later than the Chesapeake and the newly founded economy struggled, linked at first to the West Indies (whence much of its early produce was shipped). In return, slaves from the islands were brought into the region. All that changed in the 1690s with the introduction of rice. In 1698 some 12,000 lb were exported. By 1730 it had risen to 18,000,000 lb, and 83,000,000 lb by 1770. Rice was to South Carolina what tobacco was to the Chesapeake. There were other crops in the region, of course; notably indigo and naval stores. But rice (also grown in Georgia by the mid-eighteenth century) was the transforming economic activity. From the first, slaves dominated the agricultural work, in large measure because the first settlers had come from the West Indies, and had brought their slaves with them. Right up to independence from Britain in 1776, slaves were in a majority in South Carolina. Slavery quickly proved itself as the most obvious and viable of institutions, brushing aside any local moral objections (in Georgia, for example) in the rush to make profitable returns from luxuriant land, but with no obvious supply of large-scale labour other than enslaved blacks.

Rice plantations, clawed from a hostile terrain by servile gangs working in unpleasant and often dangerous conditions, reminded many contemporaries of life in the Caribbean. The work was harsh, the climate was similar and the labour force was an image of Africa. As the rice economy thrived, centred around the elegant city of Charleston (the fourth-largest city in British America), slaves were poured in by the boatload. Rice quickly established itself as a major export crop (mainly to Britain), the fourth most valuable export from British America, after tobacco, sugar and wheat.[25] In the 1720s, 600 slaves a year were landed in South Carolina. That increased to 2000 a year in the following decade. By 1740 there were almost 40,000 slaves in the colony and slavery had seeped into every corner of the colony. Though there were major slave-holdings – big plantations with very large slave gangs – two-thirds of slave owners owned only a very small number; four or even fewer.[26]

Rice cultivation needed complex systems of cultivation and irrigation and was from the first much better organized on a large-scale basis. Tobacco had, initially, been grown on smallholdings; rice needed big, labour-intensive arrangements. As the local planters prospered, their holdings – of land and slaves – got bigger, their wealth grew and they tended to retreat to their fashionable houses in Charleston, much as Caribbean planters went 'home' to England. But, unlike slaves in the Caribbean, slaves in South Carolina worked a task system, given specific jobs or quotas to fill. Sugar slaves worked in large gang-based operations. This meant, at one level, that Carolinian slaves had, from the first, a degree of liberty to organize their time, work and leisure in ways not common in the West Indies. But slave owners elsewhere in North America distrusted the task system. It seemed to undermine the strict control and discipline which they felt they needed in order to keep the whole system in its place.[27]

For all the importance of the rice slaves of the lower South, they only ever constituted a small proportion (perhaps 17 per cent) of the overall population of North America. The fact that 61 per cent (144,872) of North American slaves lived in Maryland and Virginia provides a clue to the respective economic importance of the two regions. It was tobacco above all else which wagged the enslaved dog. It was normally the nature of local work – i.e. the crop produced, and the topography in which that crop thrived – which, more than anything else, determined the nature of the slaves' experience. All the objective social data of slave life (from birth and death statistics onwards) varied enormously between different slave communities. And it is clear enough that those figures were determined by the kind of work the slaves undertook. It was most risky to work in sugar; more dangerous in rice than tobacco. And these differences were reflected through the social experiences of slaves across the Americas. Slaves were also treated differently from one place to another. Quite apart from the personal quirks – one master's cruelties versus another's more humane approach – it was the *structure* of local slavery which shaped the slaves' lives. In sugar and rice, where slave gangs lived in effectively self-contained communities and where they saw whites less frequently, the relationship between black and white differed from that on smaller holdings, where they often worked together and lived cheek by jowl. Though this may seem merely a cosmetic issue, in fact it had enormous consequences for the ways in which slave communities evolved. Those living and working close to the whites quickly absorbed the habits of their owners – their languages, their styles, even their way of child-rearing. But slaves who were left to their own devices, living at some distance in 'African' villages, were less easily acculturated to local white society. Of course such cultural changes were not simply one-way – i.e. of whites influencing blacks. There developed a complex process of cultural change, as settlers from Africa and Europe accommodated themselves to each other's company and to the company of local peoples.

In communities where black outnumbered white, where most slaves lived and worked remote from the whites, contemporaries saw in the Americas a vision of Africa itself. More than that, the slaves were accorded a different treatment and status. By 1700, let's say, they were no longer merely black labourers, enduring the penalties and disadvantages, the restrictions and punishments which had been the lot of indentured labour (indeed of labour in general). Now they were sharply isolated in social and legal terms. And, unlike all others in the Americas, they were distinguished above all else by the immutable marks of race. But what role did race play in bringing the whole system into being? Were Africans enslaved *because* of their colour and ethnicity? Or were those indisputable features seized upon by proponents of slavery to justify a system which, at its inception and throughout its development, seemed out of kilter with the changes in the Western world? Slavery emerged in the Americas at a time when forms of bondage had disappeared, or were under attack, in Europe itself. There seems little evidence that, in establishing slavery in the Americas, Europeans were simply continuing, in exile, what they knew at home. And, in any case, why should slavery come to be the fate of the African – and not others?

Some of the founding scholars in the study of slavery were content to see in African slavery a form of labour which was climatically suited to toil in the tropical and subtropical regions of the Americas.[28] Few, however, would seriously make that case

15

today. After all, as we have seen, the initial, pioneering work in a number of regions was undertaken by white, not black, labourers. Early planters in both Barbados and Virginia were happy to develop their holdings with white indentured labour. The fact that they switched, in a short space of time, to servile African labour tells us little about physical suitability of black or white; rather it tells us about the changing costs and availability of black and white labour.

The English, it is true, had traditionally viewed the African as less than an equal human being (though that was true of their attitudes to many others). Blackness was a defining characteristic; a colour which had powerful cultural associations familiar to all sorts and conditions of white people. Black was dirty, sinful, impure; white meant beauty, virtue, cleanliness. Africans were also 'uncivilized' in most ways which Europeans recognized, though this too was not peculiar to Africans and could, at one level, simply be a way of defining outsiders.[29] They were above all 'pagan', believers (if they believed in anything) in 'superstitions' which bore little resemblance to religions recognized by Europeans. Again, this was hardly unique to Africa. The Indians and Chinese, for example, fell into this category, as did ever more people encountered by the Europeans as they encroached on distant regions and societies.

English-speakers thus brought to their encounters with Africans a host of cultural attitudes which served to shape their subsequent relationships. Yet the problem is much more complex than many historians have allowed. How do we know, for instance, that the attitudes of an intellectual élite (those who wrote and read about the issues of race, of foreign peoples and their cultures) were shared by ordinary folk – by the rough-and-ready venturers who formed the bedrock of white colonial society in the Americas? The very great majority of white emigrants were poor, rural people with little to offer but their own brute strength. What sort of intellectual baggage did *they* carry into the Americas? What attitudes did *they* bring to bear when they encountered Africans for the first time? There is a lot of evidence to show that relations, in the short term, were more equitable than we might expect (not least because our expectations have been shaped to a marked degree by the later history of slavery, and by the violence and bitterness of black–white relations).

For a start, black and white worked side by side. Small groups of workers toiled together in the fields, scrabbling together some form of viable habitat and agriculture from a fertile but resistant wilderness. Black and white might (and often were) at opposite ends of the same saw. In frontier societies, there was little room for the social (and racial) niceties which emerged in a more complex community. Men (and, to a lesser extent, women) needed each other in simple, physical terms; they needed to be able to rely on each other merely to survive. There was a crude sense of camaraderie in frontier life which flowed from the stark needs of human survival. Faced by hostile native people, surrounded by an unforgiving and often unyielding natural habitat, pioneers – black and white – leaned on each other; not, perhaps, from a shared sense of equality or humanity, but in order to survive.

There was a world of difference, as Philip Morgan has shown, between black–white relations ('race relations', for want of a better phrase) in a slave-owning society and a slave society. The former, where slave owning was common but not predominant, the latter where slave owning was the overwhelming and pre-eminent form of social relationship.[30] Nor was the physical treatment of Africans, in those early days of pioneering settlement, noticeably worse than other labouring people. Both at home and in the colonies, the labouring sort were accustomed to physical maltreatment, crude conditions and corporal punishment; labourers and apprentices, wives and children received their own share of blows as a matter of course and as part of a disciplining process which assumed that corporal punishment was an important tool in keeping inferiors in place. For most people, life was nasty, brutish and short.

But the key to relations between black and white in the English-speaking world was not simply this cultural legacy of seeing black as deeply, and perhaps immutably, inferior, or that labouring people were traditionally maltreated, but the fact that Africans had – and *for some time past* – already been enslaved and shipped across the Atlantic as chattel for the economic benefit of white settlers. English-speakers settled in the Americas knowing that Africans were slaves already.

More than a century before the English settled their own colonies in the Americas, the Spanish, Portuguese and Dutch had been turning to Africa for labour. Indeed it was imported African ailments as much as European diseases which blighted the native peoples of the Americas so much in the first years of encounter.

17

And in the key economic developments in the Americas – i.e the first sugar plantations in northeastern Brazil – imported Africans had been crucial. Thus, when English settlers made their first tentative foothold in Barbados and the eastern Caribbean, they turned to the Dutch for help; the same people who had perfected the links between imported African labour and the lucrative production of sugar in the Americas. If any single fact sealed the fate of millions of Africans, it was the rise of the sugar industry. As European taste was transformed – edged towards sweetness in many things – the Africans became indispensable. Their fate was sealed as slaves. Few, however, could have predicted the enormity of what was to follow. The subsequent enforced migration of Africans from their homelands into the Americas was on a scale never seen before.

2

BUT WHY SLAVERY?

By the mid-eighteenth century, Africa had become a cornucopia which conjured forth, in abundance, humanity and profit (for Europeans). Few doubted that the African slave trade was 'the main spring of the machine, which sets each wheel in motion'.

It yielded large numbers of Africans 'without whom our plantations could not be improved or carried on . . . ' To many, it seemed obvious that the African trade 'is so beneficial to Great Britain, so essentially necessary to the very being of her colonies, that without it neither could we flourish, nor they long subsist'.[1]

Those who watched the rise and rise of Atlantic prosperity based on African labour were sometimes bemused by what they saw. Writing in 1764, John Hippisley noticed that 'it has often been asked with astonishment, how Africa has been able to supply them with such prodigious numbers'.[2]

Observers of the Atlantic slave trade were inevitably impressed by its geographic enormity, providing mid-eighteenth century traders with a coastal trading system from Senegal to Angola, and delivering Africans 'from nearly the utmost extremities of Africa'.[3] Contemporaries had every reason to believe that the slave ships would continue to find good trade at some point along that vast and varied coastline; 'Africa not only can continue supplying the West Indies in the quantities she has hitherto, but, if necessity required it, could spare thousands, nay, millions, and go on doing the same to the end of time.'[4]

A full century was to pass before the Atlantic slave trade was staunched.[5] Even then, Africa continued to haemorrhage its peoples (on a much smaller scale) via the East African slave trade to various states in Arabia.[6]

19

However, it was in the Americas that Africans made their most dramatic and most visible impact. Those millions who survived the Atlantic crossing were in effect the labouring battalions flung ashore to make possible the European invasion and exploitation of the Americas. Clearly the Africans were not alone in this, and in some regions (notably in some of the northern colonies) they played only a minor part. But not until Europe began to unleash its own waves of transatlantic migrants (from the 1820s onwards) were the Africans and their descendants dislodged from their key economic position. When we consider the overall figures for transatlantic migration to the Americas, Africans were the dominant and most important settlers until the early years of the nineteenth century.[7] Of course, in comparison to others, Africans were not voluntary migrants. They were slaves – bought, sold and violated long before they stumbled ashore (naked or near-naked) in the Americas. The Africans landed with nothing – no material possessions, no family and with a fair chance of dying soon after arrival.

Others, too, landed in the Americas less than free; notably thousands of indentured labourers. Through all these twists and turns, the cultures of the native peoples of the Americas collapsed before the ailments introduced by Europeans and Africans. At critical points in these various collisions between peoples in the Americas, Europeans realized their need for labour to tap the economic potential. There were simply not enough Europeans (free or bonded) – and effectively no Indians – to undertake the work required. There were, however, legions of Africans (who were already been used as slaves, in Africa, Europe and the Atlantic islands).

From small, *ad hoc* and uncertain beginnings there evolved a massive global business; a multiheaded hydra which transformed three regions of the world. African labour opened up lucrative New World developments, and the fruits of African labours – notably sugar and tobacco (and, much later, cotton) – transformed the tastes (and, in part, the economies) of the Western world. The labours of enslaved Africans, and of their local-born children, created prosperity on both sides of the Atlantic, helping to refashion the physical face of the landscape in the Americas. Most significant of all, of course, was the simple human fact of the black presence in the Americas. From the slave quarters of the hemisphere there emerged those diverse and varied black communities which characterize society in the region to this day.

The consequences for Africa were, of course, of an utterly different order. The loss of population, the violence and dislocation caused by the Atlantic slave trade, the upheavals within and between African states and societies attendant of the slave trade – all and more sent damaging seismic waves throughout the affected areas. Historians are still not fully able to tabulate the enormity of the changes brought about by the Atlantic slave trade.[8] Recently, some historians have been anxious to locate the slave trade in its much broader context of African history, not to minimize the slave trade but to place it in perspective. Humanity was not the only commodity traded from Africa.[9] It remains however Africa's best-remembered export, and for very good reasons.

Africa became a seductive target for slave traders of very different social and religious backgrounds. But the Europeans were not the first to buy and sell Africans. Arab and Berber caravan routes long predated the hesitant arrival of European sailing ships.[10] And long after the European and American slave traders had left, long after they turned their aggressive attentions to other profitable forms of labour, other outsiders turned to Africa for supplies of enslaved humanity. African slaves continued to be shipped into distant cultures well into the twentieth century. By then, however, there were many more Africans held in bondage *within Africa* than there had been in the Americas at the height of the major American slave empires. Again, the wheel had come full circle. Africa, once the prime supplier of slaves to a voracious international slave-based economy, was now home to massive slave systems.

Atlantic slavery can deceive. The Atlantic slave ships were largely filled with men, and planters commonly begged for African males. Yet women quickly took their place in the most demanding of physical labours in the Americas. Slave owners wanted healthy slaves, yet the system they brought into being was riddled with sickness and death. Slaves were needed primarily for brute, manual work, but they soon developed a wide spectrum of skills. Slavery, built on the backs of alienated and violated Africans, was a crude, violent system, yet it clearly worked best when slaves were granted freedoms and spheres of independent activities. Yet their descendants, born in the

21

Americas, quickly developed crucial family and communal structures. Slave owners came to recognize the value of stable slave family life and communities, yet so often they seemed intent on destroying that stability. Personal violence, predatory sexuality – the capricious ups and downs of material success and misfortune – all and more could sunder slave happiness and tranquillity at a stroke.

Through all the travails of slave history, slave women bore a disproportionate number of burdens. Triply disadvantaged – as workers, as slave mothers and often as victims of casual sexual approaches – they supported the greatest weight of communal slave needs and expectations. The bonds they established with other, non-slave women – white women – were too often delicate and fissured by the pervasive chasms of class and colour to be more than the most temporary of helps. Colour (or 'race', to give it an inaccurate expression) was all – but that had not always been the case.

Across the slave societies of the Americas it came to be assumed that to be black was to be enslaved. Freed slaves generally had to prove their freedom (by producing the appropriate documents in the face of incredulous and doubting critics).[11] The polar opposite was certainly true: to be white was to be free. And, as free people, whites came to refuse the work – even the proximity – of blacks. Thus, black slavery drove a wedge between black and white. The passage of time, however, created anomalies inside all American slave societies. Growing numbers of blacks were indeed free, and sizeable black communities developed, especially in major urban areas (which proved more congenial and flexible to black freedom than the restraints of rural life). It was easier to retreat into a fraternity of black fellowship in a city than it was to do so in the countryside. New laws had to be implemented to count, and thus control, the number of slaves living in towns.[12] This did not mean that a life of freedom (or freedom of any kind) necessarily brought enhanced material comforts. In very different social settings – in London in the 1770s and Philadelphia in the 1830s – defenders of slavery pointed to the material poverty of free blacks as proof of the foolishness of black freedom.[13] As useful as this political ammunition seemed, it ignored the other critical fact: that we know of no ex-slave who wanted to return to bondage – however miserable the conditions of freedom. Indeed, one reason

22

why the organizations found it so hard to recruit free blacks in London to 'return' to Sierra Leone in 1787 was the communal black fear of enslavement and slavery. Freedom – in poverty – was preferable to slavery.

This was the central paradox which slave owners everywhere found impossible to resolve. Planters were particularly fond of telling the outside world of the esteem and even the affection in which their slaves held them. Plantocratic literature is peppered with such claims, yet it would be wrong to think of these claims as mere plantocratic delusions. Slaves became remarkably adept at dissembling: conveying one impression while harbouring another. Which side of this varied personality was the slave owner to believe? For their part, slaves played out the role which best suited their own interests. Theirs was an adaptable life, learning at a tender age the adult qualities of adaptation. So many of those personal and social qualities valued by whites as the basis for successful social life made little sense to slaves. Truthfulness, industry, application, comprehension, alertness – all and more held hidden dangers for the slaves. There thus evolved that slavish character trait (rather, a host of traits) which so many – then and since – interpreted as inherent personality. At its most basic, all this meant was that slaves behaved slavishly. But not always. In their own social and economic spheres slaves sprang to life, exhibiting that full range of qualities and attainments which slave owners searched for in vain when slaves were under their command.

When hostile commentators wrote about slaves (and hostility was invariably accentuated whenever slavery was under attack), they rarely spoke about the slaves' areas of independent life, i.e. their attainments. They pointed instead to their shortcomings *as slaves*. As slaves they were of course property: things which were at once chattel and yet – obviously – human. The paradox, sometimes minimized by scholars, confronted slave owners and their backers throughout the history of slavery in the Americas. Yet it was by no means inevitable that chattel slavery would develop in, or be transplanted to, the European settlements of the Americas. After all, European migrants came from societies which, on the whole, had turned their back on slavery. Within a very short space of time, however, those same Europeans had 'perfected' forms of slavery which hinged on the property status of imported Africans.

There was a Western tradition of viewing the African as an object of curiosity. Africa was known as the home of people who were utterly different from anything familiar to Europeans.[14] Their blackness had powerful cultural associations which predisposed English-speakers to view the African as a deeply inferior being, well beyond the pale of contemporary English sensibilities and sympathies. But there was nothing in the relationship between the English and Africans to suggest that Africans should be *slaves*. By the time the English began to seek labour for their early settlements in the Americas, however, other Europeans had already made extensive use of African slaves. Economic convenience, not cultural (still less racial) bias edged the English (and other Europeans) into using Africans as slaves. In the words of Robert Bisset, writing in 1808, 'With the Negroes they might raise and reap the crops which that country [America] bestows upon industry, but *without* Negroes, the discovery of those regions would have been unproductive to Europe.'

It seemed clear enough in retrospect (though much less so at the time) that Europeans were 'totally unfit for hard work in a tropical climate, and the natives in any climate. Necessity, therefore, and the example of Portugal, gave rise to an English traffic in Negroes from Guinea.'[15] As sugar planting slipped from one English colony to another, trade, industry and prosperity boomed as never before. Even the North America colonies – which supplied much of the food and hardware for the West Indies – flourished on the back of sugar-based slavery. Few doubted that the African slave was the very basis of this remarkably diversified material well-being (shared by other European colonists as well as the British). Thus, in daily economic practice, and later in legal definition, the African slave was reduced to the level of property: to be bought, sold, bartered and exchanged much like any other item of trade. The problem remained, of course, that they were also human.

The economic use of Africans required rationalization and justification. There was a need to give the slave systems a legal structure and definition. Both in the laws which came from London (governing navigation, settlement and trade), and the legislation which emerged from colonial legislatures, the slave was defined and rationalized. To ship Africans, to trade for them on the African coast, to regulate their daily lives in the slave settlements, laws and legal conventions developed which provided a justification and rationalization for an institution which was out of kilter with contemporary practice in Europe. The basic point was a simple one: 'Chattel slavery required, in common with other manifestations of the commercialization of society, decisions as to how the account books were to be kept.'[16] Fortunately for the slave lobby, cultural assumptions compounded economic change: 'Our statesmen and lawgivers of those times regarded Slaves as articles of property.' More precisely, one legislator after another 'proceeded upon the principle of human and divine law, that SLAVES ARE PROPERTY'.[17] Beginning in Barbados, colonial acts specified the African's status as property. By the end of the seventeenth century a consensus had emerged, on both sides of the Atlantic, that African slaves (and their local-born descendants) were property;

> Not merchants only, and planters, but the statesmen and lawgivers of England, sanctioned the idea that Negroes might be subjects of property, and that it was both expedient and necessary to employ them; the whole nation agreed in the same opinion; and at the same period of an ardent zeal for English freedom, no opponent of arbitrary power ever questioned the justice of Negro slavery.[18]

Notwithstanding a degree of exaggeration here, the basic point was valid.

If contemporaries had their doubts about chattel slavery, they were rarely mentioned. Indeed, proponents of the slave trade made great play of the fact that throughout much of the eighteenth century few of those British statesmen and politicians involved in contemporary debates about political liberties so much as *mentioned* the iniquities and inconsistencies of the slave trade. The only real objectors were 'those laughable but innocent fanatics, the Quakers'. The reason was simple enough. The British people 'liked sugar and rum; and when they could afford these gratifications, never had any scruples of conscience, because these palatable wares could not be effectively raised without the labour of Negroes.'[19] Few criticized slavery because so many people benefited from it – even the humblest of labouring folk whose labours often went into the Atlantic trade and whose tastes were sated by slave labour.

Through all this welter of detail it is easy to miss the logical leap. The sugar colonies and their associated trades had clearly become economically (and strategically) critical to British well-being. So, too, had the trade to and from West Africa. But why was the labour involved *necessarily* enslaved? And why was that enslaved labour African?

The American colonial system had developed a momentum, a dynamic force, which seemed both natural and unstoppable. It hinged upon a supply of labour which, though fashioned in an earlier era, had created its own economic culture on the African coast and into the interior. Demand for Africans had set in train major changes within Africa that became addicted to the continuing enslavement and trade in Africans. Whole societies and regions were transformed by the need to find and to sell other Africans. The Atlantic trade thus became a major force for change within Africa itself. Slave systems took root and flourished in response to factors so far removed from the area as to be unimaginable. Even when the Atlantic slave system had ended, its consequences lived on, often in catastrophic form, in distant interior regions of the continent.

After the 1860s, black chattel slavery survived in the Americas only in Cuba and Brazil. But by then, too, millions of people had passed through the slave systems of the Americas. Here was a phenomenon – black slavery – which had been conjured forth, in small-scale, embryonic form, to fill a labour vacuum faced by European settlers in the tropical Americas. Its success was not simply in developing regions of the Americas, but in creating major patterns of material consumption which demanded ever more products from the Americas. And the whole process required an ever-increasing number of Africans. As it did so, slavery spilled out, from its early beachheads in the tropical Americas, to take root in regions (and in work) for which its pioneering importers gave no heed. In the north, slavery became as American as apple pie (even the apples were introduced into the Americas by the English). It seemed basic, indigenous and natural; but it was no such thing. It was in origin haphazard and fortuitous. Its evolution was capricious and unpredictable. But its consequences were utterly fundamental and revolutionary (for Africa, the Americas and Europe).

One of slavery's most persistent insidious consequences was the link forged between slavery and colour. The issue of 'race' sunk deep in Western life, with the result that the culture of slavery continued to resonate throughout the Western world long

26

after slavery had been forgotten. The broader story of racism is, of course, more complex and debatable but black slavery was seminal in its evolution. Slavery generated and bequeathed a number of important myths about black humanity; most notably the idea that blacks were in essence lazy and would work only under compulsion (despite abundant evidence to the contrary). Slave owners everywhere asserted that blacks would resort to their native, innate indolence once removed from the compulsions of slavery. In the words of Robert Bisset (1808), '... Negroes are inefficient, useless, and burdensome members of a community, unless they are Slaves and compelled to Labour.' This same author accused abolitionists of wishing 'to exempt Black labourers from the necessity of working, and leave them to idleness and wickedness'.[20] Such ideas recur throughout the literature, but they tell us only about the slave-owning mentality. The economic vitality of the Americas would be sapped by black freedom, by removing the incentives to work. Only slavery, with all its apparatus of compulsion, could be relied on to keep blacks at their various tasks. To admit evidence to the contrary was to detract from the slave owners' case: that blacks (among other vices) were incorrigibly lazy. In a world which prized industry above sloth, this was an important defence of slavery.

It was also untrue, and part of a much broader ideology which promoted slavery as a civilizing, progressive force. Far from being the retrogressive, self-interested (and, increasingly, un-Christian) cruelty alleged by opponents, slavery and the slave trade were portrayed by its more assertive supporters as the very stuff of enlightenment and salvation. It plucked unfortunate Africans from the cruelties and barbarities of Africa (where, as prisoners, they would have been slaughtered), to rear them up in the disciplines, skills and religions of their New World endeavours. There, in more civilized environs, they were enabled to acquire the more rounded abilities and attainments of civilized people. Most important of all, in the Americas they were exposed to Christianity.

Looking back, it seems bizarre to claim that slavery was a civilizing force. Such claims (condensed here from a complexity of arguments) stood reality on its head. But a critical point was made which few contemporaries were able or willing to challenge: namely that slaves in the Americas were more 'civilized'

27

than their African forebears; that the slave societies of the Americas were themselves more civilized than the African societies from which the Africans had been initially brought.[21] This aspect of slave-owning ideology had a superficially persuasive appeal to all sorts and conditions of people, most of whom knew only a garbled concoction of mythology about Africa.

Such arguments were mere self-interest masquerading as social ideals. They were, again, part of a slave-owning ideology which sought to justify the continuation of slavery itself. The kernel of that ideology was, of course, economic. Slaves – and slaves alone – could undertake work which generated such levels of material well-being.[22] In origin, and at its death, slavery's simple rationale was economic. Who else would do the work?[23] It seemed, at the height of slavery in the Americas, that so much depended on slaves.

3

VARIETIES OF LABOUR

The early European settlements in the Americas were not dependent on African labour. Though certain regions developed without Africans, few eventually managed to remain untouched by the presence or influence of slavery. It was, to a degree, a matter of numbers. The sheer number of Africans landed was astonishing. Taking British America as a whole, the tide of black migration began to swamp the trickle of white migration. By the time of American independence, many more Africans than Europeans had settled in British America. Between 1630 and 1780 some 2,339,000 blacks had settled there as opposed to 815,000 whites. Of course the actual *proportion* of black to white population was the reverse of these figures. So destructive were the demands of slavery, so consuming of humanity were the slave regions of the Americas, that the social and demographic health of slaves was sapped and undermined. Whites fared better; living longer and reproducing more successfully than slaves. The simple result was that the black–white population (as opposed to the figures for immigration) favoured the whites. In 1780, despite the waves of Africans landed in British America, the black population stood at just over 1,000,000; the white population was more than 2,250,000.[1]

The only reason for this black presence in the Americas was work. That was also true, of course, for many white settlers. But whites had migrated for a variety of reasons, some to seek freedoms denied them in Europe. Others sought, in the risky opportunities of Atlantic migration, the prospects for both personal freedom and material advancement unavailable in the more restrictive societies of Europe. It is true that many, in the early days, travelled to the Americas as bonded people; tied by

29

indentures to a miserable, unrewarding life of servitude.[2] But even their prospects were quite different from the slaves. For a start, their bondage was finite. With luck it would come to an end. Indeed it was freedom at the end of indenture which made that form of labour so unattractive a proposition to their masters; they had a labour force harbouring the real expectations of freedom. Slaves could have no such hopes. Unlike servants, they bequeathed their slavery to their offspring. Chattel slavery throughout the Americas was, like family traits, passed down from generation to generation. Occasionally, this cycle was broken. The lucky, the attractive or the strong might break their bonds and secure freedom, in return for gratitude for good service, a personal liaison with their owner or their own ability to escape. But these were, by and large, rare in societies which, across the hemisphere, kept millions of slaves locked into a perpetual bondage.

It seems unnecessary even to emphasize the point that the sole reason for maintaining this system was to extract work from the slaves. After all, the language of slavery has entered the modern vernacular. Anyone expressing unhappiness with their work is likely to resort to images of slavery – 'working like a slave', 'being a slave', 'to be enslaved'. The words are normally sufficient to make the point: that here is a labouring condition beyond the bounds of human endurance. Of course – and like many other modern usages – the language and imagery of slavery does a gross historical injustice to the real slaves. Yet it captures an important point which needs further exploration.

It is widely assumed that slavery was/is the worst form of human condition. But it would be wrong to suggest that the degradation of slavery lay solely, or even largely, in terms of material experience. There were, as we shall see, slaves who enjoyed ample material conditions; some who prospered and a few who thrived. It is perfectly possible to point to free people enduring material conditions (of work, of domesticity) far worse than those endured by some slaves. It would be hard – to offer an obvious and much-quoted example – to fare worse than the Irish peasantry in the 1840s. And how do we incorporate those recent wretched scenes of mass starvation, from the Horn of Africa, among people whose sole freedom seemed to be the freedom to starve? Yet to focus on material conditions as a defining characteristic of slavery is to misunderstand the problem. It is true, of course, that economic circumstances often drove people into slavery. Debt slavery, the handing over of hungry children, the consigning of women and children to bondage to relieve family hunger – all and more were (and are) forces which propelled untold legions into slavery. But slavery is not, and cannot, be merely (even largely) a debate about levels of economic deprivation. At times slaves *did* find themselves at the bottom of the economic heap. But the real definition of their status was that they were normally at the bottom of every *other* heap as well. More often than not they were also denied formal access to any local social structures. They were, so often, non-people. To be a slave was to be denied those basic rights which distinguish mankind from lesser creatures; they were, in fact, stripped of humanity and rendered dehumanized. It is, in the phrase coined by Orlando Patterson, to be reduced to social death.[3]

Work in itself was not a definition of slavery. But work was the rationale for black slavery in the Americas, and in many regions slaves came to dominate certain kinds of work. Custom came to decree that only slaves could undertake certain jobs. It was not that free people or white people could not, physically, do the work, but rather that particular work had become the unique cultural lot of the slave. Slave work involved, then, a complexity of issues which touch on the very nature of slavery itself.

When Africans began to arrive in the Americas in large numbers – when white colonists came to realize that African labour made better economic sense than persisting with Indian or European labour – the die was cast. William Byrd, the Virginian planter, was worried about the increase in the number of slaves in Virginia in 1736. Among the 'bad consequences of multiplying these Ethiopians amongst us', he complained that slaves, 'ruin the industry of our white people, who seeing a rank of poor creatures below them, detest work for fear it should make them look like slaves'.[4]

That switch was intimately linked to the history of sugar and the development of plantations. As demand for sugar in Europe grew, as supplies of Africans were shown to be regular and relatively cheap, and as the organization of sugar production became ever more efficient, it was the African labourer who became the key ingredient in an extraordinary international exchange of peoples and goods. The Atlantic sugar economy hinged on the African.

It is easy to see why the myth came into being that the African – and the African alone – could undertake work in the sugar fields. It is worth recalling, for instance, that some 70 per cent of *all* Africans imported into the Americas were destined, in the short term at least, to work in sugar. There was a simplistic parallel between the two regions: the tropical areas of Africa, and the Americas. In fact, African slaves came from diverse geographical regions: from deserts, from savannahs, from cooler, higher altitudes. They also came from a remarkable range of societies: from pastoral and agricultural, from artisanal and warlike. Men came from communities where women undertook field work. Yet, despite the variety, the assumption developed – and was rehearsed down the years by any number of white commentators and apologists – that here were people ideally suited by their African background to harsh physical labour in tropical settings. Some were – but many were not.

This environmental explanation for black slavery was, as often as not, a smokescreen; an ideological argument on the part of vested interests who needed to justify the use of African labour. In the late years of the eighteenth century, when the British slave system found itself under attack from a growing body of abolitionists, the slave lobby needed to justify slavery. Planters and slave traders needed to convince the dubious (and the swelling ranks of the hostile) that black slavery not only made economic sense, but was the sole way of continuing the essential business of sugar production. Africans and their descendants were alleged to be the only, obvious and irreplaceable, source of labour for the sugar fields, blessed by nature with all those physical characteristics (hair, skin and a host of other physiological attributes) best suited to labour in the tropics. The literature of the abolition campaign, pro and con, is steeped in a crude, reductionist anthropology which, in drawing upon personal experience, hearsay and cultural fairy tales, created a case for African uniqueness. This was an argument which was more a 'polemical imperative' than an unassailable thesis.[5]

By the late eighteenth century the environmental association seemed unbreakable. For the West Indian planters, in the words of James Dunbar, 'blackness, and slavery, are so blended, so twisted together in their minds that they may be supposed as utterly incapable of separating them'. Abolitionists despaired of breaking the link: 'features and complexion, regarded as the natural badges of inferiority, seem to mark them out for slavery ...'[6]

It was widely accepted that black skin responded better to the sun than fair skin. But what had that to do with slavery? There was, understandably, a great deal of confusion in the debate about race/slavery/labour. In retrospect, it is much easier to see through the confusion of issues. Clearly planters and their supporters came to believe what they said and wrote about black humanity. But their arguments masked a much deeper economic self-interest. If they were to lose their supplies of Africans, or their slaves, who else would undertake the work for them? Environmental arguments were thus at one level a plea for self-interest.

From these various beachheads in the Americas – Brazil, the Caribbean, North America – black slavery seeped throughout the hemisphere. The Africans went, against their will, to undertake field work which, increasingly, the white host society decreed that blacks alone could do. But wherever black slavery was established, the nature of the work quickly changed. Invented to provide the beasts of burden for the production of tropical staples, slavery, and its attendant labours, soon spread into most corners of the local economy. Though intended for back-breaking field work, slaves quickly proved themselves economically (and socially) indispensable in a host of ways undreamt of by the pioneers of the Atlantic slave system.

Africans – and Africans alone – seemed able to tap the potential of the Americas. As the Atlantic system evolved, however, a number of contradictions began to emerge. First, slave owners throughout the Americas preferred healthy (and preferably younger) Africans. Yet the process of enslavement and transatlantic transportation ensured that most slaves were sick on arrival. More than that, a substantial number died *en route*, and others died within the first years of settlement. The ability to work was thus undermined by the ailments, the diseases and the impairments created or worsened by the Atlantic slave system itself. Second, planters showed a marked preference for young African males. Slave owners preferred young men to women – initially at least – assuming that the muscle power of the young male was the key to agricultural success. Yet slave women were soon turned over to many of the physically demanding tasks in and around the slave properties. In fact, this ought not to be so surprising. Many African women came from societies where female labour, in the fields, with cattle and in the villages (to say nothing of in and around the family units) formed the economic bedrock of local life. Third, though slaves were prized (and priced, initially) for their physical strength, maturing slave societies required a more complex and sophisticated range of labouring and skilled abilities than mere muscle.

The early days of settlement required a great deal of brute strength which was afforded by varied mixes of labourers; enslaved, free and indentured. Africans, Europeans and Indians were flung together to scrape a precarious survival from a hostile environment. Building homes, defences and cultivable plots required cooperative strength – and a great deal of good luck. Many, of course, did not succeed and many did not survive. Often, they scrapped through by learning from the people they feared most (the local Indian peoples), notably about local foodstuffs, but in those early days there was little scope for distinction between shades of freedom or slavery. At first, though, life was marked by the crude but simple necessities of communal self-preservation. Much the same pattern persisted in a host of communities as the frontier pushed westwards. In time, however, the rigidities of divisions, between enslaved and free, and the consequential racial divides, were intruded throughout the Americas. As circumstances changed, as local crops thrived and exports to the metropolis enabled planters to expand and to buy ever more slaves, Africans began to arrive in large (but sickly) numbers. And therein lay the central problem – for the slaves and for their owners. Sick slaves were expected to undertake difficult and strenuous labour. But any effort to explain what happened to African slaves at work in the Americas must begin with what had happened to them in Africa and on the Atlantic crossing. They arrived, and were set to work, with the ailments and the miseries of another continent, compounded by the terrors and physical damage of the slave ships.

The process of enslavement and transportation has become part of the popular cultural memory. The visual images which survive, and which were used for decades as powerful tools in the abolitionist armoury, are of coffles of Africans, driven to the white traders on the Atlantic coast, thence packed, sardine-like, between decks, before rolling and pitching their tormented way to the slave auctions and dockside sales of the Americas. This

34

image has become a caricature, but it does contain a kernel of sustainable reality. In simplifying, however, it overlooks the diversity of slave experiences, and ignores some salient African experiences.

From first to last, the Africans were violated. Africans became slaves through acts of violence; by-products of war, of raiding parties and the like. Their movement to the coast was a long, tortuous trip down river systems and pathways, often being sold or bartered *en route* – and all before falling into the hands of white traders and merchants on the coast. The process of violation then took on a new dimension: there they were inspected, scrutinized, generally in the most intimate of fashions, before being herded into the crowded quarters on the slave decks.

In the contacts with Europeans on the coast, but more especially in the squalor of the slave decks, slaves were mixed into a disease environment of peculiar potency. Though the white traders and crews died in horrifying numbers, so too did the slaves, succumbing to imported and indigenous ailments but, on the slave ships, contracting illness from the polluted filth which dominated their lives on board ship. The further the distance, the worse the weather, and the more miserable the lot of the slaves. Losses varied, but there were few slave ships which escaped loss of life among their human cargoes.

At landfall, the full human cost was counted. The dead were a lost investment; the survivors were often not much better, reduced by months in a disease-ridden ship to incapacity or weakness. The vendors, however, needed to make them appear fit and healthy, so they were washed, shaved, oiled (with palm oil), plugged (when sick with dysentery) and given tobacco to cheer them up, Africans were thus paraded, virtually naked, before potential purchasers. Planters and their agents, however, quickly learned the slave traders' tricks. Richard Ligon reported from Barbados in 1657 that local planters 'buy them out of the Ship, where they find them naked, and therefore cannot be deceived in any outward infirmity. They choose them as they do Horses in a Market . . . '[7]

The sickest and most disabled slaves (people who, in Africa, had been thought worthy of purchase and shipment, i.e. their deterioration had taken place on the ship) could scarcely walk. The most common complaint was the disabling humiliations of dysentery. One batch, so plagued by their ailment, were, on landing, 'obliged to stop almost every minute, as they passed on'. It was for these – the very sick and the dying – that planters and slave traders coined the phrase 'refuse slaves'. The phrase entered the vernacular of the Atlantic slave system; a simple turn of phrase which revealed the mentality of the slave-owning world and which captured the wretchedness of untold legions of Africans. Time and again, planters railed against slave traders who brought them only 'refuse slaves'. Planters did not want such slaves at any price, because they knew that they were unlikely to survive.[8]

Slave owners became accustomed to the fact that most survivors were sick people. Even where their health seemed more robust, they were often spiritually fragile – their resistance, even their stability, corroded by the experience of the past months. Few emerged from the slave ships unscathed, even when their health held up. Yet these were the very people required for hard physical labour in the fields throughout the Americas. Some indication of their enfeebled state can be gleaned from the fact that many newly arrived Africans did not survive long in their new homes. In the West Indian sugar islands in particular, many Africans died soon after arrival. Planters came to accept that, from any batch of Africans, they would lose a sizeable proportion within the first few years. Of the Africans who survived the crossing to the Caribbean, one in three died within three years – and we need to recall that by 1775 some 1,500,000 had been imported into the British islands. The slave trade thus destroyed Africans even though it seemed that the system was the only way of providing suitable labour for the Americas.

There is a temptation to think that slaves were killed by their work. In truth, those who died, in their prime, were more likely to succumb to the range of illnesses imported from the slave ships, and from the after-effects of that debilitating experience – but all mingled into the new disease environment of the Americas. It would be wrong, of course, to eliminate work as a source of their troubles. Sugar in particular was cultivated in generally hostile and harmful climatic and physical conditions. The sugar plantations simply devoured Africans. In Barbados, the Codrington estates need to replace 5 per cent of their slaves each year until the mid-eighteenth century. On that island, where conditions seemed much better than, for instance, in Jamaica, some 35,000 slaves were imported between 1764 and 1771 – but

36

the overall population grew by a mere 5000.[9] This pattern was to characterize the British sugar islands throughout the history of the slave trade. As long as sugar dominated the economy, planters called for more Africans; and, as Africans poured in, they brought with them the illnesses of Africa and the ailments of transportation.

The slaves' working experience differed from crop to crop. In North America, the rice-growing region of South Carolina came nearest to the West Indian model of slave work and life. Here was a hostile climate where local employers preferred Africans for the strenuous unpleasantness of converting the steamy, waterlogged region to rice production. Rice took hold after 1690 and, as it spread throughout the coastal low country, the population was progressively Africanized. By 1740 there were about 40,000 Africans in South Carolina, many of them arriving direct from Africa and not, as was initially the case, via the Caribbean.

Work was organized differently between these two regions. The islands were characterized by the slave gangs. Slaves were regimented into three or even four field gangs; the strongest slaves toiling at the most difficult work in the first gang, and lighter (though no less essential) tasks falling to younger and weaker slaves. Slaves progressed up and down the slave gangs as age and growing (later, decreasing) physical strength suited them for different work. Slaves of all sorts and conditions – young and old, strong and weak – could be fitted into the patterns of work in the sugar fields. Thus it was that women came to play a crucial role in the toughest of physical tasks in the fields; work which planters initially had imagined was best/ideally suited to male slaves. In the rice fields of South Carolina, however, work was structured around a task system. Slaves were given specific jobs and, when the task was over, their work was complete. For feebler, less nimble slaves, task work would be no less troublesome, for they had to plod on with their work long after others had finished. It was unpleasant work in an unpleasant environment, beginning before sunrise. In the Caribbean, too, slaves were summoned from their huts before sun-up to be in the fields at first light.

Tobacco demanded different routines again. Slaves in tobacco fields worked in small teams, often alongside local white workers and employers, planting the staple from seeds around Christmas and carefully tending them throughout the year in small beds before transplanting them. The plants needed a watchful eye and trained hands as they progressed. It was persistent, detailed work quite unlike the back-breaking toil in sugar or rice. But when the dried leaves were packed and loaded in huge 1000lb barrels, slave strength was important. By then, fifteen months on, the new plants were already spouting. Tobacco offered an endless routine to its slave labour force.[10] But the slaves of the Chesapeake were thinly scattered throughout the region. Unlike West Indian slaves, they were not grouped in large gangs or villages. Indeed their numbers remained relatively small; certainly much smaller than in the Caribbean. Initially brought via the Caribbean, from the 1680s onwards they were imported direct from Africa. Between 1700 and 1740, 54,000 – the great majority of them Africans – were imported into the Chesapeake. As late as 1775, most Virginian planters owned five slaves or fewer; the average in the Caribbean at the time was 240.[11]

In all slave regions, society matured from raw frontier communities to more complex social organizations which required a range of skills from its labour force. Each of the major slave crops, for instance – and most of the less important ones – required specific skills for successful cultivation, processing and shipping. Slaves were trained in the specialized skills and techniques of sugar, rice and tobacco cultivation, knowing precisely when and how to tap the boiling sugar cane and to pick the leaves. Such slave skills were vital, a fact easily measured in the higher prices paid for skilled slaves in the slave auction place. Costly skilled slaves in effect formed the élite of slave society, whose labouring majority formed the broad base. On sugar estates, the skills and experience of distillers and boilers transmuted the raw produce into exportable, profitable sugar. But even their work would have been to no avail without the related skills of carpenters, masons, coopers and smiths, all toiling to maintain the physical fabric and machinery of the sugar plantation. Labourers were kept at their demanding tasks by the physical strength (often by the brutality) of gang-drivers and overseers. Slave women prepared the food, made the clothes, delivered and nurtured slave babies, cared for the sick and taught the young. Each slave was thus expected to contribute to local economic life according to his or her skill or strength.

Each industry spawned its own peculiar, necessary skills. And each skill, in time, was taken over by the slaves. In tobacco, the early skilled occupations tended to be white and free. As the eighteenth century advanced, however, skilled slaves tended to take over. White craftsmen were hired to supervise and train skilled slaves. Eventually, slave artisans took over. Though they learned their skills from whites, they tended to bequeath those skills to their families and offspring. Thus, in time, the best way to acquire a skilled slave position was to be born to an artisan father or a skilled mother.

Slave societies everywhere spawned a remarkable number of domestic slaves. It was as if slave owners needed to surround themselves with servants for their every need. Visitors to the Americas were frequently struck by the profusion of servants; they filled domestic space with their chattering presence, seemed inescapable and, through their gossip, made public what many whites would prefer to keep private. From the making of clothes and the routine of (often lavish) meals, from the tasks of daily cleaning and domestic preparation, to the more intimate demands of the planter's bedroom, all and more were serviced by domestic slaves. Young girls, often following their mothers, were 'trained up' as domestics, acquiring those necessary refined habits of obedience, service and attention. Such work may have avoided the sweaty unpleasantness of field work, but it took place under the watchful eye of often imperious white women. Complaints of the minute scrutiny and the aggressive management of white mistresses were legion. Locked into the inescapable intimacy of daily domestic life, black and white women lived in a social environment of potential friction. Slave women 'invariably found themselves the butt of the mistress's impatience, dissatisfaction, and frequently of her unevenly applied standards'.[12] Yet the plantation mistresses often had their own serious difficulties. They, too, were victims of the cruel conditions of plantation life, removed by distance and environment from much that they regarded as a civilized, home environment. On isolated properties, white women missed their distant families, especially the company of other (white) females.[13]

Yet, as difficult as domestic life might often seem, it was unquestionably an improvement on life in the fields. Significantly, one punishment for a domestic was relegation to field work. Planters in the West Indies came to view their domestics as more intelligent than the Africans toiling in the fields, though of course it was largely a matter of socialization. Domestic slaves possessed the skills, refinements and those acquired social graces needed when living and working at close proximity to the slave-owning class. Domestics were expected to display their refinements, field hands their strength and durability. The habit of employing black domestics quickly spread to Europe and, as early as the mid-seventeenth century, fashionable society in Britain and France was characterized by the presence of black servants.

The maturing of American communities inevitably spawned more complex social systems among local slaves. In the eighteenth century, for example, the proportion of skilled slaves increased throughout mainland America, especially in those regions where whites were few and far between.[14] They were most obvious in those ports and cities which thrived as the entrepôts for vital imports and exported staples destined for Europe and beyond. By the last years of West Indian slavery, some 10 per cent of the population lived in towns. Kingston's population, for example, was more than 12,000.[15] It is understandable that slaves were drawn to the towns – to work as domestics and in the varied trades which serviced urban life, as vendors and hagglers, ferrying and selling rural produce to town-dwellers; as washerwomen, workers in the taverns and inns, prostitutes or jobbing labourers. 'Negro yards' grew up close to white residences, and from these slave quarters growing numbers of slaves spilled forth each day to ply their various urban trades and jobs. Here, in an urban setting, a slave society emerged which was quite different from life in rural settlements. At its simplest, urban life bestowed a freedom of movement and behaviour which was more striking than among rural slaves. Such slaves, though outnumbered by whites, moved around with ease, often beyond the control and ken of their owners.

There were more skilled slaves in major towns than in the country, covering all the trades of urban life – butchers, bakers, craftsmen serving local shops (carpenters, smiths – including goldsmiths and silversmiths), watchmakers, printers – plus the various occupations associated with maritime trade, e.g. sailmakers, caulkers, shipwrights. Not surprisingly, there were large numbers of black sailors employed both in the short-haul local trades along the coasts and rivers and between the islands, and the long-distance trade which linked the colonies to the distant

European ports. There was always a risk that slaves might effect their escape by boat, and in 1784 Virginia stipulated that no more than one-third of a local crew could be slaves. In the Caribbean we know that pilots, guiding ships into their destinations, were sometimes slaves.[16]

The streets of colonial America were filled with slave workers carrying and pushing, washing and sweeping, selling and buying, canvassing their goods and foodstuffs from door to door, carrying food and produce from the country to their favourite spot for selling, wending their way back home after a long day in town. In all this they displayed an independence which their owners – and other whites – often found irksome. Here was a degree of latitude – an area of freedom – that sat uncomfortably with the broader system of slavery, which demanded immobility for most slaves. But truth, as we shall see, was that the slave systems could not really function *without* such latitude. Slave owners – and others – needed some slaves to be mobile and peripatetic; *needed* the labours and the produce, the finished produce of slave enterprise and freedom. And those accomplishments would not be forthcoming without a tolerance granted to slaves. But it sometimes created discomfort for slave owners and those who controlled and directed the affairs of slave societies.

Many of the slaves who enjoyed the freedom of economic and social movement were women: washerwomen, domestics, hawkers. The latter were important, for they were the conduit for the transfer of goods from the countryside to the towns. Indeed, scenes of slaves, overburdened with agricultural produce heading for market in the towns, provided some of the most vivid impressions for visitors to the slave colonies. With the food they had grown, the animals they had reared, the artefacts they had shaped and fashioned, slave vendors became a major landmark in urban life of the Americas.

Slaves could be found in a host of other occupations. Throughout the Americas, musical slaves were everywhere. It was widely accepted that Africans and their descendants were innately musical; naturally attuned, by their African background, to whatever rhythms their homemade musical instruments could conjure forth. It was partly true (music clearly did play in important role in African societies – and provided slaves with a cultural link to the world they had lost). But it was also an enduring and self-fulfilling myth on the part of the whites. Everywhere in colonial America, whites encouraged slaves to play, to sing and dance (though often restricting some musical forms – notably drumming – thought to provide a rallying sound for troublesome slaves). Favourite slaves were selected for musical training; hence in the Americas and Europe black musicians were commonplace, many of whom were slaves.

There were in fact few jobs which were not served by slaves. Barbers and nurses, 'slave doctors' and cowboys, messengers and clerks, cooks, fishermen, shoemakers, butchers and jewellers – slaves could be found in all these jobs. But most slaves toiled in the fields which yielded colonial America's primary economic wealth. The rhythms and patterns of work changed from one locale, from one crop to another. Everywhere slaves were held in the grips of agricultural regimes which were reinforced and kept in place by a mix of material inducement and physical threats. Some work was, in itself, harsher than others. And the harsher the work, the harsher the regime required to keep slaves at their tasks. Women and children, as well as strong young men, felt the blows administered freely in order to keep the process of cultivation and production moving. As we shall see, the threat – and reality – of physical punishment was a universal of slave society. It was thought to be essential, as the lubricant of all slave systems: the final resort of management forever goading its labour force to undertake tasks it clearly did not want to do. Work was invariably accompanied by physical punishment, and it is worth asking how far slavery itself was unworkable without the spectre of physical pain.

By the early nineteenth century, British observers of slavery (growing in numbers by the year, thanks to the efforts of the abolitionist lobby) became ever more squeamish about the punishments meted out to slaves. They were especially unhappy about the violation of female slaves. This was, of course, one aspect of a changing sensibility; not merely about slavery, but about unnecessary suffering in general. It was also an aspect of the changing attitudes to women. Yet slavery needed the hard physical labour of women in the fields. And that labour would not be forthcoming, in the form and at the pace required, unless slaves were goaded and threatened. There were, it is true, exceptions, particularly with the passage of time. Pregnant slaves and women with large numbers of children were spared the worst rigours of the local slave system. But these concessions came late and were driven as much by economic self-interest as by tender feelings. It came to be appreciated that harsh treatment might be economically counter-productive.

Female slaves had fewer opportunities of advancement than men (though the term seems odd when applied to slave systems). Apart from the obvious opportunities of domestic work, most women were restricted to labouring work – and much of that, as we have seen, was crude, heavy and sweaty. More and more plantations, and their associated holdings, employed a growing number of domestic slaves as the eighteenth century advanced. In fact the occupational distinctions between slaves was often blurred as slaves slipped from one occupation to another (especially on smaller holdings) with seasonal changes and by their own maturity or physical decline. Moreover – and this seems so obvious as scarcely to need repetition – women moved from the demands of the fields to the demands of the home. Work for the master was normally replaced by the essential demands of domestic and communal life. Spare time, in the evenings and on Sundays, was consumed by the chores of household life and work in the slave gardens and plots.

The economic demand for slaves in the English-speaking colonies was uneven, faltering in one region while it began to pick-up or be transformed in another. Though slavery had made possible the development of key areas of mainland America (the Old South), with its revolutionary crops of tobacco and rice, North American slavery is best remembered because of its association with cotton. In the early years of the nineteenth century – when the British abolition of the Atlantic slave trade had severed the supply of Africans (though many continued to be shipped 'illegally'), and in the very years Caribbean slavery came under ever closer scrutiny and criticism – slavery in North America (now the USA) boomed, expanded and began to seep into vast, new areas of the continent. As with sugar and tobacco earlier, the key to the expansion of American slavery was a particular crop; cotton, in this case. By 1860, slavery had intruded into nine new states and had spread 'more than halfway across the American continent'.[17] By then, however, many viewed it as an anachronism. Essential in the eyes of Southerners and the cotton lobby, to ever more people in the North – and to European eyes – slavery seemed out of kilter with the times and ill-fitting in a society which was forged by the ideals of equality and democracy.

43

Despite a host of moral, theological and political objections, cotton slavery continued to make economic sense. Thus, more and more slaves found themselves locked into the labouring and social rhythms of a system imported into the Americas for the production of very different commodities. Yet the formula remained the same: American lands, tapped by the strength and skills of alien (and alienated) blacks, for the betterment of local white élites and for the material advancement of distant societies. The cotton from the American slave states ultimately clothed millions the world over, thanks in large measure to that other dynamic revolution – the textile revolution in Britain.

The number of North American slaves increased dramatically. In 1790 there were 697,897, but by 1860 there were almost 4,000,000. The slave regimes of North America sought to improve the lot of their slaves (largely for reasons of good economic sense), but they also made great efforts to tighten their control over both free and unfree blacks. Material improvement went hand in hand with more rigid control. Both were needed, not least because of the remarkable expansion in the number of slaves. There were more slaves in North America after 1830 than in all the other slave societies in the Americas combined. And they worked overwhelmingly in cotton.

Thanks to Eli Whitney's cotton gin (1793), cotton production in the South boomed. The paltry 3000 bales of 1790 had increased to 178,000 in twenty years. By 1860 it stood at more than 4,000,000 bales. By then it was far and away America's greatest export and underpinned the initial development of industrialization in the USA itself. And this whole, extraordinary phenomenon hinged on slaves in the cotton fields. As the frontier moved west and south, about 1,000,000 slaves were moved from the old slave settlements. There was, in effect, an internal North American slave trade, with all the dislocation, family breakup and personal agonies familiar in the earlier maritime slave trade. Though never approaching the physical damage caused by the Atlantic crossing, this new American slave trade left scars of its own, though many were unnoticed because they were so deep and so psychological. Once again, the demands of territorial expansion and economic betterment (for the whites) involved mass suffering and long-term damage to their black underclass. It was, however, a profitable trade. The economic need of the frontiers offered rich pickings to those traders who scoured the slave communities of

44

the Old South and moved coffles of miserable slaves westwards. They were moved on, in the main, towards the new cotton plantations, and all the evidence suggests that this trade would have continued to thrive long into the nineteenth century had it not been for the eruption of the Civil War.

Whatever the statistical debate about this internal American slave trade,[18] slave voices speak of the anguish of upheaval and resettlement. Slaves uprooted from family and loved ones, those left behind, those scattered to the remote and wild corners of American frontier settlement: all and more left their distress on the historical documents. And this was as true of the eighteenth-century Atlantic slave trade as it was of the nineteenth-century movement of slaves within domestic America.

Slaves in the new slave states worked in that range of occupations familiar in the east; again, their lives shaped by the particular locale and the specific kind of work. The variations in slavery continued in new settings, between town and country, between small- and large holdings. There were, however, some broad, general patterns across the South. Slaves formed about one-third of the population (unlike the West Indies, where they had greatly outnumbered whites), though certain regions were predominantly black and enslaved. Cotton was the driving force behind the expansion of slavery but even then there were variations. Cotton was grown on both small and large plantations. However, only a tiny number of slaves lived on very large plantations. Most were owned and worked on properties containing fifty or fewer slaves, and most of them lived close to their masters and owners. The whites tended not to be absentee, choosing instead to live on the land, keeping an eye on their slaves even when not directly responsible for their daily management. On smaller estates, whites worked in the fields side by side with their slaves.

The bigger the estate, the greater the need for overseers – the field management. It was here that large slave gangs emerged, with work divided among slaves according to physical strength and the demands of the work, in a pattern similar to the sugar gangs of the West Indies. The great majority of cotton slaves worked as field labourers. There were many, it is true, employed at other tasks, from the most basic of frontier developments through the skilled jobs spawned by a maturing local economy. But there was a notable decline in the number of slaves in

45

artisanal manufacturing skills, partly because of pressure from local whites, but partly because many goods once made by slaves could now be imported cheaply from the North.[19]

The crop once again dictated the nature of local slave work, with the sugar planters of Louisiana coming nearest to replicating the harsh regimes of the Caribbean. But, whatever its local peculiarities, work was the rationale and the leitmotif for slaves everywhere, and work everywhere was accompanied by the threat of the lash. Physical violence was as important a management tool on the nineteenth-century plantations as it had been in the sugar-cane fields of the eighteenth and seventeenth centuries.[20] The pain and sound of the lash, like the pain of upheavals and separations, entered the folk memory of the black populations of the Americas, resurfacing time and again right up to the present day: the scars of their forebears continue to pain the sons and daughters of slavery. The crop also provided breaks for the slaves: weekends and slack periods, out of crop, all allowed slaves to work at their own activities or to enjoy themselves as they saw fit.[21] For many of the slaves who seemed at first glance to enjoy material benefits – notably better clothing, food and housing – there was often a price to pay. Many of them were, for example, domestic workers – who were also supervised more closely than field hands. Though materially better off, their lives were often subject to an intrusive control and supervision. Again, the pattern resembled that in the eighteenth-century Caribbean.

Beneath such generalities about slave labour, however, lay a myriad exceptions. On smaller properties slaves had to double up, and undertake whatever task was demanded of them. The smaller the property, the less likely it was that slaves could prosper – poorer owners held poorer slaves. To confuse slave life even more, the planters' habit of selling slaves when they needed cash – or when they had surplus hands – could, at a stroke, plunge personal and family life into utter confusion. Equally, the practice of hiring out slaves to distant properties was disruptive. Again, slaves found themselves cast hither and yon, by forces beyond their ken and control, with all the disastrous consequences for their peace of mind and their social lives. Like the lash, removal and upheaval was a persistent threat – even when it failed to materialize.

Life for the North American slave followed many of the working patterns of slaves elsewhere in the Americas. Labours began early in life and continued until either old age or infirmity intervened. Slaves were shifted from job to job, as age, strength, skill or demand required. Slaves showed marked preferences for certain kinds of work but few slave jobs were without their pains and troubles. The sweat and discomfort of the cotton fields might sometimes seem preferable to the strict, minute supervision of the domestic slave. But, whatever form of work the slaves were engaged in, however much it changed throughout the life cycle, and however modified by the slaves' own rhythms and pace, it was a working life, which was dictated by an alien white management and élite. Slave life was fissured by layers of distinctions – between crops, place, age and gender. Ultimately, however, to use the words of Peter Kolchin, despite 'the multiplicity of slave experiences, much more united the slaves than divided them'.[22]

From first to last, the black slave was the beast of burden used by different white élites to shape the economic development of the Americas. It was a form of labour which was readily adaptable to different locales and different crops. The regiments of resistant Africans – flung, like an invading army, at the unwelcoming Americas – were in time replaced by their local-born descendants whose toils were directed at a string of tasks unimaginable to the pioneers. The broad pattern remained the same, however. Africans – and their offspring – formed the task force for the economic exploitation of land throughout the Americas. It was their manifold labours – reluctant, enforced and at incalculable personal and social cost – which profited their owners and the societies they brought into being. Slave work brought only the smallest crumbs of material comfort to the slave quarters of the Americas. But few doubt that slave work was an engine which drove forward the economic settlement and development of vast regions of the Americas. More than that, it powered key sectors of a much wider global economy. This central economic fact was perhaps more difficult to appreciate when viewed from Europe. But it was more easily grasped – because so close and tangible – when viewed from within the Americas. Yet the material evidence of slave labour was there for all to see – and to enjoy.

The labour of slaves had transformed the habits of the Western world. This was especially true of the remarkable rise of sugar and tobacco consumption. The cotton slaves of nineteenth-century America made it possible to clothe people the world over in cheap cotton goods. Of course, the labours behind those products were only one aspect of a much more broadly based global economy. Nonetheless, slave work was the hinge upon which so much of the modernizing world turned. In time it came to be appreciated that labour could be organized in other ways; that staples could be profitably conjured forth from a hostile environment by other forms of labour. But, for a critical period in the history of the English-speaking world – from the early seventeenth to the mid-nineteenth centuries – black slave labour was the key to the development of the English Americas and proved vital to the consequent wealth and development which transformed societies on both sides of the Atlantic.

4

DOMINATION AND CONTROL

Keeping slaves at work was no easy matter. They were, from first to last, an alienated and (as long as Africans survived) an alien people. They were originally imported great distances, often relocated from one place to another, kept at their lifetime's routine – and all against their will. Keeping them in their place was difficult. Indeed slaves posed a series of overlapping and reinforcing problems for the slave-owning class. At its simplest, the basic problem remained: how to maintain slavery itself. How to sustain a precarious balance between keeping slaves in submission and yet persuading them to give of their best. Most slaves were needed for their physical strength, but that very strength could pose a threat. Moreover here was a physical presence which needed to be shaped and directed towards goals which the slaves generally found alien and unattractive.

The obvious way to induce and perpetuate discipline – at work or in the slave quarters – was by physical punishment. The lash had obvious limitations, however. It could be counter-productive, it might breed resentment and a desire for revenge, and it could actually harm the slave. Furthermore, for many forms of slave work, the lash was quite inappropriate. It could not easily or readily be used in a domestic setting (but blows and cuffs were just as frequent), though there was a complexity of disciplines at work in slave societies and slaves were in fact kept at work by a host of disciplines and rewards, ranging from the threat and reality of pain through to the prospects of material rewards (however trivial). But it would be wrong to minimize or ignore the importance of physical punishment as an essential lubricant in the operation of slave systems throughout the Americas.

Like much else besides, the physical assaults on slaves began long before they reached the Americas. The Atlantic slave system was conceived in and nurtured by violence. Slaves were acquired by violent means. They were driven towards the African coast by overlapping systems of violence against them. They were herded, corralled and marshalled in the slave barracoons by the most violent of means. And all this before that most horrific of institutional violence – the Atlantic crossing – heaped unimagined levels of suffering upon their communal heads.

From the first days of black slavery, whites assumed that only repressive force could be guaranteed to keep slaves in their place. On the African shore and on board the slave ships, Africans were kept in subjection by ferocious conditions and were permanently under the nose of awesome weaponry. Here were unusual ships; ships which trained their guns, not on external enemies, but on their own human cargoes.[1] Of course it did not always work, and the history of the Atlantic slave trade is peppered with slave rebellions and violent outbursts against the white violators. More often than not, however, such slave revolts were unsuccessful and rebellious slaves were forced to learn the bloody lessons of defeated resistance. Here was a lesson which they needed to recall periodically (and hand down to their American-born descendants): that to assault their captors and owners – and to fail – was to invite excruciating pain and death on an almost medieval scale.

It is easy to caricature the process (and some of those caricatures have stuck in the popular mind) but we need to recall that every African shipped across the Atlantic (and more than 11,000,000 Africans survived the ordeal) had been violated physically. They had been held in chains, often branded, kept for weeks on end in the most wretched of seaborne conditions, and all under the nose of threatening weapons and crew. There could have been no doubt in the minds of transported slaves about the nature of the white man's power over them. It is true, of course, that slaves were humbled by other factors, most notably by the inexplicable forces of illness and debilitation which sapped their strength, gnawed at their resolve and thinned out their ranks as they pitched their miserable way across the Atlantic. But this was all of a piece. They were held subservient by white men, who reduced them to unimaginable levels of suffering, who threatened them with weaponry of the most fearsome kind and who appeared to bring inexplicable ailments and death to the slaves

50

huddled in their own filth on the slave decks. It was indicative that one slave captain remarked that 'we receive them on board, from the first as enemies'.[2]

They were, however, *unusual* enemies, for they were intended to bring profit at the end of the journey. Slave captains therefore had to tread a delicate line; in maintaining a necessarily-severe physical regime, yet also seeking to maintain their slaves in sellable condition. It was a task made all the more difficult because it was administered by the lowlifes from their own crew; by men who cared little for the slaves beyond their temptations of sexual gratification. Here, on the Atlantic crossing, was forged the essential relations between black and white which survived long after the ending of the Atlantic slave trade itself. The experiences of the crossing were dominated by violence. Indeed, the whole system was violent in its very essence. Africans shuffled ashore, at the myriad landfalls throughout the Americas, apprenticed to a violent relationship which, though shifting its contours and forms, was to remain basic to their lot for the rest of their enslaved lives.

Though the Atlantic crossing was unique, it was followed by a series of subsequent adjustments to enslaved life in the Americas which, again, were partly designed to make clear the nature of the relationship between black and white. From the point of sale, through the onwards journey to their new home, and to the initial introduction to local life and labour, the nature of local discipline was plain enough. Slaves were prepared for landing by the most humiliating and intimate of processes; inspected, poked, cleansed and spruced up ready for the sales. Some were sold on board ship, others were sold on shore, sometimes in a 'scramble' (when purchasers rushed forward to secure their desired slaves by physically grabbing the terrified Africans). It was a scene of pandemonium, the terror visibly etched on the slaves' faces.[3] And, even then, their agonies had not ended, for they now faced the trek to their new home; into the interior of a Caribbean island, or along the rivers which formed the communication systems for South Carolina or the Chesapeake. A century later, they trekked still further westward, sold on from the slave settlements of the old South, to the new cotton states on the brink of North American expansion.

This confusion of movement, the sequence of one painful, violent and threatening event after another, was a prelude to a

51

life of bondage. But we need to recall that, throughout the Americas, a very high proportion of newly arrived Africans simply did not survive the first two or three years. They died from a number of ailments and weaknesses acquired in that brew of disease and stress which was the Atlantic crossing.[4] Africans made landfall in the Americas sick and weak; alone, without kin, with no worldly possessions. They carried with them the scars of the past few months, the haunting nightmares of transportation and, of course, the memories of their various African homelands. They entered the Americas as violated victims of a system which, from the moment they had passed into the hands of white men on the African coast, had made painfully clear the nature of the relations between black and white. In time, life in the slave quarters served to counterbalance many of their problems (most notably by providing communal strength and resilience).

Whatever the crop, wherever the region, African slaves underwent similar processes of discipline. It took the simplest – but most fundamental – of forms. European settlers were keen, for example, to give the Africans a new identity by renaming them; removing them as far as possible from their African backgrounds. Simple first names, Classical names (Caesar, Pompey, Venus, Jupiter), pet names which were sometimes ridiculous – anything other than the complexity of African names. Thus did Olaudah Equiano ultimately become Gustavus Vassa. Understandably, Africans did not like this renaming, often keeping their own names. But in time they – and even more so their locally born descendants – became acculturated to European customs, accepting European names (a process hastened when the slaves were converted to Christianity). Understandably, slaves sometimes kept their new names (even more bizarre – especially classical – names), because they were an affectionate way of linking generations; of naming children and grandchildren after revered older relatives.

Though imported Africans were renamed, slaves chose the names for their own children, part of the emergence of an independent slave community and culture. Slaves kept some African names, maintained others they had been given, and often sought (at least in North America) to avoid the names of the whites around them. Here at least they were able to distance themselves from the people who sought to control their every move. For their part, whites wanted no reminder of Africa (save for the physical strength of the Africans). It was sometimes possible to accommodate aspects of African culture (to allow African slaves to enjoy the cultural pleasures remembered and imported from an African past), but slave owners commonly assumed that most things African were inappropriate; out of place in the developing communities of the Americas. Once physical survival of the newly arrived slaves had been secured, what was needed above all else was the establishment and imposition of a new labour discipline. New slaves may well have been cowed, for the time being at least, by the horrors of transportation. But it was quite another thing to lick them into some sort of economically useful shape for work in the Americas.

Slave owners everywhere complained about their slaves' inability to adapt to the local regimes of labour. Though this was understandable among new Africans – unaccustomed to most of the types of work expected of them – it may seem harder to understand when alleged of slaves born in the Americas. As we might expect, there are layers to the problem. Complaints about slave stupidity, about their apparent failure to grasp the basics of even the simplest labouring tasks, tell us as much about slave owners as about slaves themselves. Indeed, the process of labour discipline created by the slave owners takes us to the very core, the essential heart, of the various slave systems which pervaded the Americas.

Throughout the history of black slavery, slave owners complained about their slaves' shortcomings: slaves were slow to pick up ideas, slow to carry them out, slow to deliver what their masters demanded. But why, we might ask, should they be otherwise? As we shall see, there was a slavish style – a mentality – which sought to impose a rhythm on whatever work was to hand; a rhythm which was of the slaves', not the masters's, making. Though we need to be suspicious of masters' complaints, they do provide a useful entrée to the world made by the slaves. Yet, even before that was possible, slave owners were faced by imported workers who needed instruction in the most basic of tasks. They had to be 'broken in'.

Slaves often did not know how to effect some of the tasks expected of them in their early days in the Americas. But many jobs were similar to the work undertaken in their African homelands. The pattern is, then, confused and we need to know which Africans came from particular regions – and who among them had experience of the kind of agricultural work confronting them in the Americas. But even the simplest of jobs were often too much for many Africans. Many were too sick to work at all. Time and again, owners had to withdraw their new Africans as they began to wilt; not from the difficulties of work, but from the ailments they carried with them from the slave ships.[5]

The problem was even worse in the tropical colonies. A Jamaican doctor explained the problem to the local Assembly: 'a very great number of newly imported Negroes are lost by Diseases, the predisposing Causes of which they bring in this Country along with them'.[6]

On Worthy Park Estate, Jamaica, of the new Congolese slaves bought in 1792, more than a half were dead within four years. The owner, alarmed at such a rate of attrition, moved the survivors to a healthier location, ' . . . for a change of air . . . '.[7] Thereafter the death rate declined to more 'normal' levels. We need to remember, then, when discussing the development of labouring disciplines, the seminal and unavoidable facts of illness and death among the Africans. Their first, immediate struggle was not to comprehend the tasks demanded of them, but simply to stay alive or keep well. This sobering fact formed their entry to a lifetime of labour in the Americas.

On smallholdings – in the early days most holdings were of necessity small – the slave owner worked with and supervised the training and the breaking in of the new slave. But as time passed, as estates grew in size, the day-to-day management of slaves fell to delegated officers; to overseers and drivers. In the Caribbean, these were also slaves, normally in charge of a particular gang. In effect they were the sergeants of the systems, carrying out the orders of their own superiors, enjoying better conditions than the rank-and-file slaves in return. But for that, they had to keep slaves in line and make sure they did what was required of them. They beat out the rhythm of work (often on the slaves' backs). The driver got them into the fields on time, made sure there was no slacking, spending the day among the field slaves, encouraging where necessary, instructing when needed. But he was always – always – willing and ready to cuff and beat the reluctant and the backslider. It was the driver who carried a rod or switch for instant or more considered punishment.[8]

Slaves had little interest in working hard – or working at all. Few doubted that physical force was an essential ingredient on any slave-holding; the necessary lubricant of a tough system. All slave societies developed their own conventions about corporal punishment – how, when and by whom it should be administered. It was also widely accepted that punishment which was wrongly or capriciously meted out was both counter-productive and possibly dangerous. Flogging – specified numbers of lashes for certain offences – was the most common punishment, and it was the most widely discussed punishment debated by slave owners and their supporters (especially when, as the nineteenth century progressed, ever more outsiders found the process increasingly distasteful). Local laws normally defined the nature and limits of floggings, but such restrictions were often to no avail on distant properties where whites in effect exercised complete control over their black charges. Even then, the limitations placed on punishments (for example, thirty-nine lashes in a Trinidad law of 1800) seemed outrageously severe.[9] Where planters controlled the local legislatures, restrictions on floggings were hard to enact and harder still to implement on the ground. It was clear enough that planters, at least in the sugar islands, preferred to use the whip regularly (though lightly) rather than authorize the more severe regime of whipping which accompanied the more extreme backsliding.

Planters had to tread a delicate line, knowing that too much, or too little, whipping did not serve their economic and social purpose. Outrageous punishment of slaves was as dangerous to the white cause as no punishment at all. Yet the history of slavery could be written in terms of the story of physical punishments, sometimes of the most sadistic kind, to which there was no appeal, apart from dangerous slave retaliation and resistance. Slaves were familiar with the sight of the driver and overseer, whip and knotted rod carried about his person, pacing or riding through the slave lines, cuffing and chiding his way through the working day. In the words of William Beckford, the whip was an ' . . . instrument of correction in Jamaica, whether it be in the hands of the cart-man, the mule-boy, or the negro-driver, [and] is heard, in either case, to resound among the hills and upon the plains . . . '[10]

Slave owners did not expect their slaves to work well or persistently unless goaded. In the words of another Jamaican planter,

A planter would as soon expect to hear that sugar-canes and pineapples flourish the year round, in open-air, upon Hounslow Heath, as that Negroes when freed would be brought into the like necessity or disposition to hire themselves for plantations work.[11]

Planters throughout the Americas were united in similar views. A Virginian planter remarked in 1772, 'I find it impossible to make a negro do his work well. No orders can engage it, no encouragement persuade it, nor no punishment oblige it.'[12] Most agreed that slaves were lazy (again, this was part of the ideology of slave owners everywhere) and could be kept at their tasks only by a carefully modulated regime of threats, violence and rewards. But, because slave owners were wedded to the idea of black indolence, they were also attached to corporal punishment.

Slaves were not, of course, the sole victims of physical punishment. It was assumed, for example, that good child-rearing habits needed the occasional (even the regular) blow. So too did management of apprentices – and even wives. This pre-modern world made lavish use of corporal punishment; to secure obedience, to inculcate good habits and to extract performance. But the punishment of slaves in the Americas was of an entirely different order. In the words of one commentator, 'The fear of punishment is the principle to which we must and do appeal, to keep them in awe and order.'[13]

The lash was basic to the relationship between slave and slave owner (though normally doled out by others). Corporal punishment was not, of course, the only means of exerting authority. But it was the most obvious, visible and stinging manifestation of slave owners' power. It could be counted in any number of ways. It was enshrined in local laws and regulations. It was recorded, often in shocked tones, by any number of visitors to slave colonies and it could be seen in the scars and 'stripes' carried by the miserable victims. Most eloquent of all, it entered slave culture. It was remembered, discussed, denounced from one slave generation to another. It became part of the demonology of the slave quarters, as slaves told others of what had happened to them, forming a crucial lesson which parents told their children. The lash entered the collective consciousness – popular culture – as a reminder of the profound wickedness of slavery.

We can gauge some sense of the physical effectiveness – or the memory – of physical punishment by what slaves and ex-slaves recollected. Africans were especially prone to beatings, partly as a way of moulding them to the slave owners' needs, but partly because they did not understand the world around them (and how could they?). Most fundamental of all, of course, Africans often could not understand instructions in English (or other European languages) until they had acquired the local patois, or were helped by other slaves. Incomprehension at instructions and orders barked out in an alien language were too often interpreted as stupidity or wilful refusal. But what sense, for example, could a sick Congolese or a newly arrived Ibo, make of threats and instructions bellowed by a Scottish overseer or a Jamaican-born driver? Not surprisingly, whatever spark remained in the newly arrived slaves occasionally flared: they reared up, struck back, ran away or similarly bridled at the last of the painful straws heaped on their long-suffering backs.

As slavery moved into the new states of early nineteenth-century USA, corporal punishment was transported to the edges of American settlement. The era of the slave-based cotton boom was, of course, very different from those pioneering days of settlement on the seaboard two centuries earlier. Now, for instance, there was a powerful anti-slavery lobby in the Northern states, quite apart from the irritating attention which the British paid to such things. Having spent the best part of two centuries pioneering their own lucrative slave system, from the 1830s onwards the British had become aggressively abolitionist and sought evidence of outrages against slaves wherever they could find them. This all served to heighten awareness of the lot of American slaves. It was not that slaves in the cotton states were violated more outrageously than slaves in earlier communities, but rather that the whole business was acted out in an entirely different context. There were many more people in the Western world alert to slaves' sufferings. Nonetheless, the cotton planters of the nineteenth century, no less than the Jamaican sugar planters of the eighteenth, felt they could not do without the lash.

American slave-holders in the nineteenth century had learned a great deal about slave management from the older systems. The fact that slaves were owned and controlled in relatively small numbers also meant that, unlike the large Caribbean sugar plantations, whites in the cotton regions often knew their slaves quite well. But they also locked them into a tight framework of regulations covering slave management. West Indian planters, though they too had manuals by the end of slavery, had learned the process of labour control and discipline by trial and error. Of course one crucial difference in nineteenth-century USA was the virtual absence of Africans. American slaves were American; transported, not from Africa, but from the old slave regions in the east.

Like all slave owners, the cotton men assumed they knew what was best for their slaves. Holding the slaves in conditions of permanent thraldom, trying to provide them with everything they needed – from food to clothing and housing – many planters sought to be the fathers to their infantilized slaves. At its most extreme, theirs was a paternalistic world which justified its existence by the state of permanent underdevelopment of the enslaved labouring force. Though viewed by the whites as little more than children, the slaves – unlike children – could never grow up and reject the paternalistic environment. But, like children, they were in need of regular chastisement and correction, even when tempered – where possible – by affection. Such sentiments now seem a bizarre account of what was, in essence, a brutal system. Yet nineteenth century American planters embarked on a great deal of self-justification couched in just these terms. In part of course it made them feel much better, operating as they were within a system which was patently hard to justify to an increasingly sceptical outside world. Moreover, such sentiments, repeated time and again across the face of the slave states, provided a fig-leaf of comforting self-deception when planters had to turn to sterner measures to cope with their slaves.

In many respects slaves were no easier to control in mid-nineteenth-century USA than they had been two centuries before in Barbados. Then, and earlier, there was always a need for vigilance and physical assertion. Indeed, planters assumed that slaves *expected* their masters to be tough when circumstances required. James Henry Hammond, who owned 147 slaves at Silver Bluff, South Carolina, devised an amazingly detailed code of rules and conventions for every aspect of their lives. He even decreed that when slave couples separated each should receive up to 100 lashes.[14] Once again it is impossible to understand the realities of slave life without confronting the ubiquity, the inescapability, of physical punishment. There were, it is true, some slave owners who steadfastly refused to beat their slaves; who sought to encourage and cajole with material bribes and humane treatment. But such men were unusual; though so, perhaps, were the sadists for whom the torture of slaves was a way of life. Somewhere in between lay the great bulk of the slave-owning community.

Slaves assessed their masters – how good or bad they were – on the scale of the violence measured out to them. Outsiders also knew who were the good, and who were the bad, slave owners. This was not simply a question of tenderness. Excessive violence was corrosive. It bred resentment among all slaves and was likely to undermine the efforts of those who used it sparingly. Management manuals specified the limits on violence. One decreed,

> The object of all punishment should be 1st for correction to deter the offender from a repetition of an offence, from the fear of the like certain punishment; and 2nd, for example to all others, showing them that if they offend, they will likewise receive certain punishment.

We have certain indices of slave floggings. Account books spell out which slaves were flogged, and when. On one Louisiana plantation, between 1840 and 1842, half of the male slaves were flogged.[15] We can sometimes even count the resulting scars. Excessive whippings normally scarred slaves for life, and advertisements for slaves (for runaways or for sale) often specified their number of scars. When assessed alongside other forms of evidence, a clear picture begins to emerge. Slaves were flogged and beaten regularly. And, even if they were lucky enough to avoid such a fate, their security was never guaranteed. They were permanently under the *threat* of physical pain; be it from a simple cuff or a comprehensive and damaging assault.

Here was *the* central fact in the disciplining of all slaves; a seminal truth in the complex relations between black and white in all the slave societies of the Americas. Time and again, slaves recalled the pain they had suffered, weaving the experience into the communal tales and folk memory of the community, offering their experience as a cautionary tale to young slaves: 'Don't done your task, driver wave that whip, put you over the barrel, beat you so blood run down.'[16]

One slave remembered, simply, that 'The whip is all in all.' When North American slaves looked back over their lives, they invariably recalled the whip. Even the lucky ones testify to the ubiquity of the whip: 'I did not get many whippings because I always did what I was told, in a hurry.' Another recalled the advice of a grandfather: 'To keep the whip off your backs, you know . . . children, work, work, work, and work hard. You know how you hate to be whipped, so work hard.'[17] From their earliest days, slaves were told about the whip and how to avoid it. Later, they were in no need of such storytelling because they could see and even feel it. Slave owners everywhere found themselves unable to thrive without the lash. What else would compel slaves to work hard (even to work at all)? There seemed to be no obvious incentives as there were with free labourers; 'we cannot substitute that which makes the English labourer industrious, namely, the fear of want'.[18] We know, however, that on their own plots and gardens, slaves *did* work hard. But there they were working for themselves.

The supervisors of slaves normally carried the instruments of punishment in the fields. They wandered through the slave ranks displaying the symbols of their power; a physical reminder of the proximity and immediacy of pain and punishment for any backslider. In the West Indies, drivers carried two whips, one long, the other short. But they also used pieces of wood, sticks and twitches depending on what sort of pain they wanted to inflict. Slave manuals specified that drivers should carry their whips, 'emblems of [their] rank and dignity'. This same guide argued that, even among the children, working in the 'weeding gang', the woman in charge should be equipped 'with a pliant, serviceable twig, more to create dread, than inflict chastisement'.[19]

The whip stands, then, as the emblem of slavery throughout the Americas. This does not mean that all slaves were flogged (though it seems likely that, in the course of an enslaved lifetime, most were). But it represented more than the formal punishment of slaves, for the violence done to their persons might take a number of forms, ranging from the isolated blow, delivered in anger, through to the more ritualized and sadistic tortures of the extreme cases. At times, it seemed that planters plunged the depth of their own demented imaginations to devise physical punishment for slaves. Who could even *devise* the torture of forcing one slave to defecate into another's mouth?[20]

The West Indies seemed to encourage more of these vile punishments than North America, a fact which may be related to the different ratio between black and white, and the fear of isolated whites when confronted day and night by overwhelming armies of sullen and reluctant Africans, themselves scarcely controlled or assimilated to whatever passed for local life. During the era of American cotton slavery, the slaves were American, however powerful and influential their African background and cultures. Caribbean slave history, until its last generation, was dominated by large numbers of Africans. Not until the 1820s did Africans begin to play a diminishing role in the shaping of Caribbean slave life. It was in facing Africans, as opposed to their local-born descendants, that slave owners had the severest of troubles in maintaining their control without resort to the most punitive and physical of systems.

Slaves were kept in place primarily by their owners, the drivers and overseers. But there were other agencies designed to encourage acceptance and tranquillity among the slaves. Masters and their assistants might administer local punishments. But it was the local *legal* system which tended to exact the most savage of tolls from transgressing slaves. All slave colonies devised laws – and punishments – to control slaves. Colonies, later states, copied the codes and legal practices from more experienced communities. But everywhere, slave discipline was thought to be a central concern of the law itself. When John Reeves summed up the British slave laws in 1789, he asserted that the principle of 'the Negro System of jurisprudence' was simple; that 'Negroes were *Property*, and a species of Property that needed a rigorous and vigilant *Regulation*.' Some nine-tenths of the initial seventeenth-century colonial laws were concerned with regulating slaves; laws which (conceived in Barbados) were then copied in other colonies. Not surprisingly, those laws reflected the severity of seventeenth-century penal and social thought, but by the late eighteenth century they had come to look distinctly old-fashioned and contrary to changing values.

Slave laws prescribed especially severe physical punishments. What slaves actually *saw* of the law was the way it was implemented against them through an array of fearful corporal punishments. Reeves summed them up accordingly: ' . . . Banishments, of slitting the Nose, branding in the Forehead with hot Iron, cutting off the Ears, and in some Islands, even that of taking off a Limb'.

61

Though such outrages were unusual – and were effected normally only after serious slave trouble – they were, increasingly, out of kilter with the rest of the Western world. As the British penal system, for example, made ever fewer sacrificial offerings of criminals (preferring to transport rather than execute), the suffering and death of slaves offered a chilling reminder of a world that was in rapid retreat. Caribbean slave owners seemed worse than their North American counterparts. William Byrd remarked, 'We have nothing like the inhumanity here, that is practised in the islands, and God forbid we ever shoud.'[21]

The Caribbean islands, with their overwhelming slave populations and small white minorities, were especially bloodthirsty towards transgressing slaves. Execution was decreed for a host of offences (as, indeed, did the law in contemporary England). Slaves were denied a jury and could not give evidence against white people. Even with the benefits of late eighteenth-century changes, the principle underlining slave law was clear enough in 1789: 'the Rights of a Master be every Thing, and those of the Slave nothing'.[22] More than that, for our purposes, it was a system which made clear, from first to last, the awesome power which white people had over their black slaves. In practice, most slave owners did not need to resort to the process of law in their day-to-day dealings with slaves, for the law sanctioned their behaviour, even in its more extreme and bizarre forms. The law, for slaves, was merely a continuation of their daily routines; of white domination and the threat and reality of physical punishments.

By the late eighteenth century, the British imperial Parliament and its officers, alert to changing sensibility at home, sought to persuade colonial bodies to ameliorate the more outrageous punishments. Time and again, their complaints and suggestions were ignored or deflected and, in the last years of the eighteenth century, reports about the violations of slaves in the Caribbean began to influence British feeling. A new breed of missionary, making the first effective forays into the West Indian slave quarters, sent back to their sponsoring churches and supporters tales of plantocratic violence and barbarities which both offended and puzzled British congregations. Here were men (the white slave owners) who argued that they and their methods of discipline stood between the slaves and barbaric anarchy. Yet it was increasingly unclear who were civilized and who barbaric. Even in the first decades of the nineteenth century, after legally approved slave punishments had been scaled down, reports of the most obnoxious violence filtered back to Britain. A Wesleyan missionary to Jamaica reported, in 1828, the excessive flogging of a young male slave. That done,

> a female, apparently about forty years of age, was laid, her stomach upon the ground, her clothes were most indecorously turned up and whilst two persons held her hands and one her feet . . . the driver inflicted stroke after stroke.[23]

Colonial legislatures (normally in the hands of planters) resisted amelioration from London. In Barbados, the only restriction they accepted on flogging 'was that the indecent exposure of a woman's body should be avoided'.[24] At the same time, it was recognized that acts of violence against the slaves should only been administered as 'the act of cool deliberation'.[25] Corporal punishment *did* decline in the last years of British slavery, though slaves always faced the risk of painful punishments at the hands of their owners and employers. Curiously enough, it was in precisely the same years that corporal punishment became a political issue in Britain. For that first generation of industrial workers, especially for children in the textile trades, beatings were commonplace and formed one of the strongest objections levelled at the emergent industrial system. It seems that physical suffering and industrialization went hand in hand. Clearly, it was not the same, nor on the same scale, as violence done to slaves. But it is a reminder of the ubiquity of corporal punishment and of the fact that large numbers of people in authority – in factories or plantations – simply assumed that a blow, a beating or a whipping were essential elements in the manuals of contemporary management.

The pattern of the West Indian islands was replicated in North America. As slavery slipped its moorings in the older established eastern states, and drifted westward with the frontier, new laws and codes were established to give local forms of slavery a necessary legal framework. Again, as in the Caribbean, the slaves were denied the most basic of rights (a fact that was all the more pointed in a nation forged through democratic debate about human and social rights in the 1770s and 1780s). From one state to another – and notwithstanding variations between the laws and codes – legal practice was similar. Slaves were subjected, in law, to a fearful range of corporal punishments familiar through-out the Americas. They faced a litany of offences for which they could be executed, another list for which they would be flogged (the exact number of 'stripes' specified for each of-fence). The Alabama slave code of 1852 specified that a slave who committed perjury should be branded on the forehead with the letter 'P'.[26]

From one slave colony and state to another, local legislation specified what should be done to keep slaves in their rightful place. And time and again the concentration was on physical dis-cipline. Of course the most excruciating penalties were reserved for the most violent of slave behaviour – especially rebellion. There was often a mismatch, however, between the law as it was enacted and the law as it was implemented. But the law of slav-ery is important, for it provides an important indication of 'how authorities *wanted* it to function'.[27] Laws across the South were designed to prevent slave movement, to secure their loyalty, to prevent their escape (physically or through manumission) – in general, to undermine the emergence of a black population that was anything other than utterly subservient and enslaved to the masters' will. The law also specified, it is true, the obligations masters had towards their slaves. But such clauses tended to be inoperable, particularly when we recall that slaves could not legally testify against their owners. And, in any case, most slaves were disciplined not by the law – caught by white patrols and dragged before a local court – but were dealt with on the spot, where they lived, by their owners and drivers.

Viewed through slave eyes, it must have been difficult to see the distinction between the law and local white management. This was especially true in the Caribbean when planter, court of-ficial and politician might be one and the same man. Where did the abstractions of law begin and the power of the local slave owner end? What most slaves recognized, in all slave societies, was that they were caught in a system that was stacked against them. Whatever improvements were introduced to secure their interests (designed to lessen the arbitrariness and the old cruel-ties of the law) must have seemed distant and theoretical; mere detail which scarcely tipped the balance their way. What they *did* experience, on a daily and unavoidable basis, were face-to-face dealings with white people which were physical, arbitrary and often cruel and capricious. The law clearly gave slave owners a framework of control and domination in societies which seemed, for much of the time, precariously balanced and insecurely wrested from nature and hostile peoples. But the crucial forces which disciplined most slaves – the forces which drilled slaves, of all sorts and conditions, into a grudging acceptance of the world around them – were local and specific. The disciplining of the slaves was achieved through the imperatives of local labour and the threatening violence of slave management and ownership.

Having said that, slavery clearly could not be maintained solely through physical control. Slave owners were in a paradoxical position. On the one hand, they were dealing with a labour force they had defined, and treated, as non-people – chattel to be bought and marshalled like other objects. They also sought to deny their slaves many of the areas of freedom most people (even the poor) took for granted. The freedom to enjoy life independent of the owner, to be able to move and act freely, to acquire material artefacts independent of the owner, to conduct social and family life untrammelled by the slave owner's intervention – all this served to strain slavery's fabric. Independence seemed corrosive of the compliance and subordination which slavery demanded. As slavery settled in the new cotton states, local laws were introduced to restrict slave freedoms, tightening up on those areas of free choice and movement, on and off the property, which slaves in older states had come to accept as normal. Restrictions on manumission, on slave movement, on literacy and marriages – all and more testified to the slave owners' intention to keep as tight a hold as possible over their charges.[28] Yet most experienced slave owners – and sharp-eyed observers – came to appreciate that slavery thrived best when slaves were not utterly dominated and controlled, but where they were accorded areas of social and economic freedom.

Slave laws, codes and convention (the last most important of all, because most slaves were controlled directly, not so much by the law as by the conventions of their immediate owners) determined what benefits slaves should receive. Owners were ordered to provide slaves with a ration of food, clothing and shelter. The working days were regulated and free days and holidays became an accepted part of their working year. This was especially notable with the passage of time. The mid-nineteenth-century slave laws of the American South were more interventionist, more alert to the need to control master as well as man, than the early laws of the British Caribbean. Indeed the very fact of this legal intervention – the fact that the state sought to prescribe what masters could and could not do – was itself a recognition of a central fact in the history of slavery. It was clear to most that slavery did not thrive well solely on subordination and repression.

That slavery was a repressive system is axiomatic. But slaves could not have been kept in place simply or solely by force or by the threats of force. Force had its obvious limitations. To take an obvious example, the physical mutilation of slaves – allowed and specified in many slave laws of the Americas – might horrify the other slaves and caution them against misbehaviour, but it also disabled a valuable labouring asset. Too much flogging would bring on debility and lack of production. Slaves rendered miserable by punishment did not work well. The need, then, was to achieve a balance in the management of slaves; to keep them securely in line but to allow just enough leeway to breed acceptance, if not contentment. It was a precarious balance that could be easily disturbed, often by forces beyond the slave owners' control. Food shortages, poor weather, economic hardship, a new, cruel white overseer, the ravages of disease – all these and more could tip the balance and throw slaves into a truculent mood of foot-dragging, non-cooperation and even resistance. Anyone could try to keep slaves in place by violence and by threats. It took experience and an eye for problems to get the blend right.

Slaves needed rewards to be at their best. Slave societies accepted this fact in the regimes they devised for rewarding slaves. The structure of work itself recognized this fact. Work in the slave fields, as we have seen, needed more than just brute strength. Those slaves who were skilled, those who held responsible positions within the local slave hierarchy, were invariably better-rewarded. Just as the field gangs in the Caribbean provided planters with a perfect tool for socializing slaves to a life of labour, so too did the prospects of promotion, however distant and limited, serve to wed some slaves to the labouring system. Most, of course, rose up and down the labouring structure only as far their physical strength allowed, finding themselves in old age doing the same, simple, undemanding tasks they had undertaken as children. A fortunate few improved themselves within the slave structure, but the greatest measure of slave self-improvement was to be seen not in the slave owners' time, but in the slaves' own plots, gardens and homes.

Slave owners everywhere assumed that slaves were lazy. It was part of the slave condition, almost a defining characteristic. And it was a perceived indolence which could not be broken solely by force. Incentives – rewards of food, clothing and free time – were the lubricants of all slave systems. Of course, all slaves had to be provided for, to be given the basics for human survival. But those items could be donated and withheld at the owner's discretion. They were, in effect, rewards and punishments as much as life's necessities. Slaves were the objects of a system which was itself an exercise in paternal care, a fact reinforced by the regularity with which slave owners and their supporters described slaves as children. The masters and mistresses took it upon themselves to provide the wherewithal of life itself. In return they expected the submission and obedience of a grateful labouring force. It did not always turn out as they planned, of course.

On North American properties, where the ratio of white to black was much lower than in the Caribbean (or Brazil), it was easier for slave owners to know their slaves personally. They showed a personal interest in them and their families in a way which was unthinkable on the bigger Caribbean sugar plantations, where slaves lived out their lives in distant 'African' villages, geographically and socially removed from the white people. Planters in the American South laid great store by looking after their slaves. They often wrote, privately and in public, of the need to provide for the slaves' physical and social welfare. More than that, all the evidence suggests that the material conditions of nineteenth-century American slaves were better than their predecessors in the colonial eastern colonies or in the West Indies. Historians have been able to measure this because we know what clothing and foodstuffs (even luxuries) were given to slaves in most of the slave quarters of the Americas. And it is undoubtedly true that the material circumstances of slavery improved in the course of the nineteenth century. But that was *also* true for labouring people throughout much of the Western world. The early material benefits of industrial growth, the availability of new cheap, personal goods and clothing, the slow but noticeable rise in material consumption on all hands – all this enabled slave owners, like other employers, to bestow on their slaves the kind of material benefits which the slaves' ancestors could not have dreamt of.

Slaves in the American South were healthier and bigger than earlier slaves. With regional exceptions, the material circumstances of their lives, from their cabins to their foods, were superior to those enjoyed by West Indian slaves a century earlier.[29] In addition, the slaves received medical attention (though it remains uncertain whether this helped or hindered their physical well-being).[30] These various material benefits were provided by slave owners partly from a paternal sense of obligation, but also from the acute awareness that it made economic sense to care for their slaves. It was, in effect, part of the deal they struck with the slaves. In return for providing the basics of life, slave owners expected their slaves to fill their side of the bargain: to work, as and when required. Of course, to state the arrangement in this way is to suggest a contract agreed between two equal sides, but, as we know, slavery was not a freely agreed contract. It was a system kept in place 'without consent or contract' on the part of the slaves.[31] Nonetheless, slavery needed persuasion and seduction as well as force to maintain its economic viability. Slaves worked in response to the whip *and* to the material tokens of plantocratic paternalism.

The English-speaking slave systems all displayed remarkable levels of intervention in the slaves' lives. From Barbados in the seventeenth century to Alabama in the nineteenth century, slave owners intruded into the most personal and private areas of their private and social life. It was assumed that slave owners had a right to intervene, to direct and control areas of behaviour normally left to individual choice. Yet, here again was a major curiosity, for slavery, a thoroughly intrusive institution, survived because slaves were allowed distinct (and, in some regions, increasing) areas of independence. It was clear enough that slaves valued their free time, and came to regard it as a customary (if not legally sanctioned) right. They made good the material and social shortcomings of slavery itself by the activities and products fashioned in free time. It was on their weekends, at holidays and seasonal breaks from work that slaves throughout the Americas worked for themselves, cultivated foods, tended animals, made clothing, improved their homes, visited friends and relatives and generally took their pleasures. We will return to these issues later, but their significance here is central, for the slaves' free time was integral to their acceptance of the harsher side of their lives. Free time was granted – and expected – as part return for a life of labour.

Slave owners widely recognized that they could reward their slaves in a number of obvious ways. They could, as we have seen, promote them or give them better or more material rewards. But they could also turn them loose from their drudgeries to do whatever they wanted (within the obvious restraints of any slave system). For all the exceptions and the gross violations, it is clear enough that slave owners recognized that free time was as useful for them as it was important for the slaves. At its simplest, slaves who enjoyed their free time were better suited to returning to the fields. Outsiders were frequently taken aback by the efforts and zest which slaves invested in their free time, especially on the more elaborate high days and feast days. It all seemed such a marked contrast to their generally listless and grudging performance for their owners. Yet it was accepted that one could not exist without the other; the concession of free time was the concomitant of enslaved work itself. It seems a paradox, certainly a curiosity, that slavery seemed to work only because it embraced significant degrees of freedom accorded to the slaves. Here was a system which, though all-intrusive and consuming, required certain liberties to function adequately.

The point is underlined when we recall that much free time served to wed the slaves to their locality. Simply to cultivate their plots and gardens, to commit themselves to the varied activities of their local community, strengthened their commitment to property. It was another element in the socialization of slaves to their local community. They owed no loyalties to masters and their regimes of work. But they developed a sense of local identity and attachment which, unconsciously, served the masters' interests. When slaves were firmly ensconced, with family and community, when they had fashioned their own routines of free-time labours and pleasures, they had in effect become wedded to a local way of life. It was, however, a way of life of their own making, which was important. But even that could be destroyed, at a stroke, by the unpredictable; by random violence, by a slave's intemperate response to provocation, by a planter's upheaval and removal of family members – in short by any of those contingent and haphazard blows of fate which threatened black slaves everywhere.

In all this – the debate about the forces which kept slaves in their place, the debate about how slavery survived apparently against all the odds – we need to think of slavery in all its confusions. Here was a system which was conceived, nurtured and sustained in violence; violence of the most persistent, ubiquitous and pernicious kind. Yet it needed a degree of acceptance on the part of the slaves simply to function. Physical force alone could not maintain a system which pitched armies of disaffected black slaves against a small white minority. Throughout the Caribbean (though less so in North America) the statistics were stacked against the whites, yet, notwithstanding periodic revolts and rumbling resistance, slaves overthrew slavery in only one major outburst (in Haiti). For the rest they were kept in place.

What ultimately kept them in place, of course, was the chemistry of violence, which spread its toxic influence from the African coast, across the Atlantic and into the Americas. Even when violence was kept in reserve, it cast a sinister shadow across all slave proceedings. But, to repeat, violence alone is not a sufficient explanation for the durability and success of the slave systems of the Americas. Slaves were kept in place by a curious mix of violence and benefits; of stinging blows (and worse) and rewards. True, the rewards were, in retrospect, meagre and the most important rewards were, on the whole, self-made. But it was the tolerance (however grudging) of slaves' independent culture, especially of their material culture and their calendar of festivals and recreations, which enabled slaves to shape autonomous spheres of activity. And it was here that we see slaves making their own lives tolerable. From the time and circumstances they were granted, or which they secured, slaves shaped an independent world which seemed to owe little to their owners.

Slave autonomy was at once disliked and yet tolerated by slave owners, who came to appreciate that it formed a safety valve in a society fraught with serious tensions. There were, of course, exceptions to this rule – men who saw no reason to grant their slaves anything but the sweat of work and painful domination – but it is surely instructive that such men were themselves often disliked and feared by other slave owners. Slave unrest and unhappiness was contagious, likely to simmer locally before spreading to other slaves. Rogue planters and slave owners were almost as dangerous to the generality of other slave owners as disruptive and troublesome slaves, for they had it in their power to give slaves cause and occasion to unite. It was important for all to grant slaves conventional rights which would complement their labours. Without those moments of freedom, labour might falter or be rendered fruitless. It may seem strange, but it is nevertheless true, that areas of slave independence played their role in the broad disciplining of slave communities. Obedience (though rarely loyalty) could not be secured simply by the lash.

5

COLOUR, RACE AND
SUBJUGATION

Slavery in the Americas was based on people who were, over-whelmingly, black. In its mature form (the timing of which varied greatly from one place to another), slavery had brought into being large black populations whose sole purpose was to serve the economic interests of small local white élites. The formula looks simple and seems easily explained. White landowners and pioneers employed Africans and their local-born descendants to break-open and develop swathes of the Americas. Slave owners also needed to explain and justify the use of slave labour. Often those justifications were couched in terms of race, asserting the unique suitability of people of African descent to labour in tropical and semitropical regions. Yet other people also worked at the same tasks, especially in the early days of settlement. Europeans, Indians, Africans – and mixes of all of them – worked side by side in pioneering labour throughout the Americas. By the time the slave economies had matured, however – when sugar dominated in the Caribbean, tobacco the Northern colonies, and cotton the US South – slaves alone were thought fit for much of the local field work. More than that, the slaves were black and it came to be assumed that blackness denoted slavery; to be black was to be a slave. But why was that the case? After all, many other slave societies did *not* distinguish their slaves by colour or ethnicity. Yet maybe the best-known feature of New World slavery – perhaps because its consequences live on to the present-day – is its link to race – or at least to colour.

As we have seen, there were enormous differences between various slave societies in the Americas. The most basic of divisions was that suggested by Philip Morgan between a *slave-owning* society, where some slaves exist, and a *slave society*, where

72

slavery 'is *the* determinative institution'. Relations between black and white varied greatly between these two types of societies. In the former, relations tended to be less formal and more easy-going (for example, in the early frontier days of settlement). Roles for blacks were more varied (they were not expected, for instance, to fulfil one particular role) and sexual relations tended to be more open. But in slave societies, strict legal and social conventions severely restricted slaves' movements and choices. Likewise their economic role – and sexual freedoms – were more strictly defined and controlled.[1] Though some societies changed from one type to another, the evolution of the major slave-owning societies in the hemisphere had implications, in time, for blacks throughout the region. Slavery became a defining institution, creating the image that to be black was to be a slave. Such a close and formative link between race and slavery had not necessarily been true of earlier slave societies.

There had been a host of slave societies where race had played an important role in defining slavery, or in defining relations between master and slave. In Islamic societies, for example, black Africans were treated quite differently from European or Turkish slaves. In Asia, a number of slave societies viewed darker-skinned peoples as inferior. It was common for slave-owning élites to decry and hold in low esteem the physical characteristics of people they used as slaves. Of course, since slaves were often imported great distances from very different societies, they inevitably looked different (swarthy, for example, where their masters were blond). Even in classical slavery, race played a more significant role than is often accepted. Slaves in classical Greece and Rome were obtained from the far reaches of their respective empires, and many of them therefore looked quite different. Slave owners also displayed racial preferences in the ways they treated their slaves, especially African ones. Naturally enough, the evidence from the classical world is sparse and sometimes equivocal, but there is little doubt that Africans were the object of dislike, disdain and a degree of prejudice.[2] But this was qualitatively different from the nature of racial relationships which emerged in the slave societies of the Americas.

Sometimes this formula (of hostility to darker people) was turned upside down. Black slaves were occasionally prized for their exotic qualities; their blackness offering a sharp contrast to the prevailing qualities of fairness prized by the slave owners.

73

Elsewhere, fair slaves were prized above black slaves.[3] But in most of these cases the key distinction was the ethnic difference between slave owners and slaves. Generally, it seems that people were reluctant to enslave people perceived to be from their own ethnic group. When they did, they categorized those slaves as outsiders; redefining categories to ensure that they, and their slaves, were distinct and separate. When that could not be done, enslaved peoples (often captured in fighting) were killed, or sold outside the region. It was precisely this phenomenon which yielded such rich bounty to the Europeans in Africa, as Africans sold their captives for movement and sale to the white slave traders on the coast.

It was in the Americas, however, that the links between race and slavery were most effectively forged. At first demand for labour in the Americas was colour-blind. As we have seen, the initial forays into the Americas – especially in the northern colonies – centred on indentured labour. Half of all the whites who settled in Barbados in the 1630s and 1640s were indentured, bound for five to seven years. Sometimes they were auctioned in the island, much like Africans at a later date. But they had rights, prescribed by local laws, and their bondage was limited – quite unlike the Africans.[4] In the same period (1630–1680), of the 75,000 white migrants to the Chesapeake (primarily to work in the burgeoning tobacco industry), between 50 and 75 per cent were indentured servants – poor unskilled youths unable to make their way in the world and propelled to the New World by a mix of desperation and hope.[5] There was no contemporary moral compulsion against indentured labour. The British – and other Europeans – accepted unfree labour as part of the normal, unquestioned 'way of the world'. Tens of thousands were consigned to bondage, as legal punishment, or by freely signing away their liberties, and few, in the seventeenth century, thought this odd or immoral. But indentured servants were *not* slaves. And, though many were Irish or Scottish (and therefore low in English social and political esteem), they were not black. Planters, however, needed labour that was more long-term; labour that could be managed more intrusively, was more durable (lasted longer – or could be replaced easily), and was cheap. For all these reasons – and more – Africans began to arrive in ever greater numbers.

In 1670 there were about 40,000 slaves in Maryland and

Virginia; ten years before there had been a mere 1,700. Over the next century, a further 100,000 Africans were imported into the region. But even these astonishing figures pale when we look at the Caribbean. In the century after 1710, a quarter of a million Africans were imported into Barbados. In Jamaica – bigger, wilder, less controlled – the figures for the same period reached 600,000.[6] These armies of Africans gave New World slavery its human face, but the British *already* had distinctive and pejorative views about black humanity, *even before* the emergence of chattel slavery in British America.

Blackness had powerful – and negative – cultural assumptions for English-speakers. Here was a colour (though, of course, it was more a spectrum of shades of darkness) which suggested dirt, sin and evil. The colour black stood in contrast to a range of cultural values associated with whiteness; with purity, goodness, virtue and beauty. Africans were black – so were sin and ugliness. Europeans were white; as were purity and beauty. While it is tempting to overstate this polarity, here was a conflict about the most deeply held cultural values which found a particular form in the apparent differences between two species of humanity, black and white.[7] Equally important, in British eyes, Africans were savage. There were few aspects of African life (such as it was known by contemporary Britons) which accorded with British perceptions of civilization. Africans were beyond sympathetic comprehension; barbarous people plucked from a barbarous continent and ideally suited to the demands of labouring in the Americas. Worse still – but important, because it served to compound other British attitudes towards Africans – they were heathen; un-Christian and therefore even further beyond the pale. Thus did the Africans provide a focus for an accumulation of cultural antipathies, serving to divide them utterly from the British (and, in different ways, from other Europeans). But, of all these distinctions, the one which was most obvious, most inescapable (and easiest to blame as the source of all other vices), was the question of colour.

This bundle of attitudes towards black humanity formed the context for the development of relations between black and white in the English-speaking Americas. Many historians have claimed that in practice the treatment of the Africans differed little, initially, from the treatment of poor indentured workers. But there *was* a major difference, for Africans were *already* being treated as slaves *long before* the development of slavery in the English colonies. English sailors had been buying and selling slaves on the African coast and shipping them into the Spanish Americas long before the early English settlement of Barbados or Virginia. It is true that those early slave ventures were speculative, small-scale and uncertain, and scarcely comparable to the subsequent massive movement of peoples. Nonetheless, the English were treating Africans as things, as items of trade, long before they settled their own colonies. Nor was this merely a matter of piratical adventurers interloping into the monopoly trades of Iberians, for those early English slave deals had the financial backing and the tacit political sanction of the English Crown and Court.

In the last years of the reign of Elizabeth I, the Queen bowed to objectors who complained that there too many blacks *in London*. There were, said the royal document, 'already here to manie'. In a subsequent Proclamation, Elizabeth ordered all blacks to be shipped out of England; they offended the English (caused 'great annoyance of her own liege people'), consumed scarce foodstuffs and, 'the most of them are infidels, having no understanding of Christ or his Gospel'.[8] During the reign of her Stuart successors, however, the small numbers of blacks in London inevitably increased as a by-product of English slave-trading to Africa. Spaniards, Portuguese and Dutch all wanted slaves, and English traders sought to oblige. In 1651, London officers of the Guinea Company asked one of their captains, 'We pray you buy for us 15 or 20 young lusty Negers of about 15 years of age, bring them home with you for London.' As a precaution, the ship was equipped with '30 pairs of shackles and boults for such of your negers as are rebellious . . .'[9] Time and again, ships returned *to England* with a small number of African slaves, to be sold and used normally as domestic servants. They were the material possessions of people for whom an African servant provided a fashionable *cachet*. There was, of course, more to this than the mere baubles of fashion. The whole edifice of fashionable domestic service hinged on the concept of the African *as a thing*. After all, most of the Africans who served in England were originally slaves.

English society was, then, predisposed to regard Africans as culturally different and inferior. Of course this could be said of many (possibly most) outsiders, including many from the Celtic fringe. But there was a qualitatively different attitude towards Africans and their local descendants. Black humanity had a special place in cultural demonology. From classical texts, biblical references, early travel accounts to Africa and, later, from the evidence about imported Africans, the English acquired concepts of black humanity which were more mythical than real. Not surprisingly, when Africans appeared in Tudor and Elizabethan drama and literature, they were generally portrayed as villains who were at once both lascivious and untrustworthy. Most notably, Africans were portrayed as especially sexual beings, blessed with a physique and passion which distinguished them from others.

When English maritime explorers made early contact with West Africa, they took with them these and other cultural attitudes about black humanity. Not surprisingly, they returned home with stories and accounts which confirmed and embellished, rather than dispelled, prevailing myths. Time and again, returning sailors, their stories published and reissued in a variety of popular forms, told amazing tales about Africans, people 'we now caule Moores, Moorans, or Negroes, a people of beastly lynyage, without a god, law, religion or common wealth . . . '. They lived in a region where it was so hot that they were 'so scorched and vexed with the heate of the soone, that in many places they curse it when it ryseth'.[10] Here was a colour, stark blackness, which represented much that the English viewed as distasteful: dirtiness, ugliness, sin and carnality. It was simple to assume that the environment was to blame, that the heat and the sun caused this human blackness. It also offered proof of the biblical story that, in Africa, there was evidence of God's curse on Ham for having gazed on his father's nakedness. Such explanations were, of course, flawed. They were not so much cast-iron, sufficient theories but rather broadly based cultural reactions which spread widely and rapidly and came to form the cultural backcloth for the rise of chattel slavery.

When the first Englishmen sold Africans to other Europeans for work in the Americas, economic opportunity fused with cultural preconceptions. At first it was an *ad hoc* affair, only taking on formal and full legal construction when the English settled their own colonies in the early seventeenth century. But the early English Atlantic slave trade formed an important cultural and trading precedence. Long before Englishmen living in Virginia and Barbados decided that their interests were best served by African labour, their fellow countrymen had *already* come to regard Africans as immutably different and inferior; people who owed little to the family of civilized mankind. It was easy to point to the Africans' colour as an explanation for that whole range of cultural differences which the English employed to justify and explain their growing reliance on slaves in the Atlantic economy. Here was *post hoc* rationalization emerging to justify economic practice. What had once been mere cultural prejudice was henceforth offered as a rationale for a vast and growing commercial enterprise. In fact, the real justification for that enterprise was profit. What made Africans ideal for the Americas was their cost and ease of replacement, not their colour. But it helped those Englishmen involved in the trade to justify African slavery in racial terms – or, initially, in terms of colour.

Of course, there were exceptions to prevailing ideas; people who did not accept the association between colour and inferiority. In 1694, Captain Thomas Phillips claimed that Africans should not be despised for their colour, 'being what they cannot help'.

> I can't think there is any intrinsick value in one colour more than another, not that white is better than black, only we think so because we are so, and are prone to judge favourably in our own case.[11]

The Presbyterian Richard Baxter told the planters in 1673,

> . . . how cursed a crime it is to equal men to beasts? Is not this your practice? Do you not buy them and use them merely to the same end as you do your horses; to labour for your commoditiy, as if they were baser than you and made to serve you? Do you not see how you reproach and condemn yourselves, while you vilify them as savages and barbarous wretches?[12]

Such critical views were advanced especially by a small band of divines, perhaps most notably by George Fox, founder of the Quakers. Another, Morgan Godwyn, a minister in both Virginia and Barbados, was fiercely critical of slavery he had seen in the colonies. His pamphlet, *The Negro and Indians Advocate* of 1680 sought '*to prove the* Negro's Humanity, *and to shew that neither their* Complexion *nor Bondage, Descent not Country, can be any im-*

pediment thereto.' Godwyn denounced the plantocratic claims that blacks could not be human because they were black:

> their *Complexion,* which being the most obvious to the sight, . . . is apt to make no *slight* impressions upon rude Minds, already prepared to admit of any thing for *Truth* which shall make for Interest . . . [13]

Such critical views of chattel slavery were outflanked by the rapid rise of the plantations and the material bounty they yielded on all hands. While planters and slave traders were the most obvious material beneficiaries, so too were the British consumers who devoured the fruits of slave labours in such growing profusion.[14] Much more strident, vociferous and successful, in the short term at least, was the argument of the slave lobby. It was, however, the sheer weight of slave numbers which clinched the planters' case. By the time of Godwyn's tract, the association had been firmly established: '(These two words, Negro and Slave being by custom grown Homogeneous and convertible . . .)'.[15] By then the association was simply a recognition of fact, for tens of thousands of Africans were now scattered throughout the English colonies.

In the eighteenth century, it was important for slave owners to deny the claims of black humanity and to resist demands that they convert and Christianize their slaves. To admit slaves to the brotherhood of the church was to accord them an equality that might conflict with the claims that they were people destined by origins and race to a humbler, less-than-human role in life. Of course, plantocratic ideology is best seen in its starkest form in the daily, brutal operation of their properties, and took its most clearly defined form in the legal system they erected around them. There was, however, a more public and metropolitan aspect of that ideology, in the form of pro-slavery tracts and pamphlets, growing in volume as the eighteenth century advanced, which was aimed at the reading public on both sides of the Atlantic. Time and again, these plantocratic tracts turned to the issue of colour and race.

It is surely instructive that the terminology had begun to change. The early terms 'Moors', 'Blackamoors' and 'Ethiopians' slowly gave way to the generic 'blacks' or 'Blacks'. In part this was obviously a result of the development of black communities born in the Americas, not in Africa. Now, when whites described, wrote about or cursed their slaves, they increasingly used the language of race and colour. It was claimed, in 1684, that slave overseers beat their slaves 'and the best words they can afford us, are, *Dam'd Doggs, Black ugly Devils, idle Sons of Ethiopian Whores,* and the like'.[16]

The key to the transmutation of the African from an object of cultural curiosity, viewed as inferior and beyond the pale, to being regarded as an object – a non-person – was the story of plantation slavery and its consequences for African enslavement and transportation. It was a process which was reflected in the changes in the law. London and colonial legislatures conjured forth appropriate legislation which left the mark of property on the African. Acts which, for example, governed the slave trade specifically designated Africans as property. So did colonial legislation, legal commentators and the common-law judgements of a host of English judges. In the words of the Solicitor General in 1677, 'negroes ought to be esteemed goods and commodities within the Acts of Trade and Navigation'.

When an Englishman mentioned a black servant in his will in 1700, he declared, 'I take [him] to be in the nature and quality of my goods and chattels.'[17] There were, however, social and legal confusions about this issue in England. How could a country committed to a concept of freedom (secured through the seventeenth-century Revolution) allow slavery to exist at home? There was no such quandary in colonial North America. The slave as property – for all the worrying problems, the inconsistencies and contradictions – was the fulcrum on which the grand design of colonial slavery turned so profitably for all (save the slaves).

This part of the historical formula is well-known. Less frequently discussed, however, is the manner in which arguments about race were used to justify and support an economic system so important to British well-being. It was understandable that planters and the slave lobby should seek confirmation for their activities in whatever evidence came to hand. And it was available, in abundance, from within the squalid conditions which they had created in the slave colonies. Each and every personal and communal slave shortcoming was illustrated and discussed; repeated in print, in political debate (in London and the colonies), and offered as evidence and proof of the slaves' predestined inability to be anything other than a slave. It was, of course a circular argument: treat people like slaves, and they behave like slaves. Planters (and their hired writers), however, were able to adorn their case with theories of race. Not content simply to describe black life in the slave quarters as proof of the need for slavery, they sought to persuade their readers that it was also proof of the slaves' immutable racial inferiority.

The plantocratic case was successful in that it won over to its side a growing body of highly influential writers and thinkers who repeated, in transmuted form, ideas about black humanity derived from stories, rumours and tittle-tattle from the slave lobby. In this way the slave lobby first secured the high ground in a public, printed debate which emerged from the mid-eighteenth century. Many of their assertions were subsequently repeated and proffered to the reading public as serious social observation by writers whose authority was greater than their expertise.

There were, it is true, voices of dissent (generally of Dissent) who refused to relinquish their belief that Africans and their offspring were human. But there were many more voices (some of them influential) adding to the late seventeenth- and eighteenth-century clamour that the African was a lesser being, destined by inferiority to a life of toil for the whites. It was most famously proposed by David Hume in 1753: 'There never was a civilized nation of any other complexion than white . . . ' Hume brushed aside rumours of a famous contemporary black in Jamaica: ''tis likely he is admired for very slender accomplishments, like a parrot, who speaks a few words plainly.'[18] By then, of course, the facts of the American slave empires were well-known and were clear enough for all to see. British life itself had, in the form of American produce, been transformed by the slaves, and thousands of blacks had found themselves cast ashore in Britain as slaves, servants and labourers.

No one could doubt that mid-eighteenth-century Britain was a society closely linked to the slave empires. Its myriad ports dispatched and received hundreds of ships each year from Africa and the Americas, British social life was lubricated by slave-grown produce, and tens of thousands of men spent time in the slave colonies, notably in the merchant and Royal Navy, in government and in trade and commerce. On top of this, there were few areas of the British economy which remained untouched, either as producers or consumers, by the Atlantic slave empire. It was virtually impossible to remain ignorant of the role slavery played in British life. Thus, when the question of slavery surfaced in the press – as it did with increasing regularity – it did so not as a topic of distant, colonial and marginal interest, but as a question with which large numbers of people were familiar, directly or indirectly.

It was understandable that Africans and their descendants should be a subject of recurring curiosity in the mid- and late eighteenth century. They were, at once, an obvious source of much British prosperity, yet they remained beyond the pale; familiar, yet distanced by a powerful cultural tradition and by the distortions fashioned by slavery itself. The forces which served to keep black humanity at intellectual arm's length (even when individual blacks were socially close to hand) were galvanized by the slave lobby, to seduce the reader with tales of black inferiority. If that issue could be kept firmly in focus – if the reader could be persuaded of the immutability of black inferiority – the ideology of slavery was safe. Thus it was, from the mid-eighteenth century onwards, that men with experience of the slave colonies began to add the voice of colonial experience to older, speculative assertions about black inferiority. Here lay the foundations of a debate about race which derived from the experience of the slave empire and was, in turn, used to promote and to defend that same slave system.

In part, the racial debate about slavery was prompted by a growing concern about the settlement of blacks – slave and free – in England itself.[19] The rise of a black population, much of it free, provided living refutation of much of the plantocratic thesis. Such people (mainly men) had shaken off the stereotypical roles of slavery, had secured their freedom and exhibited those personal qualities of civilized and socially acceptable behaviour admired by the English. Many were literate, many devout. Many served faithfully in positions of sensibility, as trusted domestic servants expected to behave with decorum and tact in the most fashionable of circles. Though there were plenty of poor, ignorant blacks in eighteenth-century London, their more sophisticated peers caught the eye and threatened to damage the basic arguments of the plantocratic lobby. Here was proof enough that black humanity was indeed educable to English norms; they could be socialized to forms of behaviour acceptable to even the most refined of English people. Blacks were not, then, necessarily destined for the inevitable and unavoidable life of helots to their white masters. The history of blacks in late eighteenth-century London revealed the flaws in plantocratic theories, and for that reason alone (though there are plenty of others) they incurred the most bitter and vituperative of racial abuse from the slave lobby.

It was a curious matter. Though there were armies of slaves scattered across the Americas, it was a small band of blacks in London which incurred some of the most hostile commentary in the mid and late years of the eighteenth century. They were, of course, heirs of a sense of hostility which traced its roots to a more innocent period of curiosity. Now, they provided a focus for a debate of a much broader significance. As that debate unfolded – with associated efforts to remove the black community from London and 'back' to Africa – the question of race surfaced as never before. Indeed, henceforth the problem of slavery was suffused with the issue of race.

Arguments about the relationship between race and slavery surfaced at much the same time on both sides of the Atlantic. They did so throughout the English-speaking world because slavery itself came under scrutiny at the same time. The philosophical and political debate about slavery flourished in both London and Philadelphia because men in both cities were forced to confront the problems posed by slavery in the same years. The most immediate catalyst was the American Revolution with its far-reaching debate about the rights of man and about theories of the nature of government. It was a debate which drew into its intellectual vortex older debates about human organization – none more pressing and confusing than slavery itself. In North America, where the revolution prompted a debate about the complex issues of social and political rights, how could slavery be justified? And, as slavery came under attack in London and Philadelphia the competing sides drew upon data from the slave societies and from existing theories about the nature of mankind, to find evidence for their case. Not surprisingly, it proved to be a confusing debate.[20]

For a start, relations between black and white were not always hostile or violent, even in societies closely related to slavery. In London, for instance, relations were remarkably flexible. But that had also been true at a number of points in the early Americas. Where slaves were in a minority, and especially in the years of settlement, black and white worked together with no barriers about who did what. In the words of Peter Wood, they 'shared the crude and egalitarian intimacies inevitable on a frontier'.[21] This communalism was gradually undermined: Africans had to be treated differently. The major distinction lay in the fact that they were unfree, and this central fact determined what could be done with them. Conversely, the fact that indentured servants had areas of freedom (and would ultimately become fully free) limited what could be done with them. Thus, there evolved distinct areas of treatment: what was appropriate for slaves was inappropriate for whites. Gradually, these distinctions were enshrined in local laws. And, of course, in those regions – most notably the Caribbean – where slaves greatly outnumbered whites, the divide between black and white became ever more stark. But the theories followed the facts. Whatever rationale was offered for distinguishing between black and white – in law, in management, in social classification – it took the form of justification for what had already emerged.

In the last thirty years of the eighteenth century the need to justify slavery became more urgent and pronounced for the simple reason that, quite suddenly, slavery seemed to have enemies on all hands. For a century and more, its critics had been voices in the wilderness; cogent, prominent and sometimes persuasive, but generally ignored as the Western world was propelled forward on a wave of slave-based prosperity and material well-being. It was the late eighteenth-century attacks on slavery, from all angles, that conjured forth pro-slavery defensive theories. And one of the easiest pro-slavery cards to play was race.

The question of race began to emerge as a *central* issue in the debate about slavery between the slave lobby and a growing band of people opposed to slavery. But this was very late in the day. Debates about race and colour had been a mere descant in the origins and spread of black slavery into the Americas. However, when – in the years during and after the American Revolution – a new language of social and human rights evolved, images of race were conjured forth by the slave lobby to counter the potent vernacular of human rights. Again, the debate took place on both sides of the Atlantic. In London, an abolitionist campaign was launched, after 1787, which secured a popular base across the face of urban (especially dissenting) Britain. The main purpose was to end the slave trade, and their main opponents were the shippers and absentee planters who, through the agency of the West India lobby, peppered the British people with tracts and pamphlets dripping with racial abuse. It was in this debate that we can see the flowering of plantocratic racism, leaving the British readership with a set of caricatured images which went well beyond most previously published material. It was extremist literature, and it was published on a massive scale.

The British debate about the slave trade prompted the most abusive plantocratic defence to date. Initially the most severe arguments were (after the 1772 Somerset case) about the need to keep blacks out of Britain. In the arguments about preserving the British from 'contamination', the pamphleteers began to stray into a debate about race. Samuel Estwick's tract of 1772 proposed a law which would 'preserve the race of Britons from stain and contamination'.[22] He was in no doubt that humanity was divided into groups and subgroups, and Africans and their descendants were at the lowest level of creation. Even more vituperative (and influenced by Estwick) was Edward Long, Jamaican planter, former Jamaican official and ferocious proponent of an early plantocratic racism. In pamphlet, and later in his *History of Jamaica*, Long provided the extreme racial interpretation of mankind. Long, like others, believed that 'the White and the Negroe are two distinct species'. Africans looked and smelt different and there was nothing about their personal or social organizations which suggested they were capable of civilized life. Cruel to their offspring, especially lustful, more animal than human in their appetites, they were, thought Long, closer to the animal kingdom than to humanity. Africa, he concluded, was the 'parent of everything that is monstrous in nature'.[23] Throughout his diatribe, Long spoke about 'the Negro race'[24] and simply assumed that his readers would accept his categories of mankind (even if they did not share his political conclusions).

In the flurry of tracts in the last two decades of the eighteenth century, and as the British slave lobby stumbled to marshal its case against the early abolitionist attacks on the slave trade, such arguments were thrown at the British reading public in growing abundance. Colonial officials, returning planters (of whom there were plenty), contemporary writers – all and more joined in the publishing rush to defend Britain's vast investment in the slave economy by denigrating the slaves. To concede black equality was to undermine the very basis on which so much British well-being depended. Thus did the political germ of racial thinking, asserted in the 1770s, blossom in the 1780s and 1790s into a more recognizably familiar phenomenon. The case was simple enough: if slaves were freed, they would take over the plantations and, like planters before them, eventually set up home in Britain – with all the dire social consequences debated in the 1770s. Black freedom – the end of the slave empires – would undermine British prosperity and transform the British people by the process of 'contamination' between the races. It was to 'preserve the race of Britons' from such intermingling that the slave lobby's supporters advocated a ban on black immigration. Throughout the debate, however, the classification of 'race' had become unquestioned. It was a category of mankind accepted by both sides as relevant and unchallenged.[25]

There was a curious twist to this argument, however, because, since the early days of colonial settlements, whites had fathered children by their slaves throughout the colonies. Distinct social groups had emerged, especially in the Caribbean, from the relations between black and white, and the compilers of demographic data had to count the 'coloured', as well as the white and black, populations. Acceptable perhaps in the unusual circumstances of colonial life – especially when local life was dominated by slavery – such arrangements were unimaginable in Britain. It is true that there had been various attempts to prohibit sexual relations between black and white, and by 1750 all the mainland slave colonies had legislated against it. In all the colonies it caused tension and concern. Yet the West Indians were more at ease with the phenomenon, as Edward Long remarked in 1774:

> he who should presume to shew any displeasure against such a thing as simple fornication, would for his pains be accounted a simple blockhead; since not one in twenty can be persuaded that there is either sin, or shame in co-habiting with his slave.[26]

Visitors to the two slave regions – colonial North America and the West Indies – were struck by the differences. Americans slept with their slaves in great secrecy, whereas West Indians flaunted the fact that they did so.

Planters disliked in theory what they enjoyed in private. Keen to seek physical pleasure with their slaves, they were less keen to concede the right to others (and were revolted by the idea that white women might find similar comfort with slave men). But,

86

whatever the social realities, relations between black and white were presented, as a *racial* issue, in the debate about black freedom which ebbed and flowed in Britain between 1772 and 1838. Increasingly the debate was couched in terms of race and a language of race evolved – much of it in code – derived in large part from the assumptions of planters and providing a rich vein to be tapped by subsequent writers and theorists. In the debate which flickered and flared in the campaign for black freedom, especially in the 1820s and 1830s and in the tortured aftermath of British emancipation (from 1838 to the mid-1860s), race was a central issue.[27]

Firmly established in the last decades of the eighteenth century as a central plank in the slave lobby's defence, race remained a critical question long after British slavery had ended. In large part this was because abolitionists, in pitching their case as a demand for complete black equality ('Am I not a man and a brother?' 'Am I not a woman and a sister?'), elevated expectations to an unrealistic level. Remove the artificial restraints of slavery, they claimed, and black society would thrive like any other. Of course this utterly ignored the distorting consequences of slavery itself. People shipped abroad and raised as slaves knew little, in some cases nothing, of life as free industrious workers. How could they transmute themselves, at a stroke, into the hard-working free peasantry the abolitionists predicted and expected? Few recognized that black freedom would herald major dislocations and readjustments for the ex-slaves. In the event, black freedom in the Caribbean was swiftly followed by economic collapse, as the dominant sugar industry – deprived of imperial protection – slid into an apparent terminal decline, leaving ex-slaves clinging as best they could, as free peasants, to the wreckage of the system their forebears had created and made profitable. When the ex-slave lobby and the critics of black freedom looked at the British West Indies in the mid-nineteenth century they saw confirmation of everything they had predicted: that blacks were indeed fundamentally flawed. Former slaves, they felt, had proved themselves incapable of application, industry and civilized life, preferring instead the easily acquired fruits of tropical living. The West Indian black peasantry of the mid- (and late) nineteenth century provided living confirmation of the confused racist assertions of the old slave lobby. And, to add strength to the plantocratic elbow, new 'scientific' theories were to hand to lend plausibility to older arguments about race.

The nineteenth-century rise of modern science, and especially the evolution of anthropology, with its particular interest in the categorization of mankind, drew upon many of the issues embedded in the earlier pro- and anti-slavery debates. Various European scientists absorbed existing data when they devised their own classifications for the animal and human kingdoms. Anatomists and anthropologists, botanists and naturalists – all, and more, scrutinized humanity and drew their own particular conclusions about the distinctiveness of different subgroups and subspecies. The more they looked, the more it seemed clear that blacks were utterly different, removed by physiology and social organization from the general fraternity of mankind. Of course there was a rich and often confusing variety of views and findings. But there was a pronounced consensus that black humanity occupied the lowest rung of human evolution, qualitatively removed from white society by inherent inferiorities which were a function of their racial grouping. These origins of scientific racism were to haunt intellectual life for the rest of the nineteenth century, and were to become a potent and destructive force in the twentieth.[28] Indeed, the scientific and intellectual credentials of scientific racism were not utterly discredited until the mid-twentieth century.

At crucial points, these developments were inextricably linked to slavery. It was the Atlantic slave economy which provided a focus and an inspiration for many of the ideas and debates about race which surfaced at a much later date. Of course, slavery was not the *only* issue involved. European expansion and imperial control had brought white society into contact (and conflict) with a host of societies around the world, and all posed problems of explanation for the growing band of scientists and polemicists interested in race. Slavery, however, posed unique problems, not least because, in essence, many of the justifications for slavery were at heart questions of race; problems defined by the classification of black mankind as distinct, separate and inferior beings, inevitably anchored at the base of the human family by their defining racial characteristics. It was the *purpose* of the slave lobby to ensure that black humanity – in the form of their slaves – would indeed remain anchored at the base of society. Slaves were the very foundations on which their

commercial prosperity depended. If the slave lobby could persuade outsiders – especially that growing body of British people who were increasingly interested in slavery – that slaves
were inevitably trapped by race, the case for slavery would be
more easily secured. It was to be an extraordinary paradox that,
even though politically defeated (the slave trade was abolished
in 1807, slavery in 1838), this plantocratic racism was to prove
more durable and more influential than its proponents ever
imagined.

As we have seen, it was no accident that slavery in North
America came under scrutiny at much the same time as the West
Indian variant. For much of its early history, slavery in colonial
mainland America provoked little moral debate. There were, of
course, the inevitable problems – notably legal conflicts – which
raised worrying questions. But few challenged slavery's right to
exist in the fledgling societies of North America. American
Independence inevitably prompted more serious debate, not
least because the rights claimed by Americans in their dispute
with the British might be applicable to black as well as white.
When slavery was critically examined in the political upheavals
of the 1760s and 1770s, it was understandable that slavery's proponents should argue their case strenuously.[29]

This American debate was, of course, part of that more
broadly based debate about rights and representation which,
rooted in Enlightenment writing, rippled throughout the
Western world. In the process, a gulf began to open up between
Old World habits and assumptions, and modern, 'enlightened'
ideas. Cruelty and pain of all sorts (public executions, cruelty to
animals – and slavery) found themselves under critical scrutiny
as never before. Many of the old patterns of social organization
seemed flawed, few more fundamentally than the dependence
on slaves. Despite what the slave lobby had claimed for decades,
slaves were clearly people capable of higher things. More than
that, prevailing economic orthodoxy itself might be flawed.
Perhaps it made greater economic sense to use free, not slave,
labour? The publication of Adam Smith's *The Wealth of Nations* –
whose plea for economic freedom was congruent with the wider
freedom extolled by other Enlightenment writers – coincided
with the American Revolution. Stated crudely, freedoms of all
sorts were on the political agenda as rarely before. Nor was it
coincidence that the first organized activists against slavery were

Quakers, a sect attached to industrious and individual free enterprise, for whom freedom to worship was of a piece with their
freedom to work and trade as they saw fit.[30]

There were, then, a series of converging forces which focused
criticism on slavery in North America. Slavery had surfaced as
a moral, religious and economic question. And that question
was debated as never before during and after the convulsions of
the American Revolution. Warfare enabled slaves to flee, to join
the British side (the more unlucky ones ending up as free blacks
in Nova Scotia, London and finally Sierra Leone) and to settle
old scores. The Revolutionary upheavals severely shook the
foundations of slavery in North America. During the
Revolutionary War, imports of slaves had stopped, a number of
states had outlawed slavery, and elsewhere abolitionist agitation had made great political strides. More and more Americans
agreed with the Attorney General of Maryland who claimed in
1788 that slavery was ' . . . inconsistent with the *genius* of *repub-
licanism* and has a tendency to *destroy* those *principles* on which
it is *supported* . . . '[31]

Such views proved to be a false abolitionist dawn. Within a
generation, slavery had emerged stronger than ever. Henceforth,
slave owners were more willing and more capable of defending
their rights to own slaves and found it persuasive to pitch their
claims on racial grounds. Of course, such arguments were often
mere symbols for claims of a different order; of power based on
overweening economic strength, on the need for social control
and discipline. But it was easier – simple, and rooted in a familiar intellectual tradition – to couch the arguments in racial terms.
The end result of the Revolution was that both sides 'helped to
make race the central excuse for slavery'.[32]

Despite the debates about slavery in the Revolution, the suc-
ceeding years saw an expansion of slavery in the USA. In 1790
there were 697,897 slaves, but twenty years later this figure had
increased to 1,191,354. On the eve of the Civil War, the figure
stood at almost 4,000,000, by which time slavery had seeped
halfway across the continent and had been adopted in nine new
states.[33] The South was enslaved (when the North was free) and
it was a slavery which thrived on, and enabled the lucrative cultivation of, cotton. It was, however, a slavery which was out of
step with the rest of the hemisphere – with some notable exceptions – and certainly out of step with the abolitionist sentiment

throughout much of the English-speaking world. Under attack from Northern critics and from the British, whose earlier slaving instincts had, after 1838, been transmuted into a vigorous and self-righteous crusade for global abolition, the slave-owning South effected a defence of slavery which, once again, made lavish use of old racial stereotypes. And from the old ideas about race, transformed by the demands of the new cotton economy, there emerged a form of racism which, though rooted in and focused on slavery, was to establish a malevolence which was to disfigure American life thereafter.

The intellectual and political momentum against slavery flagged under the weight of the undeniable material bounty which flowed from the cotton fields. Nor was the USA the only beneficiary. Britain's textile industry absorbed much of the slave-grown cotton. But criticism persisted and, in its turn, evoked a defence of slavery which embraced many of the themes familiar to any student of the Caribbean two generations earlier. From the 1820s onwards, slavery in the South found itself attacked on all sides, but especially from the North. Slavery seemed to its critics to stand in the way of the development of the South, its denial of freedom of labour flying in the face of the prevailing economic orthodoxy of freedom in all things economic. The South seemed frozen in time, a reminder of a world that had vanished in all but the most retrogade parts of the world. By the early and mid-nineteenth century, slavery was an institution which was out of step with the prevailing social and political sensibility of the modernizing world.[34]

Slave owners were now obliged to defend their system as never before. The simplest line of defence was necessity. Who else would do the vital work? And what would happen to slaves if freed? It was unthinkable that they should be released as free agents into a 'white man's country'.[35] Here was a plea to a sense of basic racial unease which was to prove a potent force during and after slavery. What role could black humanity play in a society fashioned for white people? This was very different from the Caribbean, where blacks were in an overwhelming majority and where they, not the whites, formed the demographic core of local society. There were other defences of slavery, most notably religious (understandably, since much of the criticism of slavery came from Northern churches). But, above all else, it was *race* which proved the most frequent and most ubiquitous of Southern pro-slavery arguments.

In common with the pattern in Britain, the racist support for slavery quickly appropriated the latest twists and turns in scientific thought. It was as if the new sciences had emerged with slavery in mind, for so much of their data – both physiological and social – seemed to address the question of slavery. Medical evidence was offered to prove that blacks were innately different from whites; their each and every physical response differed from white people's. And, as if taking their cue from late eighteenth-century plantocratic racists, some American scientists thought the black closer to the animal kingdom than to humanity. They looked different – their colour, physique, posture and hair – therefore they *were* different.

It is tempting to overstate the *influence* of the specific claims of the new breed of scientific racists. Many of their arguments were demonstrably absurd (as many slave owners, close to their slaves, privately admitted). But the importance of such claims lies not so much in the empirically proven or disproved data so much as the intellectual and social climate they helped to create. They added a veneer of scientific respectability to long-held prejudices about black humanity: here were people so far beyond the pale of civilized behaviour that it was folly to think of conferring full civic rights on them. They would be unable to survive as independent beings in a free, industrious society. Only the restraints of slavery could persuade them to labour. This, in effect, was the slave-owning ideology: they, and society at large, needed labour. And black labour could only be extracted by the coercion of slavery.

More than that, slavery was presented as a civilizing force; shaping uncivilized beings into useful and productive workers. Nor, claimed the slave lobby, was slavery the brutal system outsiders alleged, for Southern slaves enjoyed levels of material care and paternal consideration far superior to that found among workers elsewhere. Were Irish peasants or Lancashire textile workers (the very people dependent on slave cotton) really better off than Southern slaves? It was a curiosity that the British debates about factory reform and the vernacular phrase 'factory slaves' played into the hands of Southern slave owners, for it suggested that there were millions of workers, ostensibly free, whose material lives seemed more blighted than slaves in

92

the South.[36] Black freedom would undo everything and, furthermore, would release millions of blacks into a white man's world. Of course this image – of a benign slave system, steered by a caring paternal ownership and populated by industrious and grateful slaves – ignores the more brutal aspects of slavery. And nothing seemed more outrageous and indefensible, to outside critics, than the regular regime of violence needed to keep slavery in place and the regular tearing apart of slave families.

In the defence of slavery, then, the vocabulary of race played a key role. It was not a separate and distinct argument, nor was it always the main line of defence. But it *permeated* the debate; a backcloth against which all other issues were played out and discussed. Scratch the surface of many of the arguments about slavery and the question of race emerged. What made race so potent an issue was not so much the way it was marshalled by the pro-slavery lobby, but the chord it struck among all sorts and conditions of white people. In the South, large numbers of whites who did *not* own slaves often had an indirect stake in the slave system (and were generally keen to be able to own slaves). The white South was more united on the issue than we might expect. Moreover, even many Southern whites who disliked the planters were agreed that black freedom was unthinkable. And in any case, Southerners tended to unite against critics from the North and from abroad.[37] They evolved that laager mentality, familiar in other parts of the world, which pitched Southern whites into a united, isolated fraternity, encircled by the local hostile black population and assailed by criticisms from afar. Southern whites of all classes viewed black freedom as an absurdity and as a betrayal; an end to Southern prosperity, a threat to Southern life – and a disaster for the slaves themselves. In the end, of course, that freedom came via the bruising Civil War. Though it destroyed the institution on which the South was based, it did not eradicate the Southern culture which had been shaped in large measure by the peculiar relations between black and white. And at the heart of those relations lay questions of race which themselves survived, in transmuted form, into the years of black freedom and Reconstruction after 1865. The line of descent was clear enough, and direct: from the slave-owning South, whose ideology pivoted on race and which spawned a virulent racism, through to the racism which afflicted American life, in the South and North, in the years after black freedom.

There was, then, a congruence of attitudes on both sides of the Atlantic on questions of what contemporaries viewed as race. In Britain and in the USA, race became a key ingredient in the arguments about slavery from the 1770s onwards, though it was generally one strand in a complex intellectual and political debate. It emerged most strikingly from the need to defend slavery when the institution found itself under attack. The lines of defence which stressed race as a justification for slavery informed and fed into broader discussions about colour and race. In time, the findings of new empirical human and natural sciences picked up many of the older arguments about race, adding to them the superficially plausible findings of science. Thus did one of the themes dear to the heart of slave-owning élites – black racial inferiority – enter the utterly transformed world of the mid-nineteenth century. The line of descent of these ideas about race, from slavery to freedom, was uneven. They were also part of a much broader debate about race which, in the British case in particular, was informed by dealings with native peoples in all quarters of the globe (especially India).[38]

In all this slavery was central, for it offered the best case study, the largest body of humanity, against which these varying attitudes to race could be directed, fashioned and reshaped for use at a more general level. It is, of course, perfectly possible to see the questions of race which surfaced in the English-speaking world after the 1770s as merely a smokescreen; a camouflage of words designed to hide more fundamental issues of power and economic self-interest. To the degree that the question of race cannot readily or easily be abstracted from those other issues of slavery, such a criticism has a degree of truth. But the question of race – the potency of the language of race devised in the century before 1850 – developed a power and momentum all its own. However deceptive it may seem, however intellectually flawed it now appears (when the concept of race itself finds few serious intellectual proponents), the debate about race proved to be one of the most durable of slavery's legacies. And the proof of that point lies in the burdens of racism, fashioned initially in the heyday of Atlantic slavery, bequeathed to the descendants of slaves on both sides of the Atlantic. This is not to claim that slavery alone created racism as we know it today. But modern

Western racism was in part a distinctive function of the virulent justification for the economic domination of black humanity. The need to explain why black labour had to be enslaved proved more durable than slavery itself. Long after slavery had gone, free blacks continued to suffer the racist barbs designed initially for their slave forebears.

6

MEN AND WOMEN

In the early days of settlement, the slave owners of the Americas wanted healthy young African males for the demanding task of opening up their settlements. And from first to last they wanted – or at least they got – more males than females. However we assess the confusing statistics of the slave trade, it is clear enough that more African men than women crossed the Atlantic. This was true for all the European slave-trading nations who came, in turn, to dominate the trade. Overall, twice as many males as females were transported. The exact ratio varied greatly from one era to another. By the last years of the slave trade, in the mid-nineteenth century, the Atlantic trade consisted overwhelmingly of young African males. The slaves landed in Cuba in that period, for example, were 70 per cent male. By the same time, a very large proportion of the transported Africans were children. Between 1811 and 1867, more than 41 per cent of the human cargoes were children. Indeed one historian of the phenomenon has claimed that by the nineteenth century 'The Atlantic trade had become a trade in children'.[1] Most slaves ships normally carried many more men and boys than women, and this demand for males in the Americas was reflected in prices. Female slaves were universally cheaper than comparable males – with the obvious exceptions provided by age and ill health.

The data for the Atlantic slave trade was characterized by oddities. On the African coast, the *export* of slaves was predominantly male. But there was an *internal* African demand for female slaves on the coast. This had the effect of greatly distorting the sex ratios of African populations on the slaving coast of Africa – with all the human and social consequences that historians are currently assessing. No serious student of African slavery now doubts that the simple consequence of these massive migrations (compounded, we need to recall, by flourishing slave trades from the Horn of Africa and from the East African coast) was that the population of tropical Africa was retarded. Enforced annual exports of 100,000 people for a prolonged period, plus the death of untold numbers of others in the process of migration, had a deeply corrosive effect on life throughout the region; on population, kinship ties, economic well-being and political stability.[2]

Africans enslaved in the interior were, if they survived, sold in two distinct ways. About half of the women went to African purchasers to be used as domestic slaves. But most male captives were sold on, to Europeans on the coast, for shipment across the Atlantic. It was a formula dictated by economics. The Europeans paid more for males, the Africans more for females. These variations reflected, of course, the different importance attached to male and female on opposite sides of the Atlantic, but whatever the reasons, two males left Africa bound for the Americas for every female. Most were young; within the 15–30 age group. The Atlantic slave trade also sponsored a powerful slave-trading industry on the African coast itself, spreading a large class of slaves along the west coast and confirming power in those groups and in men who could control the supply of slaves.[3] This system was not really challenged and destroyed until European invaders began to place different demands on Africa and ordered an end to slaving in the nineteenth century.

While New World slave owners preferred males, they might have changed their minds had they realized the economic roles played by women in their indigenous homelands. There were, naturally enough, great variations. But it was clear enough that African women, from the catchment area for the Atlantic slave trade, undertook a whole range of labouring, domestic and skilled labours. Throughout the region, a majority of local slaves were women, and African slave-holders expected them to perform a remarkable range of demanding tasks. Domestic work itself was tedious and often hard. Cleaning, cooking, food preparation and washing, the heavy chores of fetching firewood and water – all fell to the women. On top of that, in a number of regions, African women were important in agricultural work, and this was especially true when men were in short supply because of warfare or enslavement. Women were also the beasts of burden, carrying items, big and small, throughout the area. They

97

manufactured cotton goods, worked in heavy dye industries and, in a few celebrated cases, rose to high rank or military standing. But these were exceptions. As Patrick Manning has observed, African women's work was overwhelmingly 'first in the fields, then in menial domestic work, and only a very few female slaves achieved other occupations'.[4] Moreover, there was a curious – though predictable – consequence of the massive export of male slaves. Because the ratio of men to women declined on the African coast, women found themselves driven into areas of economic activity once preserved for men. In Central Africa, the Bight of Biafra and the Gold Coast, for example, where women had previously been agriculturally active, the loss of men to the Atlantic slave trade forced women to take over agriculture almost completely. In other regions the fall in the male population drove women more into commerce than cultivation.[5]

If there is one theme which emerges clearly from this welter of data (drawn across a long period of time and from geographically diverse regions), it is the economic importance of women in a number of labouring activities. Whatever the slave owners of the Americas may have felt about the different capacities of men and women in the slave fields of the Americas, those reservations were not shared in the Africans' homelands. Indeed the sharp gender imbalance which was reflected in the Atlantic shipping data, and in the purchases of slaves in the Americas, was quite unlike the patterns to be found in Africa. To make historical discussion even more confusing, with the passage of time and, notwithstanding the fact that female slave prices generally remained lower than those for men, female slaves began to undertake much of the physical work thought best done by men. By the time the various slave societies reached their mature form, female slaves could be found throughout the Americas toiling in the most laborious of conditions, doing work which slave owners so often claimed was men's work. Before we can grasp how that came about, however, we must, once again, confront the issue of the impact of the slave trade itself.

African women arrived in the Americas sick. The physiological after-effects of transportation lived on long after their settlement in the Americas. We simply cannot tell precisely what the full effects of the crossing had on the survivors, but we can gain some insight into their conditions from the problems they suffered with reproduction.[6] They entered the Americas sick and enfeebled. They settled on properties where men, at first, were in a majority and where illness and disease were rife. African slave women consequently did not conceive or give birth to healthy babies, as women of their age might be expected to. The pattern varied from one slave region to another: slaves in the Caribbean were notoriously less fertile than North American slaves. North America therefore had an early and continuing natural increase in its slave population, whereas most of the West Indian islands continued to depend on Africa for new slaves. The more Africans arrived, the more the ailments and diseases of Africa and transportation were infused into the slave quarters. It was a vicious circle. Death rates remained high and rates of reproduction remained low in those regions which continued to import Africans.[7]

Slaves were very different from one region to another. Slave women in the Caribbean (with the exception of Barbados), as mentioned earlier, were not as fertile as they should have been, and the combination of illness, poor diet and hard work produced noticeably lower birth rates. They also breast-fed their babies longer than slave women in North America, suckling their babies for three years rather than twelve months. Time and again doctors and commentators complained of the time West Indian women devoted to breast-feeding, with its natural prophylactic consequences.[8] West Indian women retained their African cultural habits (of which this was one) longer than North American slaves. In part this was a result, again, of the different ratios between black and white. North American slaves lived closer to, and were influenced by, the habits and instructions of local white women, and were more quickly socialized to different (white) habits. But this is only one of a host of factors in an environment in which women endured deprivation, harsh work and treatment, and poor diet.

Pronounced differences began to emerge among slave societies. In some, local-born slaves came to form the bulk of the local population. Elsewhere, notably in the Caribbean, planters continued to need fresh African imports. In the Chesapeake region, slaves had begun to increase naturally as early as the 1730s. With more locally born women, the slaves began to marry younger and have their first babies younger. Gradually, but noticeably, an indigenous slave population began to emerge. North America no longer had to rely on African imports for the expansion of the enslaved labour force.[9] It was very different in the Caribbean. There, the plantation records and planters' paper speak of a dismal story for slave women and their babies. Miscarriages and abortions, and all their traumatic consequences, recur time and again in the plantation ledgers. A large number of the newborn died in the first few months. Eighty per cent of such deaths occurred within the first two weeks. The one major exception to this trend in the British Caribbean was Barbados.

There the slave population was balanced, from an early date (unlike in Jamaica, where men greatly outnumbered women throughout much of the history of slavery). Even by the 1670s (when Africans were pouring into Jamaica) women outnumbered men in Barbados. This continued into the eighteenth century, with all the obvious consequences for natural population growth. Barbados could produce its own slaves and did not need to rely on the slave ships to augment the labour force. At the apogee of West Indian slave-grown sugar, Barbados had a slave population which was predominantly indigenous.[10] Such (creole) slaves were better suited, by birth and circumstance, to life on the plantations. They did not bring with them the ailments, grievances (and stories) of Africa and the Atlantic crossing. They were healthier, better able to adapt, to reproduce normally, and had fewer of the physical problems so characteristic of African slaves. Quite apart from the effects that this change had on slave culture – making it more local and creole rather than African – it had profound ramifications on the structure and development of the slave population.

There was a striking female presence among Barbadian slaves, in part a result of conscious policy by local planters: 'We buy them so as the sexes be equal; for, if they have more men than women, the men who are unmarried will come to their masters and complain, that they cannot live without wives.'[11]

Certainly, women were cheaper than men, and many planters claimed to find them more biddable and pliant. But they also had the added advantage, from their owners' viewpoint, that they might – with luck and good management – produce future generations of slaves. From the woman's viewpoint, this involved compound oppression: being treated both as a labourer and as a reproductive asset for their owners – all in addition to the dangers of casual sexual attack, to which slave women were invariably exposed in the course of their lives on slave properties.

Slave women toiled at the toughest of jobs on Barbadian plantations. They were to be found in their greatest concentrations in the field gangs, moving up and down the gang system according to physical strength and age, with some women in Barbados even rising to the rank of gang driver. Visitors to the islands professed to be shocked by some of the hard work expected of slave women – including women well-advanced in pregnancy. (But much the same could be said for the labouring poor throughout contemporary Europe.) Nor did pregnancy shield women from the lash, which was often administered in the most debasing of circumstances.

Slave women had few chances of advancement into other areas of slave work. There was, of course, a range of domestic work dominated by female slaves, but the myriad skilled jobs on and around a property remained primarily a male preserve. The end result was that slave women were primarily a manual labouring force. Wherever we look, when slavery was in its mature form in the Caribbean, women were in a majority in the cane fields. In the 1790s, on Worthy Park in Jamaica, about 58 per cent of the estate's field slaves were women. On the eve of emancipation, the figure had grown to more than 65 per cent.[12] Whatever ideals white society might have about the appropriate treatment for women, and their role, those ideals had no real application for slave women. (Such ideals had no real relevance for the world of plebeian women either, of course.)

In all the North American colonies, men were in a majority until about 1730. In Virginia the ratio was two to one, though the ratio was much higher in frontier regions. There, as slaves worked with whites and Indians to push back the frontier and convert the wilderness to fruitful production, women were rare, and men faced a lifetime's labour without the company of women. But as the ratio between the sexes levelled out, stable families began to emerge. From about 1750 onwards in North America, slave families, rooted in local slave communities, settled into a distinct fertile pattern, able to produce relatively healthy babies to African-American slave women who were marrying noticeably younger than their mothers. Thus slave reproduction became another form of exploitation for slave women, for they were not only expected to work and to contribute to the well-being of family and community, but their owners came to expect them to produce future children to add to their stock of slaves.

Much of the discussion (of American slavery) has been about slave 'breeding', a word with unfortunate farm-stock connotations.[13] It might be argued, however, that in a way this was the precise point. Did slave owners treat their slaves as stock, encouraging their propagation by providing adequate material conditions in the hope that the resulting children would add to their own well-being? However slave owners might seek to encourage slaves to reproduce, the slaves – like people everywhere – had children for their own reasons. It is clear enough that American slave owners (and, in the last generation of Carribean slavery, British planters too) wanted their slaves to thrive and to have healthy families. They put in place a host of measures ('amelioration') – rudimentary child care, relief from work for pregnant women, material rewards for women with babies, improving slave cabins – to encourage responsible baby and child care. Ultimately, however, this area of slave life existed and evolved effectively beyond the control of the slave owner.

What could slave owners *do* to bring slaves together in conditions of personal intimacy in the hope that they might reproduce? Slaves chose their own partners (violations notwithstanding). Moreover, planters' behaviour often suggests that they cared little for stable slave families. Planters clearly wanted healthy, fertile slaves – if only for selfish economic reasons – and their best hope obviously lay in the encouragement of stable slave families. Yet it was a recurring complaint from outsiders – and a howl of despair from the slaves themselves – that masters periodically broke up slave families for profit or short-term gains. This was especially striking in nineteenth-century USA, but it was also true in the Caribbean. Slaves would be shuffled around, resold, relocated, according to the planters' needs and plans, rather than with an eye to family or personal stability. The slave was an economic pawn to be pushed into whatever corner the planter saw fit.

One major, unavoidable theme in the lives of slave women throughout the Americas was sexual exploitation. From first to last – as long as their physical attractions endured – they were exposed to that predatory white sexuality which haunted the womenfolk of the slave quarters. Some made the most of the opportunities of sexual liaisons to improve their material lot (and that of their children). But such cases were relatively rare. Even when not the sexual playthings of the masters and managers, slave women were discussed as mere 'breeding stock'. Slave women were the agents who might (or might not) enhance their owners' material fortunes by the fruits of their own bodies. Of course the fertility of female slaves was a function as much of external factors as it was of deliberate management and personal choice on the plantation. Much depended, for example, on the nature of the slave property. In North America, the bigger the property, the lower the fertility rates. And cotton slaves had lower fertility rates than those on older tobacco properties.[14] Such variations were also true of the West Indies, where Africans were less fertile than creole slaves and where major fertility differences existed between slaves working on different crops (primarily because those crops were cultivated in different locales and employed different black–white ratios).

To discuss fertility in this way is, however, to abstract the data from its social reality. Indeed, the data *itself* is utterly abstracted and removed from the slave women themselves. Such evidence was collated primarily by the plantocracy for their own economic purposes (later, by the abolitionists for their political purposes). So often the historical debate has taken the form of a discussion about data, which is itself utterly remote from the women concerned. A new generation of (mainly) female historians, however, has sought to redirect our attention back to the slaves. For slave women, their own reproduction involved a different set of circumstances and experiences from those recognized by many scholars. For the slave women, 'fertility' was a matter of intimate, private relationships with partners of their own choice (or forced on them through acts of violation), and the tribulations and pains of childbirth and child-rearing. 'Fertility' also involved issues of the slave women's own physical and mental well-being, as they worked at demanding tasks through the months of pregnancy, followed by the difficulties of childbirth and child care in generally harsh conditions. Through all this, slave women were afflicted by a range of ailments, and by the sickness (and too often the death) of their babies. Thereafter, with luck, they faced the difficulties of rearing children in a hostile social environment. It was up to them to teach their children the harsh lessons of slave life; to implant the social skills and lessons for survival in a society which was like no other. A slave woman's surviving children were hers – yet they also 'belonged' to her owners. Slave owners tried as far as they could not to separate mother and children.

But, like other forms of enforced separations among the slaves, it *did* happen, along with all the consequent grief. And, throughout, the slave woman had her own labouring duties, where she might be exposed once again to the problems of demanding field work and vulnerable to the renewed sexual demands of men around her.

Demands for the reappraisal of the history of slave women are not, however, merely a plan to correct an obvious imbalance. Clearly, until recently, the history of slave women was, by and large, ignored or minimized.[15] But the importance of 'engendering' history goes well beyond the mere filling of gaps.[16] Not to recognize the central and decisive role of slave women within the broader slave society is to omit a crucial element in the historical chemistry of slavery. Gender – and distinctive gender relations – were at the heart of slave society throughout the Americas.

The data provides the raw evidence; and it shows the great differences between the lives of male and female slaves. Yet those differences form the very substance of slavery itself. Take, for example, the study of runaways. Female runaways were less common than male ones. Women were too attached to their children and families to be able to flee, and when they did run, they often escaped *to* their loved ones. Here, as with the question of fertility, we are confronted by historical data which is, at once, revealing and yet deceptive. It is evidence which needs to be handled carefully. Equipped with a new sensitivity to these problems, and influenced by a perception shaped by broader historical awareness of women's history, a new generation of women historians have helped to revise old notions.

For too long slave women were presented as powerless people; victims of each twist and turn of the externally imposed conditions in a hostile slave regime. Yet it is perfectly clear that slave women exercised previously unrecognized levels of influence at all levels: over their loved ones, and even over many of the whites around them, within the slave quarters and the local economy. Slave women were inescapable as domestics, and their most obvious influence was to be seen within white households. Slave owners surrounded themselves with enslaved domestics. Even when times were hard and when slaves might have been better employed on other parts of the owner's property, domestics were retained to deal with each and every creature comfort, from food, clothing and cleaning to sexual services.

The life of the slave domestic was unlike that of other slaves. Though domestic work had its own pains and penalties (to be under the watchful eye of a spiteful and perhaps vindictive mistress was no easy task),[17] it was generally regarded as an improvement on life in the fields: the surest way of punishing an errant domestic slave was to relegate her to menial work in the fields or around the property. Within white homes, black and white lived and worked in conditions of close familiarity; sometimes the slave women shared her mistress's bedroom. Domestic work was hard, its pace orchestrated by white superiors and measured out by the rhythms of household life – from lighting the first fire of the day through to closing down the house at night. Of course, slave women developed their own stratagems for coping with the difficulties of life under the planter's roof.[18]

Visitors to slave settlements were surprised by the number of domestic slaves. It seemed impossible to escape from them; from their presence, their noise and from the knots of their friends and relatives who gathered in the yard and at the back door (where they picked up those important spare crumbs which fell from their master's table). Every aspect of domestic life for the slave-owning class was undertaken by slave domestics, from cleaning up their domestic mess through to raising their children. Slave women nurtured and, in some cases even breast-fed, white children. Not surprisingly, those children became greatly attached to their black nannies. They grew up with the slave domestics' children and quickly picked up the games, the routines and even the accents of the slave quarters. Masters often complained that their wives allowed slave women to take over and corrupt the white children. Yet it was a two-way process, for resident plantation mistresses often took it upon themselves to take an interest in – to educate and win over – their domestics' children.[19]

White homes posed particular dangers for slave women, however. They were permanently exposed to whatever pains and punishments the whites chose to aim at them – sometimes for the most bizarre and trivial of reasons. Examples of malicious penalties, capricious pains and open fights between black and white women within the household are legion. Though relations in the better-run houses were cooperative (both sides recognizing their need of the other's efforts), too often domestic life was an area of friction, a scene of tense dispute, as women with different interests clashed and competed over the same space and roles. Yet, despite such frictions, each side was clearly greatly influenced by the other.

Domestic slaves might have copied the styles of their mistresses (and incur the irony and irritation of other slaves for doing so), but often whites also took on the styles of their black domestics. Hostile witnesses disliked the 'black habits' displayed by white women. Physical posture, manners of speech, an interest in slave pleasures (especially dancing and music) – all these and more seemed to many to be reminders that slaves could unduly influence the whites. But how could it be otherwise when black and white lived in such daily and intimate proximity? For many women, black and white, these domestic circumstances were often stressful, more so when the women shared the same men. Domestic life was often an uneasy no-man's land where women jostled for space, for primacy, for control of territories claimed by another.

At its worst, life for the female domestic was intolerable. For ever the object of unreasonable scrutiny by a hawkish mistress, the same slave domestic might also be exposed to the predatory sexual approaches of the men in and around the household. Male slave owners living alone often slid into a trough of brutish domestic behaviour, filthy in their personal routines, expecting their slave women to keep them clean, nourished and sexually pleasured – whenever and however they felt inclined. Sons of the owners quickly acquired the habits, assuming, like their fathers before them, that domestic slave women were there for their sexual pleasures whenever the fancy took them. Time and again, planters' papers speak of a persistent and apparently timeless tradition; of domestic slaves being regularly sexually exploited, often in the most grotesque of fashions. Not surprisingly, these predatory assaults frequently led to friction and conflict between black and white women, and between black and white men.

Visitors to slave regions were struck by the licentious attitude of white males towards slave women. Not surprisingly, relations between black and white might become confused, the complexities of class and race compounded by the entanglements of affection and lust, and completed by a confusion of blood ties. The offspring of white masters and slave women became servants to their white half-brothers and -sisters, the blood lines normally being ignored by the more crucial imperative of colour and economic domination. It is easy to see how, in this confusion of relationships, white domestic life in slave regions could become a crucible for the most confusing and volatile of human emotions. White women saw their menfolk enjoying the (reluctant) sexual favours of the same slave servants who tended the mistress. And, from a distance (or from the yard at the back of the house), the whole confusion of events might be watched by the husbands, lovers or menfolk of the slave women at work in the owners' homes.

Clearly this was not the lot of all slave women, though the threat of sexual intimidation cast a shadow over slave women everywhere. We know of female slaves being sexually violated in the fields, on the roadside, at work in the kitchen, and in and around the house.[20] Whether domestic slaves were more prone to such sexual aggression it is difficult to know. Perhaps their dealings with white men, in the privacy of domestic life, left them more exposed to such assaults. Sometimes – how often we cannot tell – a slave woman effectively set up house with her white lover, in effect becoming the man's common-law wife. In more remote settlements, where black and white lived distant from neighbours and relatives, the powerful conventions which operated against explicit relations between black and white were simply inoperable. This was especially striking in the Caribbean, where planters and their white underlings commonly set up home with their enslaved favourites and their inevitable off-spring. Again, visitors were struck by the boldness of such arrangements. On a visit to the Hope Estate in Jamaica, Lady Nugent found the Scottish overseer living with his 'cher amie . . . a tall black woman, well made, with a very flat nose, thick lips, and a skin of ebony, highly polished and shiny'. She was, said Lady Nugent, 'the favourite Sultana of this vulgar, ugly, Scotch Sultan'.[21] Thomas Thistlewood, who described his frequent and various sexual couplings with slave women, took a favourite, Phibbah, effectively as a common-law wife, though that did not prevent him from turning to other women when the mood took him.

Those slave women who shared the sexual favours of their masters were not always merely the abject victims of violation and power. There were many cases of long-lasting affectionate relations between black and white, but this is not to deny that the ultimate force which forged sexual relations between the two sides was power; the institutional, physical and economic power of white men over black women (and black men, of course). It was a power which some slave women could turn to their own ends, securing from their reluctant submissions a few material and family rewards: gifts and payment, a few material items, preferment for family and children. Such rewards were, however, bought at a very considerable price. In addition to the physical damage to the women involved – a damage measured in the high levels of venereal disease among slaves – there were depths of psychic pain which served to compound the personal and communal anger and resentment against the particular men involved. Occasionally it flared into open anger and violence, but aggrieved slaves knew that their anger needed to be kept within acceptable bounds.

Such liaisons had been basic to slavery since its inception, but they acquired a new significance in the nineteenth century, in part because of the nature of the abolitionist campaign against slavery. Much of the abolitionist inspiration came from religious organizations whose hostility towards slavery stemmed in part from the human and religious outrages so endemic in the slave systems of the Caribbean and North America. The slave lobby could hardly admit in public what anyone familiar with slavery knew to be the case: that sexual relations, and sexual violations, were commonplace. For their part, many slaves were understandably troubled by the idea of having their unhappy experiences paraded in public. These overlapping layers of reticence were compounded by other forces, not least the contemporary refusal to discuss explicitly the sensitive matters of human sexuality. Codes and hints were more common than specific detail. Behind the whole debate lay deeper, troubling questions of 'race'; of contemporary (though changing) attitudes about what was, or was not, appropriate behaviour between different 'races'. At the heart of the issue lay the even more confusing problem of miscegenation. In effect, the issue of human sexuality in the slave societies of the Americas provided abolitionists with a powerful weapon with which to attack slavery itself.[22] But it also posed problems of delicacy and convention. Propagandists and preachers, diarists and politicians – all and more knew the realities of sexuality in slave societies. Critics of slavery knew, though were hesitant to say so, that slave women were simply not safe from predatory white sexuality. A new generation of female writers and abolitionists were often bolder than most in spelling out the problem, and the voices of slave women, represented in the occasional memoir and autobiography, added a powerful and eloquent tone to the debate.[23] Those with eyes to see knew what was happening in the slave communities, not least because there was tangible proof of relations between black and white: their offspring.

Slave women working in white homes – the very ones most likely to be sexually oppressed – provided an important bridge between the separate spheres of slavery and white social life. Domestics were privy to the most intimate of white family secrets. They listened in to the daily conversations of family life, overheard the arguments and saw the friction between man and wife, and supervised the upbringing of white children. It was domestics who eavesdropped on conversations between the family and their white guests, learning about their views on contemporary life and politics. News from the outside world – even news from the other side of the world – filtered back to the slave quarters via attentive domestics. Thus did up-to-date information and gossip seep into the slave communities, among people who were formally illiterate. Slaves came to know about the words and policies of distant politicians. They learned that people, thousands of miles away, had started to interest themselves in their condition. And much of that information came via domestic slaves.

Female domestics could always be relegated (as punishment) to field labour, but not all field hands were suitable for domestic services. The refinements and conventions of white domestic life required a particular set of personal and labouring qualities. In bigger houses, a distinct hierarchy of female slave labour emerged, from the humblest of trainees to the most trusted of senior female domestics. The training and style, and a lifetime's labour, sometimes served to distance domestics from other slaves. But these distinctions can be overstated. Moreover, these women had relatives – husbands, children, sisters and brothers – who toiled at humbler slave work. And domestics moved back and forth, from the owner's house to their local slave community. Slaves' sense of status did not always correspond with their owners'; slaves did not esteem other slaves in their midst who were most valued by their white owners.[24] But female domestics had an importance which transcended their own work, for they provided other slaves with an entrée to the world of the whites, on the property and further afield. But to view such women merely as the couriers of gossip and the trivia of domestic tittle-tattle is to understate the broader nature of the information they ferried back and forth between their domestic workplace and the slave quarters.

To add to the complexities, women of the slave-owning class – white women – were themselves locked into a peculiar set of relationships of race and class, their identity forged by the constraints of property and by colour. They had a host of connections with slave women, forged especially within their shared domestic environment. Black and white women shared the same domestic space, cooperating in, and often disputing, similar roles as mothers, child carers, providers of material comforts for the white men of the household. The routines of daily life – set out and determined by the resident white women – were frequently subverted by domestic slaves. As often as not, the two sides of this domestic equation – white mistress, black slave – fell out over the simplest of problems, though such minor irritations often represented much more fundamental chasms.

White women regularly complained that slave domestics were indolent; sloppy, careless and apparently bent on testing the patience and tolerance of most mistresses. This criticism was of a piece with the parallel complaints about the shortcomings of field slaves, and such complaints were in effect part of that ubiquitous slave-owning ideological descant about slaves. Lies and petty thefts, inadequate cleaning, food improperly prepared, clothes badly washed – each and every facet of domestic work was likely to be criticized.[25] Attempts to reprimand and correct were widely held to be worthless. It was also assumed that permanent vigilance and regular rebukes were needed to maintain the white woman's authority. Nor did kindness seem to help: indeed, slave owners frequently complained of the 'ingratitude' of slave domestics who were likely to bite the hand that fed them. Such complaints were the domestic (white female) element of the broader plantocratic ideology. But they also represent an insight into the domestic dimension of the slaves' culture of resistance. Servants no less than field hands had their own distinctive ways of subverting daily routines to their own ends and rhythms.

For their part, white women played a varying role in slave societies. In Barbados, they formed a majority in the overall white population throughout the eighteenth century,[26] and their pres-

110

ence throughout the island is generally thought to be responsible for the less brutish habits of local white men. In other parts of the West Indies, however, where white women were less numerous, white men slid into cruder habits, especially towards their female slaves. Yet even a white female presence was no cast-iron guarantee of decent male behaviour towards female slaves. We know of the plantation mistress's frequent denunciation of her husband's indiscretions with the slaves, or of the mistress's consequent anger and revenge – not on her husband but on the unfortunate slaves. It was a bitter irony that the slave woman, already defiled by the white man, might then be punished by her angry white mistress.

Geography – physical isolation – created extra problems for white women in slave societies. On remote or isolated properties, on the edge of settlements, in the rugged and remote interior of Jamaica, white women rarely saw other white women. Not surprisingly, white women often fled from such isolation, to seek the guaranteed companionship (of other women) in the nearest urban centre – in Spanishtown or Charleston, for example. The problem persisted, of course, as the North American frontier was pushed westward. In 1853 one white woman told her sister, 'I seldom see any person aside from our own family, and those employed upon the plantation. For about three weeks I did not have the pleasure of seeing *one white female face* . . . '[27]

Those women anchored to a remote slave property, distant from towns or other settlements, often felt marooned on a landlocked island, surrounded by alien people, their daily contact and social relations shaped by dealings with black servants. For all the elements of shared female experience – most notably pregnancy, child-rearing and domestic management – white women often felt lost in a world of alien people. Whatever they shared with slave women was fissured by the massive divides of race and class.

One reason white women fled from the slave properties – to the nearest town or city, and even back across the Atlantic to Europe – was the absence of women in their daily lives. Yet they were, throughout, *surrounded* by women: indeed it was a complaint that they could not escape from them. But these women were black and enslaved. Lost in a host of domestic slave women, white women nonetheless felt bereft of female company; and the pattern was similar across the Americas. For all the specific acts of common identity between black and white women, the flight of white women from the slave properties whenever possible speaks of an isolation which was shaped and determined more by colour and culture than by gender. White women sought a more fulfilling life among their peers and equals; among women of their own class and colour.[28] Relations between black and white women were distorted by the property-status of slave women and by the gaping divides of class and culture.

Slave women also needed to escape from white homes, to find their most important and formative relationships inside the slave community, especially in the slave family. The slave families which emerged in the slave quarters were not families which easily fitted recognizable contemporary categories and provided a battleground for rival theoretical interpretations of family life by subsequent historians and social scientists. Slave families took a variety of forms, and in time a recognizable nuclear structure emerged. But all forms of slave families were fundamentally distorted by slavery itself.[29] Relations between man and wife, between parents and children, had no real basis in local law. Each family member could be removed, at a moment's notice, and sold elsewhere. Each person in the group could be violated, at the whim of a dominant white person. Parents tried to teach their slave children how to avoid the obvious dangers of slave life, how to avoid the pain and punishment attendant on any slave shortcoming. Nonetheless, a variety of family types emerged. But where the nuclear family developed, it did so on the back of slave enterprise. Where slaves had access to land and independent cultivation – where slaves had the opportunity to work for their own well-being and advancement – there developed household economies around which nuclear families evolved. And at the heart of those families were the women (often the critical worker in the family, the family plot or garden).

Relations between male and female slaves were always prone to outside dangers, however. Husbands, wives and lovers were ultimately powerless to prevent the violations which blighted and threatened slave lives. Men and women watched and listened as their loved ones took the lash or were taken in acts of sexual violation. Slaves frequently tried to intervene: men offered themselves as a substitute for their wife's punishments (though this was as likely to get both of them whipped); women pleaded to have their men's pain halted. Understandably, slaves

112

periodically bridled and reared up in momentary anger, but to lose their temper was merely to invite further and even more severe reprisals. Not able to take any more suffering – their own or their loved ones' pain – slaves often ran away. But just as often they were dragged back, in dispirited ignominy, to face further punishment.

This pattern of life for slaves was basic to the development of the distinctive relations between slave men and women. Whatever passed for 'normal' gender relations among slaves was corrupted by enslavement and slavery. The lines of authority and submission, of love and mutuality, of obedience from one generation to another – all and more were broken or threatened by the overweaning power of slave owners (men and women). Slavery gnawed at slave humanity itself. And yet, despite everything, slaves developed social relationships which provided a retreat and a haven from the outside world, and spawned institutions which formed the bedrock of slave life. Independent work and cultivation, buying and selling, manufacturing, haggling; all and more gave slaves an economic independence which itself conveyed social independence. Family life among the slaves was shaped to a marked degree by the independent work of women – in the home and outside. In its turn, the family became the fulcrum around which slave life hinged. Of course, it did so in the most trying of circumstances.

A great deal of historical debate about the dire consequences of slavery has concentrated on the nature of enslaved masculinity. Was the male slave's essential manliness stripped by the loss of his power? Slavery has been seen to strip the black male of his power over females, over children and family – even a loss of power over himself. Time and again historians were impressed by the 'emasculation' of slaves in the Americas. Wanted for his physical strength, the male slave nonetheless found his powers outside the workplace diminished. He was powerless – emasculated even – by the overarching power of plantocracy and by a system which relegated him, in the eyes of his womenfolk and children, to the role of plantocractic plaything.[30] Such a view no longer seems plausible, not least because we know so much more about the viability of independent slave economic and family life; areas where slave independent culture thrived parallel to the planters' intrusive control.

This older view rested on an assumed universal and dominant

113

masculinity. Research over the past generation, however, has revealed a more varied, diverse picture. Gender relations were much more diverse than was once imagined. More than that, gender relations in the slave colonies were at once more complex – and more in flux – than is often claimed. Chattel slavery clearly distorted 'conventional' relationships, between men and women and within families. But what were those relationships? When we consider gender roles among chattel slaves in the Americas, the question is: Which society are we discussing? Slave communities and families clearly had their own gender roles, but those roles sat uneasily with the demands of slave-owning society. There were, of course, points of contact, where black and white worked and lived together on terms of familiarity. And it was clearly at work, within slave-owning households, where black and white women shared common roles as wives and mothers. But these areas of shared gender interest were always fragile, always endangered, and permanently under threat from the imperatives of race and economic control. It is a central fact that slavery in the Americas cannot be fully understood, still less explained, outside of its defining racial determinants. And this was as true of gender as it was of other socially determined elements of slavery in the Americas.

Relationships between male and female in Britain differed enormously from class to class and from place to place. Courtly relationships in, say, the early eighteenth century were quite different from English plebeian relationships in the same period. In the attack on slavery, especially from the 1820s onwards, female abolitionists on both sides of the Atlantic made effective use of the damage caused by slavery on the fabric of black female and family life. The object was to encourage domestic arrangements among slaves which those female abolitionists accepted as normal, i.e. middle-class white relations. Clearly, what emerged in the slave quarters was quite different. And yet, for all the damage and threats of slavery, slave women carved out for themselves social roles which strengthened the very institution – the family – which seemed to outsiders to be absent or under threat. Women's independent economic role – especially in husbandry – provided the material wherewithal to create slave family bonds. The household economy became central to slave life – no matter how threatened – and it was women's work that secured it.[31]

The concept of slaves as things – and the consequent ordering and reordering of their social lives on that basis – infused into slave societies that instability and uncertainty which was itself destructive of 'normal' social life. Against all the odds, slaves managed, as we know, to construct family and communal life (the two crucibles from which flowed slave strength and stability). But here were institutions which were periodically rocked and fissured by the seismic forces inherent in slavery. The roles and relationships which developed in the slave quarters were permanently under threat from a slave-holding ideology and practice which might demand of those same people different and conflicting roles. The list of miserable prospects is long – but familiar. Vital young slaves, valued for their physical strength in field work, might have had that vitality sapped by the predatory sexual abuse of a partner. Husbands and wives might have found their loved ones violated or relocated to a distant (even unknown) place. Mothers had their motherhood corrupted by the ill-treatment and removal of their children. Siblings grieved for the rest of their lives for lost brothers and sisters. Almost three-quarters of a century after slavery in the US was ended, Anna Harris recalled the loss of her sister: 'Dey sole my sister Kate. I saw it wid dese here eyes. Sole her in 1860, and I ain't seed nor heard of her since.'[32] We need only listen to slave voices to hear the cries of outrage such actions provoked. Slaves complained, wept and grieved for years at the violations of their loving relationships. No outsider who saw or heard it ever forgot its poignancy and distress.

Separation was perhaps the most painful of all slave sufferings, worse even than the lashes borne by so many. The wounds from the lash healed (though often leaving permanent scars), but the distress of separation never went away and was a form of bereavement. It was, of course, only the most blatant of injustices which assailed slaves on all sides. They struggled to maintain a modicum of normal social life, secured for themselves affectionate relations with family and friends, and created within the slave community a haven away from slavery's threats. But slave owners were rarely far away; able, at a moment's notice to destroy or threaten a slave's role within the family or community, able to undermine relations between men and women, children and the family itself.

There were, it is true, good reasons why slave owners should nurture their slaves and encourage the benefits of happy, stable relations within families and within the communities. Contented slaves were more useful and productive than miserable ones. Most slave owners recognized this fact and many tried, as far as they could, to encourage domestic stability among their slaves. It was a recurring theme in the literature of the slave-owning class that their slaves were happy people; that they brimmed with pleasure when their masters and mistresses returned to the property from a long absence. When Henry Laurens returned home near Charleston, one slave 'Even kissed my lips'.[33] But this was often an exuberant happiness which flattered to deceive. Slaves told their owners what they wanted to hear, presenting one side of their lives in public, though keeping their own thoughts to themselves and their loved ones. Slave owners throughout the Americas suffered the persistent disappointment and irritation that the welcoming, happy slave, so pleased to see his or her master, was the same slave who ran away, was disobedient, answered back – or worse. Slave owners often despaired of their slaves; abandoning all hope of ever really knowing what went on in their individual and communal minds, preferring instead to suspect them at all times, to worry about their next move and to be prepared for the worst. Even a lifetime close to their slaves – surrounded by them in the home, working with them in the fields – failed to prepare slave owners for some of the slaves' reactions. They never really knew them.

In large measure, this was because slaves were able to keep slave owners at a distance, even while living close. For all the smiles and greetings, there simmered the deep resentment; in many cases a deep-seated, volcanic anger which erupted in acts of violence and desperation. Sparked by specific acts of slave-owning aggression – the last, violent straw – slave resistance was shaped by the frictions between their basic humanity and the demands made of them as objects. Relations between men and women in slave societies were fluid and fissured. They seemed to owe little to the recognizable patterns in other contemporary societies. Yet that was often a false impression. In truth, slaves, in shaping a world for themselves, created as 'normal' a set of relationships as was possible from the material benefits they scraped from their independent lives.

7

THE CULTURE OF RESISTANCE

Working peoples everywhere evolved their own distinct styles of resistance to prevailing forms of domination. Though the trappings of economic and political control seemed to rest securely with this élite or that, power was rarely absolute. Instead, it was contested ground, resisted and argued over. Slaves were no different. Indeed, the history of slavery is not so much the durable and persistent success of the institution itself but the story of those millions of enslaved peoples whose individual and collective efforts were instrumental in moderating and counteracting the slave owners' power and domination. Slaves (Africans or local-born) had to come to terms with their own position individually, not in the sense of accepting their allocated role (though some did) but in negotiating a personal, family or communal *modus vivendi* with the world at large.

The history of slavery is the story of enslaved resistance as much as slave-owning domination. Yet the two cannot be easily separated in this way, for they form the two polar opposites within the broader slave system. Nor should we think of slave resistance in simple terms (rebellion here, destructive reactions there). Rather, slave resistance forms the broadly defined structure of slavery itself; the very warp and weft of the slave experience across the Americas.

Slavery in the Americas faced challenges, from first to last. But, despite those challenges, it proved remarkably resistant to most of the attacks levelled against it. In retrospect at least, it seems remarkable that armies of people who were often kept in such abject conditions should not overthrow their tormentors and owners. Slave violence rarely destroyed the system that kept them enslaved.[1] Of course, there were remarkable variations in

117

the slave experience, ranging from the sick, newly arrived African scarcely able to lift a hoe, to more privileged artisans and servants who had secured for themselves a surprising degree of material well-being. No less important was the ratio between black and white; though, even in societies where black greatly outnumbered white, slavery survived. But it survived *despite* persistent, varied, daily (and sometimes bloody) resistance from the slaves. It would be wrong, however, to think of slave resistance solely – or even largely – as a violent phenomenon. Instead, it embraced a complexity of negotiations between slaves and masters – a process of adaptation, of testing, probing and redefining, which formed a culture of resistance. Similarly, it would be wrong to discuss slave resistance within the narrow confines of any particular slave society. In truth, resistance was endemic and began even before African slaves first met white people on the African coast.

It is, however, appropriate to begin with violent resistance, if only because slavery itself originated in and was maintained by violence. Among people who had been violated by enslavement, transportation and (if they survived) a lifetime's bondage, violence must have seemed the norm. Their dealings with white people, from the African coast, to the boats, to the slave sales and on to the plantations, were characterized and defined by violence. The African apprenticeship to New World slavery was a horrifying litany of physical violence. The experience of local-born slaves was of course different, but they too found themselves in the permanent shadow of threats of violence. For confirmation, we need only turn to slave folk culture and memory for evidence of slaves teaching their young of life's dangers. It was scarcely surprising, then, that when slaves responded – when they reacted to endemic violence – they too would sometimes be violent. Slave responses were normally tempered by a sense of reality: they knew that physical reactions would incur even more painful retribution and possibly death.

Slave society was structured and organized – in law, in the daily unfolding of plantation life, in face-to-face personal dealings – on the *assumption* that slaves were likely to resist. Slave owners everywhere feared the slaves' potential reaction to their manifold sufferings. Here was a society conceived in violence, protected by violence – and living under the threat of violence. Not surprisingly, the history of slavery in the Americas is pockmarked by slave upheavals. However, the revolutionary tumult which racked St Domingue (Haiti) after 1789 was unusual. More common – more typical – throughout the hemisphere was that insidious, persistent culture of slave resistance. There is a danger of inferring resistance from the most mundane of slave responses, though. This is an understandable overreaction to an older tradition which viewed slaves as passive victims; people to whom things simply happened. The findings of the past generation have illustrated the degree to which slaves shaped their own lives. They did what they could to mitigate it, to revenge it, reverse it or make it less hostile. The lives slaves shaped for themselves were both more complex and more subtle, and those who seek to explain slave responses solely or even largely through acts of violent anger and revenge misunderstand the nature and profundity of slave culture. That said, we need to discuss violence because violence permeates the history of slavery.

Slaves were dangerous and their tormentors had to be permanently vigilant. Africans were especially threatening, notably when they were herded on the African coast and when enduring the Atlantic crossing. Time and again the slaves below deck sought to break their chains, harm the crew, secure their freedom – or even kill themselves by leaping overboard. Guns on the slave ships were positioned and trained on their own decks. The abject conditions on the slave ships, the misery of the crossing, the mournful litany of dead and dying (to say nothing of the terrors of the ocean) terrified and damaged the slaves, yet sometimes stiffened their resolve. When the occasion allowed, Africans periodically rose up from the bowels of ships to visit death and damage on the crew and the vessel. More often than not they were apprehended and their resistance snuffed out before it even flared. Further suffering inevitably followed as captains and crew punished and killed recalcitrant Africans in public displays of exemplary violence. All European slavers believed that only bloodshed and extreme punishment would quell a shipboard revolt.

The Atlantic crossing, endured by some 11,000,000 African survivors, was an excruciating mix of bondage and life at sea. More than that, the slave ships formed the crucible for *the* seminal slave experience, for here, in that first prolonged encounter between enslaved Africans and white people, the relationship between black and white was forged, then sealed, through

119

violence. Survivors subsequently endured another harrowing experience, of sale and resale (with all the attendant indignities of inspection). And all this before they were shuffled off to work in their house of bondage.

African slaves had survived a series of connected acts of violence *long before* they were settled into their new homes on the plantations. Thereafter, their owners *assumed* that slaves would not work, could not be encouraged to obey, without the presence and the reality of the lash. Men controlling the West Indian field slaves paraded with a whip or a stick, and even the women in charge of the gangs of slave children were equipped with a twig. Both sides knew that violence was a conventional means of mediation between black and white; the one sure instrument to which whites resorted, from the point of sale on the African coast through to the daily toils in the fields.

Not surprisingly, slaves hit back. Their most spectacular communal act of defiance was in St Domingue – Haiti – where the debate about rights, spreading westwards from Paris in 1789, fanned the embers of discontent among a slave body which was largely African and which had been imported, at great speed and in unprecedented numbers. Between 1779 and 1792 the slave population had nearly doubled, from 250,000 to 480,000.[2] Even by standards of slavery in the Americas, theirs was a miserable story and, when slave revenge came, it was on an epic scale. Slaves took over the spluttering complaints of colonists and settlers in 1791, swept aside plantocratic control, threw out the French and destroyed a British invading army; the British alone lost 20,000 men. The Haitian sugar industry – before 1789 racing ahead to become the world's leader – collapsed in the rubble of slave resistance. Planters were destroyed, colonial government confounded and imperial armies humbled. It was, in brief, the worst of nightmares for planters and imperial government, with implications far beyond Haiti itself.[3]

Haiti became a byword for what might happen in the slave colonies; a symbol of the volcanic power and awfulness of unbridled slave resistance. As the French fled from Haiti – white, brown and (sometimes) black alike – they scattered to neighbouring islands (most of which tried to keep them out), carrying with them tales of horror and caution. Haiti was a ghastly realization of all that planters had predicted, from the early days of settlement, of what would happen if slaves were not controlled

120

with vigilance and strength. In addition, the revolutionary vernacular of 1789 and the subsequent widespread debate about the
rights of man ensured that slave societies everywhere had to contend not merely with rumbling threats from slaves, but were assailed with ideas which were utterly corrosive of slavery itself. It
was, after all, the debate about *rights* which had first sparked the
revolt in Haiti. Ideas, rumours, hints of black freedom – all and
more mingled with the realities of the Haitian diaspora to scatter
the spores of anti-slavery throughout the Americas (and Europe).
Slaves everywhere soon learned about what was happening in
Haiti. They were also quick to learn of the early abolitionist
moves in London. Careless talk among West Indian whites, overheard by black domestics, spread quickly to the slave quarters.
The word spread that Europe was about to grant black freedom.
Many slaves simply could not wait for such tales to come true.

Collective physical resistance was shaped by local geography.
Haiti was ideal guerrilla territory. So were Jamaica and some of
the smaller, mountainous islands in the eastern Caribbean.
Others were not – notably Barbados. Where could slaves run to,
gather and fight – or simply hide – in such a small, densely
crowded island which afforded few natural refuges? Jamaica, on
the other hand, was the scene of persistent rebellion, characterized initially by the Maroon settlements (free settlements of runaway free slaves). Unable to destroy or overwhelm them, the
British had to concede Maroon independence in a treaty of 1739.
Here was remarkable testimony to slave resistance: an imperial
power reaching a diplomatic accord with ex-slaves.[4] Maroon resistance flared again in the 1790s (under the shadow of events in
Haiti) and similar Maroon communities emerged elsewhere, in St
Vincent, Dominica and Honduras (and in a number of settlements in South America) but none plagued the British quite like
the Jamaican Maroons.

Planters lived in more or less permanent fear of slave violence
and revolt. They talked about it, recited rumours about it, dreamt
about it. In the words of George Cruickshank

The planter's dream doth plainly seem
To point a moral deep:
If you choose to whack a nigger's back,
You should never go to sleep.[5]

121

They found slave revolts even when they did not exist. Slave plots were more common than revolts; imaginary plans to rise up and destroy the whites. Time and again, in the Caribbean and North America, plots were uncovered, and the assumed perpetrators punished (normally in the most terrible fashion) – and all on the flimsiest of rumour and evidence. Tortured slaves not surprisingly confessed to crimes and plots. And when imaginary plots would not satisfy the planters' most paranoid needs, slaves could be relied on to provide the real thing.

Slave revolts, of varying intensity and scale, flared throughout the Americas, though normally more common and violent in the Caribbean than in North America. On the mainland, revolts broke out in South Carolina (1739), French Louisiana (1763), Virginia (1800), Charleston (1822) and, most spectacular of all, Nat Turner's revolt in Virginia (1831). In all cases, rumour and panic fed slave-owning anxiety. Sometimes their fears were realized, but everywhere the whites proved vengeful on an epic scale, slaughtering suspected slaves, sometimes after trials. However much death and destruction was done to local white society, it was visited tenfold on the slaves. It was much more than an eye for an eye. Indeed, this pattern – of violent slave resistance (normally a despairing reaction to an accumulation of grievances) and the resulting massive, intimidatory white repression – began, in time, to shock outsiders. Viewed from outside the slave societies – from, say, London or the Northern states – the vengeful power of slave owners transgressed all reasonable legal or social needs. It looked like violence for its own sake. By 1800, such displays of public blood-letting were out of keeping with the changing social tone of Western life. It began to appear that slave owners could only maintain their grip over slaves by periodic acts of ferocious revenge. More and more people asked: Was it worth it?

This growing sense of unease was made worse by the escalation of slave revolts in the British Caribbean in the early nineteenth century. In fact, the rebellious instinct of West Indian slaves had manifested itself at regular intervals since the early days. And it was this tradition which forged the planters' determination to yield little to the slaves, but to rule them largely through fear and punishment. The persistence of slave revolt can be partly explained by the continuing high ratio of Africans (the people in the most abject of conditions *and* who had known an-

122

other form of life – in Africa) and the low ratio of white to black. The Caribbean, unlike most of North America, was effectively a black society, 'an image of Africa'. It was those who had known Africa, who had survived the Atlantic Crossing and 'seasoning,' who were most likely to be at the heart of violent slave resistance and rebellion. But there were other factors at work.

The early years of massive slave imports into Barbados had yielded its fair share of plots, rumours and threats, but the island was much less troubled than its neighbours. In Antigua (1735–1736), and especially in Jamaica, a series of slave rebellions (notably Tacky's revolt in 1760) tested the mettle of the plantocracy and their supporting system. The pattern became familiar; of slave rebellion snuffed out by acts of remarkable cruelty and a subsequent tightening of the local slave regimes. As the British acquired ever more possessions in the region, especially after the 1763 Peace of Paris, more slave islands crackled into rebellion. The whole problem was made worse, from the European viewpoint, by the language of political change and of human rights which rippled through the islands after 1776. Indeed, there were a number of planters who openly thought that the islands should join North America in seeking independence from British control. They were restrained, however, by their very real need of the Royal Navy and by their dependence on British arms to keep the slaves in place. To opt for independence might have sparked a slave rebellion. St Domingue was to show, only a few years later, how easily it could happen.

The British defeat of the French in 1763, and the unchallenged strength of the Royal Navy, ensured that the formal British grip on the slave islands was strengthened, not weakened. At the same time, however, the discontent among slaves increased. It was a curiosity which many found inexplicable. As West Indian planters made conscious efforts to improve the material lot of their slaves[6] (largely, of course, to enhance their own economic fortunes), slave rumblings grew louder. More than that, the ending of the British slave trade in 1807 – which cut the supplies of African slaves (i.e. cut off the very people who had traditionally been more rebellious) – seemed to accentuate, not lessen, slave grievances. The last generation of British slavery, after 1807, saw some of the worst slave rebellions.

By then, slave society in the islands had begun to change. Firstly, the proportion of Africans inevitably declined; the slave population became more and more local-born ('creole'). Secondly, it was a population which was also more thoroughly Christian, thanks mainly to the efforts of non-conformists. British missionaries established chapels, trained black (slave) preachers, and provided slaves, through the Old Testament and hymns, with a new language and a new set of ideals. With a Christian heaven to aspire to, with an equality before the Lord, and with imagery of the Old Testament before them each Sunday, slaves began to organize, express themselves and behave quite differently. They were black Christians who were, nonetheless, still the victims of the plantocratic persecution. Their plight naturally attracted the concern of sister congregations in Britain. The network of churches on both sides of the Atlantic ensured that information about the slaves was readily available throughout Britain (which was itself changing, thanks primarily to the forces of urban growth). Thus, from the mid-1820s onwards, when the British humanitarian lobby revived its agitation for black freedom, the slaves themselves became ever more insistent and assertive. The end result was a rising tide of British interest in – and a mounting revulsion against – slavery itself. One reason for that heightened revulsion was the saga of periodic slave rebellions and their bloody suppression (by planters who claimed that their action was motivated by civilization and British economic well-being). The question was asked more and more loudly: Was it worth it?

In the years after the all-consuming Revolutionary and Napoleonic wars, the British – exhausted by two generations of costly warfare – received stories of a succession of slave rebellions. In Barbados in 1816, Demerara in 1823 and finally (and most violent of all) Jamaica in 1831–1832, slaves rebelled – and were thwarted by the most bloody of punishments. The number of slaves who died – killed on the spot or executed after trial – was chilling: 400 in Barbados, 250 in Demerara and 500 in Jamaica – figures out of all proportion to the number of white deaths. True, the material damage was enormous, especially in Jamaica, but how could deaths on this scale be justified? White élites in the slave colonies seemed scarcely troubled by death and suffering on so monumental a scale. Indeed, the legal system which supported and nurtured slavery in the islands was steeped in a punitive ethos which (again) by the early nineteenth century seemed utterly at odds with the changing sensibilities of the Western world. Yet planters and colonial agents had no problem in putting legions of slaves to death; publicly and agonizingly. The slave-owning class showed no contrition about its actions. The fate of those largely anonymous slaves seemed, to a growing British constituency, violent beyond all justification. Yet this was only the latest (though most spectacular) of a series of communal violations visited upon slaves throughout the Americas. To make it worse, such retribution did not seem to work. Repression was followed by further slave rebellion, and slave discontent simmered on. The blood-letting served to exacerbate slave anger, though it may well have diverted and bottled it up in the short term.

Rebellion was, however, only the most obvious and most memorable of slave reactions; most excruciating for the slaves and most revealing of the plantocratic mind. Slave physical resistance took many other forms. For example, slaves ran away in remarkable numbers, sometimes for a few days, sometimes for a long period. Most runaways were male and young and most seemed to be heading for loved ones: parents, siblings, children, lovers and spouses. Planters sometimes tolerated absentees. If work was slack, or food short, absent slaves meant fewer mouths to feed and fewer idle (and therefore dangerous) hands. But, on the whole, runaways were disliked and distrusted, and viewed as yet another indication of the ultimately unreliable nature of slaves themselves. Running away allowed slaves a degree of freedom – a degree of movement and a life beyond plantocratic control – which rested uneasily with the planters' need to control slaves at all times. Few slave owners (certainly on larger properties) could expect to prevent slaves from running away.

For a generation and more, historians have interpreted the lavish data about runaways as an indication of slaves' rebellious instincts. Clearly, for many this was true. But for many more it was not. Sometimes described as 'maronage' (on the model of the major ex-slave communities, which developed from runaways and thrived behind plantocratic lines), the act of running away was often too personal, too idiosyncratic to belong to a pattern. Having said that, it is clear enough that slave fugitives, however we describe them, provide an important entrée to the mentality of slaves and into that culture of resistance spawned by all slave societies.

Slaves ran away when they could no longer stand the threats, the violence (against themselves or others) when they flared up at the latest of a host of indignities. West Indian planters became so inured to slave runaways that their account books classified those at risk as runaways. One of Worthy Park's slaves in December 1787 was Strumpet, described as 'Field, Able, Runaway'. Her contemporary, Diana, was 'Able but a Runaway'. On the same Jamaican estate, in 1830, 16-year-old Hannibal was an 'Incorrigible Thief and Runaway'.[7] Despite the inevitable punishments, slaves ran away time and again. Sam, a Jamaican, ran away for six days in November 1828. Pardoned on return, he ran away within a few weeks for a further eight days. Pardoned again, he set off once more, for five days. Brought back by his mother, he took off again a few months later – seven days – for which he received thirty-nine lashes. Absent again from May to July 1829, and flogged until he was in the slave hospital, Sam ran away permanently that August.[8]

Similar stories were repeated throughout the Americas. Many slaves ran away long before they even arrived at their final destination. They escaped in Africa, *en route* to the coast, from the slave ships and, on arrival, when they were being driven to their new workplace. Runaways were frequently branded 'R' on their forehead or another visible part of the body.[9] Those living or working close to rivers or the coastline might even take to the water to escape. Slaves overcame extraordinary difficulties to flee. Some escaped into the burgeoning urban areas, where they blended with the growing black population, free and enslaved. Others passed themselves off as free people, though they were generally troubled by the lack of necessary papers to prove their freedom.

The closer historians have scrutinized runaway data (much of it buried in newspaper advertisements seeking the slaves' return), the more remarkable the phenomenon appears.[10] Some fugitives were away for remarkable periods. John Beckles, a Barbadian runaway discovered in 1805, had been missing since 1780. Another, missing for sixteen years, had been hidden by his father. In one of those bizarre curiosities thrown up by slave societies, it was alleged 'that he was stolen by his parents' when he was a child. Perhaps even more remarkable, an African discovered in Barbados in 1806 had fled six years earlier – from Jamaica. It was clear enough that slaves often knew the runaway in their midst. In small communities it would have been impossible not to know. Sometimes, even white people hid a slave. Much more common, however, slaves were cared for by other slaves; by friends, workmates or, most likely of all, by family and loved ones.[11] Advertisements often specified where a slave might be found: 'where she was born, and many of her family belong'. Another slave was sought by specifying where her mother and father lived.[12] Sometimes slaves even bargained with slave owners about their return, agreeing to come back under certain conditions (a new job, a wife, a move to another owner). The closer we look at the fine detail of slave life, it becomes clearer that slaves exercised a surprising degree of control and autonomy over their lives, negotiating formally (but more often informally) for the terms and conditions of their lives.

The pattern of slave runaways was similar in colonial North America, especially in South Carolina. The number of runaways was extraordinary. In the fifty years to 1782, 5600 runaway advertisements have been counted in local newspapers: the population at the time was 40,000.[13] Yet there were clearly many other slaves, on the run, away from their owner, whose absence went unrecorded in such data. Slaves escaped to other plantations, and some ran away to nearby towns. Most pathetic of all were the five Angolan slaves 'supposed to have gone on an east course as long as they could, thinking to return to their own country that way'.[14] Again, it was 'home' and loved ones that lured most runaways; escaping back to people and places they knew and loved. Slaves sold from one district to another tried to get back, sometimes in the most persistent and determined fashion.

What such runaways reveal is the remarkable slave networks that emerged across the face of colonial slave society. Slaves ran away knowing that they could find shelter and food from other slaves – often, of course, at great risk to the host slaves. On long trips – at night through unknown terrain – slaves needed expert local guidance. They also needed food and sustenance. Any slave carrying more than was necessary for a day's work would immediately arouse suspicion from whites in the neighbourhood. Stealing when they could, runaways travelled on, courtesy of slave donations or thefts from whites. And at each point they incurred the risk of capture – and punishment (for themselves and their protectors) for having taken the items that kept them going. The simplest escape was to see a wife or husband, a girl- or boyfriend. But, for slaves who had been scattered great

127

distances from their loved ones, running away involved placing a great deal of trust in other slaves. The fact that so many did so speaks to a slave society which provided an 'underground railway' long before the development of that system in the nineteenth century. It also reveals the levels of autonomous and cooperative behaviour in the slave quarters. However close, however intrusive the planters might be, however much they felt they had the trust of their slaves, there were areas of independence which defied their best efforts to keep close control over their slaves.

In North America as in the West Indies, local geography determined the possibilities and limitations of escape or temporary flight. In the early seventeenth century, when the frontier (and the Indians) were uncontrolled, slaves could escape and shape Maroon-type communities in more inaccessible places. But these were risky and unusual. Moreover, the wilderness posed as many problems as it solved. How many slaves were willing or able to risk the dangers of survival in a hostile natural environment, threatened by beasts and Indians and pursued by slave-hunters? Slaves wanted their freedom, wanted a respite from the rigours of slavery, wanted to go back to people they knew and loved. But the risks were sometimes enormous. And the risks were even greater for the bolder – or more desperate – who wanted to escape from the slave system entirely by seeking a haven beyond the pale of plantocratic control. To seek a loved one was risky enough, to seek full freedom was altogether a different thing. Yet it is testimony to the desire for freedom that American slaves sought it, in the most adverse and unlikely of conditions. Despite the pursuit, despite the inevitable punishments, American slaves sought to break loose from slavery.

The greatest chance came with the War of Independence in 1776. Both sides wooed the slaves, many of whom headed for the British forces (who promised freedom): 13,000 in South Carolina and 5000 in both Virginia and Maryland. When the defeated British quit America, they took with them 3000 ex-slaves, depositing some in Nova Scotia, others in London (hence the problems of the London's black community in the late 1780s). Here was a lesson heeded by slave owners everywhere. The merest chink in the plantocratic armour would be exploited by slaves, ever vigilant for opportunities to escape or run. Slave owners across the new USA therefore sought to prevent and punish it by law and local convention. By the 1850s, American laws permitted patrols to enter slave homes and search for runaways. Everywhere the law specified the lash, incarceration (and, in the West Indies, the treadmill) for runaways. Slaves who travelled – and there were many whose work took them on the road (or by water) – were forced to prove their freedom. They were required to carry and produce warrants and passes and to show them to any white person who enquired.

The expansion of American slavery on the back of cotton in the nineteenth century created new problems for slave owners. The free states to the North acted as an obvious escape route for slaves keen to flee. But to get over the border was a mammoth undertaking. Some slaves travelled with false papers (e.g. Frederick Douglass), one man had himself shipped in a box (Henry Box Brown). More used the famous 'underground railway' – that network of friends and sympathizers, black and white, who acted as staging posts for passing runaways onwards towards freedom. Most of the successful travellers on this 'railway' came from the upper South – the old slave states closest to the free states of the North. Perhaps 1000 a year made the journey by the last years of American slavery.[15]

The circumstances were different, but the pattern was similar, to that established earlier by slaves elsewhere in the Americas. Thousands of North American slaves resisted slavery as best they could, seeking to put distance and time between themselves and their captors, finding freedom (in the wild or the city), walking, riding, sailing, carrying false papers, travelling at night, relying on friends for food and shelter. And everywhere the penalties were similar: the humiliation of stinging blows, public insult and heightened white vigilance. Although other slaves saw what happened to retrieved runaways, the shame and pain of it all failed to quell the urge to flee. But in the nineteenth century, as in the eighteenth, most North American fugitives ran away only a few miles.

Like slaves in the West Indies, most headed for nearby relatives and loved-ones. Many lurked around their own plantation (fed and alerted to dangers by other slaves); most drifted back, defeated by circumstances; some were betrayed or tracked down. News of planters' search parties invariably reached the runaways before the parties themselves. The flight of slave runaways could not have happened without the help of other slaves. Runaways *knew* they could turn to other slaves for help. Networks clearly emerged; staging posts at which runaways could find help *en route*. Help, however, was much closer to hand than planters sometimes realized. When Bart, the runaway of the Virginian planter Landon Carter, returned home in March 1766, Carter was enraged to learn that the fugitive had been protected by his own estate gardener for three months.[16] Others set off on more demanding journeys. When the Virginian slave Will quit in August 1755, he travelled 100 miles from Charles to Frederick County – to see his wife.[17] But on both such ventures – living on the edges of a property or travelling great distances – slaves needed friends and contacts. Whites realized that slaves needed each other in their acts of defiance. Whites on plantations were especially suspicious. It was part of the plantocratic outlook always to assume the worst of slaves; always suspect that they were up to mischief or planning something dangerous.

Word seemed to travel faster than the runaways themselves, still further proof of the amazing networks created by slaves. News from London passed into the slave quarters, stories from the slave ships were discussed in the black community in London, warnings from the plantations passed quickly to fleeing slaves on the edges of settlements – all and more were part of the remarkable flow of information, back and forth, among slaves and ex-slaves within the Atlantic slaving empire. The black community in London was alert to the murders on the slave ship *Zong* in 1783 *even before* the story broke in metropolitan white circles.[18] Slaves in Jamaica in 1816 sang a ditty in praise of Wilberforce's efforts to free them: a man they could have known little about, save for the vituperative tittle-tattle gleaned at the planters' tables.[19] Here were largely illiterate people acquiring and using information, turning gossip and eyewitness accounts to their own ends, one slave passing on news to the next, just as they passed escaping slaves on to the next sympathizer.

Slaves used this information, gleaned from the most distant points of that vast Atlantic system, to inform, encourage and help. Scraps of gossip, half-understood rumours, All and more were power to the slaves' elbow. It became, in effect, a key ingredient in the slaves' oral culture; part of the process of learning and living which was itself basic to the culture of resistance.

Try as they might, planters throughout the Americas could never dampen the cultural instinct to resist. Nor could they staunch the flow of news which raced ahead with ten-league boots. They tried very hard indeed, of course, not sparing recaptured slaves the full weight of their own lash or the full rigours of a punitive legal system. Yet such punishments clearly did not work. However harsh and painful, however angered slaves might feel (for themselves, their friends or family), the physical threats of slavery did little more than stifle or deflect the slaves' resistance. There must have been many slaves, of course, who were genuinely terrorized by what they saw happen to runaways, and especially to rebellious slaves. Yet the broader urge to resist remained undimmed.

Enough has been said to show that physical clashes and confrontations between black and white were endemic. Though power was essentially one sided – any offending slave knew the very great risks involved – not all slaves could restrain themselves. Not all could turn the other cheek or walk away in front of taunts, punishments or threats to friends and loved ones. In the heat of the moment, slaves (understandably) struck back, attacking (and, in rare cases, killing) the offending white person. More common, though, was that brooding sense of outrage which planned to get even. Revenge might take any number of forms: harming the animals, destroying crops, stealing goods, hurting white children, poisoning the whites themselves. Fights between slaves and their white bosses were not uncommon. For here, in that heated moment, when a slave had received one blow too many, one reprimand too many – the final insult – slave tempers snapped and anger flared. Time again there were scuffles and blows. Most ended with not much more than wounded white pride.

Such incidents posed serious problems for whites and for the authorities. Slavery was a system which demanded respect (though it tended to receive no more than sullen acceptance). Violence, physical reactions, brawling between black and white – all served to corrode white authority and offered a dangerous example for other slaves. In many slave societies, especially those in the Caribbean, whites were all too aware of the precariousness of their control. They formed a tiny white minority in a sea of hostile black faces. Whites, from the grandest of planters to the humblest of bookkeepers, appreciated the volatility of the environment they

131

inhabited. Clashes between black and white could only make it more tense and dangerous; hence the need for sharp reprisals. Resistant slaves, and all who knew of their resistance, must be taught the lessons of resistance. In the words of Thomas Ruffin in North Carolina in 1829, 'The power of the master must be absolute, to render the submission of the slave perfect.'[20]

For all the punishments and reprisals – which were instant and painful (though the process of law could exact longer-term penalties) – slaves confronted their tormentors throughout the slave colonies. More often than not it was an instantaneous reaction. Planning or plotting a communal act of slave defiance had enormous dangers. Plans could be revealed, plots exposed. In fact it seems likely that more plots were hatched than realized. Whites were in a state of permanent vigilance, and could generally rely on information from loyal slaves to tip them off about impending trouble. It was easier, less risky, for a slave to go alone. Communal resistance was much more perilous than acts of personal defiance (though more common in the West Indies than North America). There were a host of ways a slave could respond, more safely, alone. Anything which involved other slaves ran enormous risks, of detection and fierce punishment. Yet even here slave cooperation was instructive.

Slaves could not be trusted or believed, and slave owners everywhere assumed that they were liars and thieves. There was, of course, a great deal of truth to their fears. Slaves needed to deceive, needed to steal, needed to be less industrious than expected, to survive in so hostile a world. From their deceptions came security (for those they protected), and from their pilfering came the wherewithal to help fugitives. What slave owners saw as vice, slaves saw as virtue, and from the slaves' ability to twist the system in these ways, slaves were able to help each other. Even the most defiant and idiosyncratic slave needed others at critical moments. The simplest need was for silence; not to tell white people what was planned or happening. Resistant slaves needed that sullen silence, that refusal to speak up which so infuriated slave owners and which persuaded them that slaves were irredeemably stupid. Yet, here again, we find a social characteristic with two faces: what the whites viewed as stupidity was often the slaves' way of masking reality.

At every turn, slave life was informed by the need to negotiate a distinct path through a world full of pitfalls. The culture of slave life was one shaped by the universal need to make the intolerable acceptable and to moderate the pains of slave life. Too often viewed by historians as alternatives (of resistance or accommodation), it is perhaps more fruitful to think of slaves generating a culture of resistance which ranged from the most overt and physical of responses to the personal pursuit of material well-being.

When we examine the details of slave resistance we can begin to detect the springs of slave actions. Their lives came to be grounded in unwritten rules; conventions which effectively bound together master and slave. When the limits of those conventions were transgressed – when whites stepped too far beyond the line of what law and custom allowed – slaves were likely to react. More than that, they clearly felt that they were *justified* in responding when their rights had been violated. For all its innate violence, for all the undoubted outrages which were part of the warp and weft of slavery, it had its clearly accepted limits; boundaries beyond which whites trod at their peril. There was, however, even greater peril for the slaves. They grumbled and complained; braver spirits spoke out openly. When free time was denied, when punishment was excessive, when work demands were unreasonable, when the behaviour of individual whites was unacceptable (by slavery's warped standards), slaves felt at liberty to resist openly. When jobs were changed, especially when slaves were expected to work below their skills or training, when families and friends were divided, when womenfolk were violated or hurt, slaves responded. More often than not it was a verbal complaint, or a sullen, foot-dragging insolence, which masked a deeper hurt.

Slaves had to be cautious in their open response, though. Many – perhaps most – nursed deep-seated grievances about their lives; most perhaps wanted an end to the system that bound them. But most also accepted that there were limits to what they could do about it. Those limits were more flexible than we might imagine, however. Only the most defiant, or the foolhardy, felt utterly free to say and do what they pleased. The penalties for violent resistance were clear enough. At their most grotesque they took the form of those public executions and dismemberings which characterized the bloody penal code on both sides of the Atlantic for much of the period. Though punishments began to moderate in Britain (fewer people were executed, despite the increase in the number of capital offences), there seemed little sign of this process in the slave colonies. As slavery seeped across the North American continent, each new slave code demanded fearful exactions of resistant slaves.

Some slaves simply could not be restrained. Slave communities everywhere, from the slave ships to the last days of US slavery, had individuals who hit back, refusing to be quiet or silent despite the range of punishments doled out to them. These were the slaves who appeared in slave advertisements as indefatigable runaways and rebels, their bodies scarred by a regular ration of lashings and physical punishments. Many paid for their resistance with their lives, on the spot, or at the hands of the local penal code. Many others were expelled; cast out from already harsh slave societies to endure the exile of life in even more difficult societies; sold to Cuba, sent to the Mosquito Coast, dispatched even to the hulks in London and, worst of all, sent as the criminal flotsam to the penal colony in Australia. Everywhere, slave owners recognized the troublesome slave who was best left alone; the slave who was more dangerous than amenable and whose responses were too aggressive for normal containment. Such slaves were exceptional, but they established a marker that was clear to all slaves: that slave owners did not always have things their own way. Such slaves helped to draw a line between what was tolerable and what was utterly unacceptable. It was only the most foolish, naive or ignorant slave owner who failed to accept this fact.

Slaves who took the most physical forms of resistance formed only one element in a much broader spectrum of slave resistance. Indeed the culture of slave resistance was then part of the very fabric of slavery itself. It helped, in many key areas, to *define* slavery. It set limits, for black and white, of the possible and the impossible. Curiously, it also enabled slavery to function, by working as a safety valve for a social system which would otherwise have proved too rigid and inflexible.

Slaves negotiated a life for themselves in what often seemed to be intolerable conditions. They often achieved an acceptable life by dissembling; by pretending and deceiving their masters and owners. Slave culture – broadly defined – embraced much more than the physical and the violent. All slaves had to negotiate a life for themselves in these intolerable circumstances. Some took the physical route – escape, violence, insolence – but all had to find an acceptable *modus vivendi*. They dissembled and pretended, always seeking to safeguard themselves without unduly upsetting their owners. Theirs was a culture of resistance which provided a defence against the most rapacious aspects of slavery's domination.

8

CULTIVATING
INDEPENDENCE

Slave owners liked to think that their power and dominion over their slaves was absolute, but it should already be clear that, in practice, slave owners' power had obvious limitations. They could not, with impunity, do as they wished, whenever the mood took them. If they took so high-handed a line, they were likely to pay a high price, not least in the form of slave truculence, diminishing returns and even open resistance. The successful slave owner was not the brute, insensitive to the needs of the slaves, but the canny manager who knew where and when to draw the line; knew how far he could push his slaves and how much he could get out of them. This does not, of course, minimize the brutishness involved but rather illustrates that economic self-interest defined many of the limits of slave-owning power. Slave owners came to accept that their slave-based operations worked best when slaves were granted important areas of freedom; spheres of independence which sustained the slaves and ultimately helped the slave owners.

As intrusive as slavery undoubtedly was, slave owners learned when to leave slaves to their own devices. But they worried about that independence, concerned that, left alone, slaves would plot against them or misbehave. Often, however, the very structure of plantation society guaranteed slave independence. In the sugar islands, for instance, slaves could not be closely monitored and regulated by the small band of resident whites, who, in any case, lived far away from the slave villages. In those huddle of huts and cabins, among the clusters of slave families that formed the network for slave communities, slaves' lives sometimes seemed untouched by their owners. Yet we need to remember that, at all turns, the independence which evolved in and around those communities survived under the threatening shadow of the changing needs and moods of the owners themselves. Families and individuals could be uprooted, at a moment's notice, and dispatched they knew not where – simply because their owner decreed it. From first to last, slave independence survived under threat.

Slaves made basic demands of their owners in order to fashion for themselves the social independence which became so important. The first generations of slaves were overwhelmingly men. They wanted and asked for women for companionship. When they did not get them – and for many years more men than women were imported – there was, inevitably perhaps, friction and fighting. In 1712 a Virginian slave, George, complained that other slaves 'had poysoned him for his wife'.[1] Their owners knew that slaves were happier, more likely to work better, when they had settled relationships. It was even better to have stable slave *families*. Thomas Jefferson was keen to encourage slaves to settle down to stable married life: 'They are worth a great deal more in that case than when they have husbands and wives abroad.'[2]

The slave family became the linchpin of the slave experience. Slaves chose their own partners, walked great distances to see and stay with them – and were utterly distraught when forcibly removed from them. Despite everything, slaves families grew and thrived, each with its own network of family scattered in the immediate neighbourhood and region, though expanding, and often breaking, as family members followed the expansion of slave society to new settlements or were driven to the US frontier.

The key areas of slave independent life grew up in and around the slave family. They embraced the simple, mundane routines of partnership and child-rearing, the daily routines of cooking, the communal habits of gossip and pleasures in and around the yards, and the teaching of children. This last was crucial, for the lessons of childhood were to inure slaves against the dangers of adult life. From one part of the Americas to another, it was the slave family that became the crucible from which slave society emerged. In places where slaves were owned in small numbers, where black and white lived close together, the slave family was more immediately influenced by local whites – especially by white women. Those slaves who lived at the back of white homes, who were only a few yards from white life, were more quickly influenced by local white cultural habits of child-rearing, feeding, cooking, religion – even literacy. Such slaves were socialized to European norms more quickly than those in large slave villages, distant from white life, where Africans remained a dominant force until late in the history of local slavery, and where white cultural forces operated at a distance. Everywhere, of course, Africa began to fade with the ending of the Atlantic slave trade. By then, however, the slave community, rooted in the family, was well-entrenched throughout the Americas.

As slave families thrived they spread throughout the Americas (and, to repeat, this from people who had landed from Africa alone, with no kin and no material possessions). The slave home became the centre of slave social life and of slave independence, and this physical centre of gravity was important. At first, slaves built their own homes. West Indian slave owners tended to provide the land, allowing slaves to build their own housing. Not surprisingly, what emerged were collections of houses, clustered around yards or compounds, which closely resembled African settlements. The huts or cabins, made mainly from wattle and daub and whatever local materials came to hand, later became more sophisticated as slave artisans (and more prosperous planters) lent their skills and facilities to improving slave homes. But they remained, throughout, the simplest form of crowded housing. William Beckford, describing Jamaican slave housing in 1790, noted that

> It is the custom now to have them built in strait lines, constructed with some degree of uniformity and strength, but totally divested of trees and shrubs; nor do I think that they are at all more mean in general appearance than those that help to form a village in some of the more sequestered and needy parts of England . . .

Planters who forced slaves to live communally in barracks soon faced slave demands for privacy. Slaves complained that, living in barracks, 'they were so much exposed to their neighbours, they did not like to let them know what they were doing on all occasions'.[3] Slaves, living in family groups, wanted privacy. And a similar pattern unfolded in North America. There, the earlier barracks (housing six men and more) of the pioneering tobacco plantations gave way to slave cabins. The urge for privacy, and the development of family life, led to the evolution of individual slave houses. But in North America, unlike Jamaica, slave owners undertook the building of slave housing, often hiring white workers but, again, using whatever materials were available locally.[4]

All this may seem obvious. Yet it contains an important general phenomenon. Given the material wherewithal, slaves constructed a physical environment that was their own, and they filled it with social activities which, in time, came to owe little or nothing to their owners. Once the ratio between the sexes became more evenly balanced, slave family and community life, focused on the slave home and the immediate group of slave settlements, provided the physical setting for the evolution of slave life. And much of that life functioned independent of slave owners. Here, then, was a social organization which seemed in many key respects independent of the plantation even when physically located on plantation land.

Slave homes were basic and possessed only the meanest of facilities; but, again, this began to change as *some* slaves began to acquire some of the material items disgorged by the consumer industries of the Western world. Cooking often took place out of doors and there, in the slave yards, a more communal slave social life evolved around the mundane routines of daily life: cooking and cleaning, relaxation and gossip, child care, and the daily concerns of people with a common set of problems and experiences. From within such slave settlements – despite their great variety across the Americas – slave cultural life evolved, with its emphasis on storytelling and music-making, incorporating themes from an African past and weaving them into the peculiarities and needs of life in the Americas. In all this, planters and others whites seemed far away, detached. In reality, of course, they were closer than slaves might like, and they could, at a stroke, intervene and sever the links between a slave, or group of slaves, and their family and community.

It was a peculiar relationship. Slave social and cultural independence was clear enough. But so was the white presence which threatened it. It is also misleading to suggest there was an unbridgeable divide between slaves and slave owners, even in those areas of slave life which speak of slave autonomy. It was, after all, slave owners who created the broader social arrangements within which slaves shaped their own lives. Take, for example, the question of free time. There is a temptation to think of slavery as all-consuming; an institution which allowed its victims no time for themselves. There were, it is true, some slaves whose lives were utterly consumed by the demands of slavery. But most slaves had free time: time off work, at the end of the working day, at the weekend, at high days and holidays, even during the day (for slaves who were able to pace themselves more independently at work). Indeed, some of the most popular surviving images – and certainly those most often portrayed by outside visitors – were of slave pleasures: the noisy and lively activities of slaves which took place in non-working hours.

Work was, of course, *the* main, central determinant of slave life everywhere. Everything else was secondary – at least in the eyes of the whites. But free time, and how best to fill it (most pleasurably and most profitably), was a feature of slave life throughout the Americas. Work varied enormously, of course, and free time itself was shaped by the distinctive mix of local work and the physical environment. Slaves returning to work after a weekly break, after the pleasures of an annual feast day (Christmas, New Year, crop-over) returned to the rigours of work in a better frame of mind. This was a variation of the European world turned upside down; of the master class allowing the lower orders their ration of pleasures, the better to get them back to profitable work and obedience immediately afterwards.

The specific customs of slaves' free time varied throughout the slave system. But free time came to be accepted, everywhere, as a conventional right which could be tampered with only at one's peril. Slave owners sighed with relief when the major slave celebrations passed by boisterously but peacefully. But such set-piece slave celebrations were the highlight of the slave calendar of free time. More frequent, of course, was that regular round of breaks – the calendar which allowed free time on a daily and weekly basis. It was, however, free time which many slaves were expected to fill to good effect. After work in the evening, and at weekends, slaves used their free time to work for themselves, in and around the home but especially in the plots and gardens. This work provided slaves with a better material standard of life, and the product of their spare-time labours – the foodstuffs, timber, animals, clothing – were sold, bartered, consumed. Thus, from such independent labours, slaves raised themselves from the minimalist conditions provided by their owners to a superior level of material well-being. In some cases, as will become apparent, these independent economic activities brought a greatly enhanced lifestyle.[5]

Slave owners granted free time knowing that much of it would be put to productive ends and thus relieve them of some of the burdens of providing for their slaves. Yet the process was important, not simply in feeding and clothing slaves, but in creating a greater sense of independence among the slaves themselves. Here was a part of their daily and weekly lives which belonged to themselves, from which they could profit and benefit.[6] And from those activities there flowed enhanced economic power. Slaves acquired a range of material goods and artefacts – for pleasure as well as necessity – from their labours in free time. Slaves' homes were improved, their clothing replaced, even luxuries acquired. They acquired things others thought worthy of stealing. We know of slaves who stole from other slaves 'sundry Goods, wearing apparel and other Matters to a large amount' in Jamaica in the 1780s. Another slave stole a clock.[7] More impressive still perhaps was the 'shelf or two of plates and dishes of queens or Staffordshire ware' seen in a slave home.[8] By the late eighteenth century, as the consumer industries of the Western world – especially those in Britain – began to disgorge ever more material items, many of those goods found their way into the slave quarters of the Americas. They helped to shape a material culture within the slave quarters which was more varied than one might expect.

Many welcomed the slaves' new-found acquisitiveness as a sign that the slaves were becoming civilized; that they were keen to acquire and consume the goods of the Western world. It was such goods, claimed Bryan Edwards, not money itself, which prompted 'the new desires springing up in [the slave's] mind, from the prospects and examples before him that have awakened his powers and called the energies of his mind into action'.[9] Thus were slaves brought to the habits of material consumption via their efforts in their own free time.

In the sugar islands, Saturday afternoons emerged as the slaves' free time.[10] Convention began to harden by the late eighteenth century (partly under ameliorationist pressure from London) and new laws specified free days. Of course, slave owners were not always bound by laws, especially those they found unfair, metropolitan intrusions. But so strong was the slave attachment to the conventional folk calendar of regular free time that only the most desperate or foolish of planters would ignore those rights. It may have been true that slaves living closest to urban areas were most alert to their legal and customary entitlements,[11] but in truth slave awareness of their rights was contagious and seeped through the slave communities. Slaves everywhere became alert to their rights, and to their entitlement of free time. Rights granted in one place were quickly adopted – or envied – by slaves elsewhere. Moreover, masters who refused to concede slave rights were likely to face trouble as truculent slaves took matters into their own hands. Plantocratic determination to enforce work on rest days or holidays might have prompted unrest and even open resistance.[12] Slaves could quite simply secure their own interests by blunt refusal. The fact that slaves periodically refused to forgo their conventionally acquired rights before the *force majeure* of their owners provides an important insight into slave mentality.

Weekends offered the most frequent break from slave work, being the time to do the string of domestic chores left for spare time. Among West Indians most time was spent on their own plots and by the last phase of British slavery slaves grew more of their own food than was provided by their owners.[13] Even here, however, slaves faced potential intrusion. When sugar prices were good, planters sometimes took back the slaves' gardens in order to plant more export crops. However, it was on the festivals of the Christian calendar that slaves lavished their most energetic efforts. Christmas and New Year were celebrated in the most extravagant fashions. Quite apart from travelling great distances to be with family and friends, slaves bedecked themselves in their best clothes and finery – often to the amazement of observers who could not fathom how slaves could afford or acquire such goods. Parades, songs and elaborate performances (in ceremonies blended from European and African elements) characterized the slave Christmas, and extended over three days or more. It was often a Christmas that Europeans scarcely recognized, though they accepted its importance for the slaves and often gave food and drink to add to the festivities.

Slave owners in nineteenth-century North America similarly helped their slaves to enjoy their free time. Keen for their slaves to establish the rituals of a Christian calendar and to celebrate the cycles of birth, marriage and death in a 'civilized' fashion, they gave food and drink, organized feasts and parties, and encouraged slaves to enjoy the major Christian feast days much like the whites. Some slaves distrusted the slave owners' motives. Frederick Douglass, for one, thought that Christmas and other holidays were a cruel fraud: 'These holidays serve as conductors, or safety-valves, to carry off the rebellious spirit of enslaved humanity . . . The holidays are part and parcel of the gross fraud, wrong, and inhumanity of slavery . . .'[14]

Though it seems clear enough that North American slave owners tried to be much more paternalistic than their Caribbean forebears (intruding into areas of slave life which West Indians were happy to leave well alone), both shared a common approach to slaves' free time. Like the property-owning and employing classes in Europe, slave owners had an ambivalence towards the free time of their labour force. On the one hand, too much of it (especially without regulation or guidance) was potentially dangerous. But suitably influenced, steered or limited, free time was a useful managerial tool. Donations of food and drink, like the concessions of free time itself, could lubricate slave enjoyment, secure slave attachments – and persuade them to return to their tasks once the revelries were over. In the words of Frederick Douglass, 'So, when the holidays ended, we staggered up from the filth of our wallowing, took a long breath, and marched to the field, feeling, upon the whole, rather glad to go . . .'[15] The world was allowed to turn upside down – like carnival, or its equivalents, St Monday or *chiavari* – on the strict understanding that it was righted the following day. Slavery was more easily managed and kept in place by allowing occasional outbursts of slave enthusiasms – loud, musical, and often drunken. The more lavish of slave pleasures, encouraged by slave owners at particular times of the year, achieved more than mere pleasure among the slaves. They clearly profited the slave owners by keeping the labour force in trim.

Slaves displayed utterly different characteristics when they went about their pleasures (and duties) in their own free time. Slaves, who throughout the Americas were denounced by their owners as lazy and incorrigibly unamenable, set about their own tasks and pleasures with an energy and application that confused owners and visitors alike. In their free time slaves were energetic and enterprising, displaying all the social and personal qualities which their owners failed to see (but which they tried to encourage) when the slaves worked at their slave tasks. They were slavish at work for their masters, but were energized and driven by application and self-interest in their free time. The obvious question that outsiders asked was: Would the slaves not be better, would they not work better, as free labourers? When slaves worked at their own plots and gardens, when they tended their own animals and made their own clothing, they faced few complaints about their laziness. Indeed, all the evidence suggests that, once turned loose from the restraints of slavery, they displayed the normal range of personal qualities seen in other communities. Slaves fed themselves from home-grown foodstuffs, sold the surplus for cash or exchanged for other goods. Slowly slaves began to acquire goods and luxuries far beyond the expectations of earlier generations of slaves. The fancy clothing, the jewellery, the cash and the animals which many slaves could boast of were all the rewards for hard work – not in their masters' fields, but in their own plots and gardens.

The results of slave independent enterprise could be seen in the gaggles of slaves heading for the local weekly market. Slave markets developed in villages and major towns, slave vendors hawking produce from gardens, selling animals they had reared, and even involving themselves in other more 'luxury' trades. In towns, slaves sold their goods from door to door, hawking their wares with that noisy, bustling confusion which survives to this day. Slaves thronged the wharves of the ports, buying and selling and generally making their (largely female) presence felt. But this buzz of slave independence made many contemporary whites, and men in urban authority, uneasy. Economic independence, and its related social freedoms, seemed to sit uncomfortably with slavery itself. Everywhere, efforts were made to restrict and control slaves' independent activities, to license their commercial activities and to keep some sort of curb on their public communal presence. But white society, especially in the towns, came to depend on this independent slave commercial presence. Servants from white homes themselves bartered and bargained with slave hawkers, and went to the local markets to buy food, meat and fish from slave higglers. Though whites might have disliked the freedoms which underpinned this remarkable slave commercialism, they also needed its produce.

Some slaves were able to acquire material possessions without moving far from the plantations. In 1760, in western Jamaica,

Phibbah, one of her master's favourite slave lovers, sold a filly to another slave for £4. 10s. She also 'sold her mare Patience to the Negro man of Col. Barclay's named Crossley for seven pounds. He paid her £5. 10s down, and is to pay the remaining 30s in three months'.[16] This is surely a remarkable fact: slaves, in a poor part of a distant colony, having enough *cash* to trade substantial amounts of money and valuable items among themselves. In fact such deals were commonplace, but they clash with many of the ideas we hold about the nature of slavery itself.

Slaves acquired hard cash in a number of ways: direct from their owners, sometimes for work, for goods, other times for sexual favours. Thomas Thistlewood frequently paid small amounts of cash when he had taken sexual advantage of slave women. Domestic slaves were especially likely to have cash, having access to the material world of the slave owners. Like domestics everywhere, they inherited goods which slave owners no longer required: the shoes and clothing, the damaged crockery, small items of food and drink and sometimes cash and gifts as a favour. Indeed, it seems likely that domestics formed the important conduit for the transfer of goods, styles and fads, from the propertied class to the propertyless. It was not so surprising, then, that luxuries began to appear in slave huts and cabins. When Thomas Thistlewood and Phibbah were about to part in 1757, he recorded in his diary, 'Thursday 23rd: Phibbah gave me a gold ring, to keep for her sake.' Later she sent him lots of foodstuffs and some soap.[17] There was, then, an important material culture among the slaves. Despite the fact that their forebears had landed in the Americas with nothing, save their ailments and their memories of Africa and the Atlantic crossing, slaves quickly acquired material objects, possessions ranging from the humblest of necessities (clothing, bedding, cooking utensils) through to luxuries which they treasured. Some of these basic items were provided by the slave owners themselves, but it is clear enough that many others flowed from slave independence and industry. Though slave possessions illustrate the rewards of individual slave efforts, they also underline an important general phenomenon. There was, within slave societies, a thriving independent slave economy which was closely linked to the broader economy dominated by the slave owners.

Planters came to accept that slaves had conventional rights to the ownership of property. Some acted as executors to slave wills, ensuring that bequeathed items were distributed as the deceased had wished. Thistlewood drew up a memorandum specifying how 'Mulato Will's goods' should be distributed:

> His wife's shipmate Silvia to have his cow; her daughter Hester, the heifer; Damsel his wife (Jimmy Hayes's wife) the filly and the rest of what he has. He desires to be buried at Salt River at his mother Dianah's right hand . . . [18]

In the cultivation, tending and sale of crops and animals slaves saved their owners considerable expense, especially in the Caribbean where many foodstuffs were imported. In time, slaves' rights to property were confirmed by law, but on the whole it was convention – and common sense – which confirmed and maintained those rights. Time and again, slave owners and outsiders remarked on the array of foodstuffs and animals maintained in and around the slave gardens. Here was the basis for slave material culture, for these foodstuffs both fed the slaves and created a surplus 'to carry to market'. In addition, planters and other local whites normally bought many of their own foodstuffs from their slaves.[19] Cattle and poultry, pigs and ducks, fruit, vegetables and fish – all passed from slave hands to the planters' tables. In return, the slave received money and an array of material items by way of sale or exchange. The surplus from their efforts formed the lubricant of their independent economy.

Access to the plots on which slaves worked was initially dictated by slave owners and, understandably, they rewarded their favourites, or the élite slaves with better or more ample land. In time, however, the development of slave families and the practice of inheritance changed the outlines of such landholdings; gardens and plots grew or diminished as family patterns changed. But, whatever their size, the gardens yielded the foods for the characteristic Sunday market. Sunday was a day of rest – or at least a rest from the slave owners' work. It involved lengthy walks to the provisions grounds, the gathering and carrying of food to the nearest market. All that was best done at night and early in the morning. Slave women carried and sold the market produce. Roads leading to West Indian markets were generally crowded with women on a Sunday morning. Thomas Thistlewood recorded in September 1753 that the road running through his property was packed 'with an abundance of Negroes', all heading for the 'large Negro market by Tony's gate'.[20] There were, of course, some slaves who did not take part, but it is significant that they tended to be the poorest of all the local slaves; a clear enough sign that slaves were able to improve themselves by access to this independent marketing culture. Those slaves who were indisputably better off tended to be people whose own efforts yielded returns from their gardens and plots.

At these weekly markets, slaves sold, bought and bartered with every conceivable class of people, from fellow slaves to planters (or, more likely, the planters' domestic slaves). But the key point remains that this independent slave economy was crucial to the broader overall economy. Islands and regions were *fed* by slave activities. Not only did individual slaves improve *themselves*, but they fed and nurtured most other sectors of their local society. Nor was this simply a matter of food, for slaves brought to the markets a range of homemade items necessary for local life – clothing, pottery, baskets, furniture, bedding, rope, matting.[21] And even when these and other items were sold by non-slave hagglers (freed slaves and people of colour), the goods had generally been purchased initially from slave producers. The whole process involved complicated transport networks, and chains of sales, from the slave plots to the urban point of sale. But the end result was that money – hard cash – found its way into the slave quarters in the remotest of plantations. Slaves were part of the local cash economy.

In Jamaica in 1774 it was calculated that slaves owned 20 per cent of all the circulating cash. The scarcity of the lowest denominations of currencies hit the slaves especially, since they were the people who made most use of them.[22] When Thomas Thistlewood took sexual favours from his various female slaves, he usually rewarded them with small change: 'Gave her 4 bits.' After an especially strenuous night with one slave, Jenny, he gave her ' . . . 2 yards of Brown Oznabrig, 4 bitts; 4 yards of striped holland, 8 bitts; and a handkerchief, 3 bitts.' After sex with Susannah, he 'Gave her 2 bits.'[23] Slaves saved their cash, sometimes giving it to another person for safe keeping, sometimes hoarding the money in their own cash box. Slaves working in towns were often paid in cash[24] and, even on the plantations, slaves received cash gifts at Christmas and holidays. When, towards the end of the eighteenth century, Jamaican planters were keen to persuade their slaves to reproduce more readily (and thus save them the expense of buying imported Africans), they rewarded them, among other items, with cash. The eight women who gave birth on Worthy Park in 1794 were each rewarded by their grateful owner with a dollar.[25] Slaves were given cash for work well done, for housebuilding, for training and helping to acclimatize new Africans, for the successful acquisition of special skills or the completion of a particular job. Some were paid when planters had to make them work on their customary free days. Not surprisingly, then, thefts among the slaves – of slave on slave – was not uncommon.[26] (Slaves who were armed to protect plantation property sometimes turned their weapons against slaves caught in the act of stealing from fellow slaves.)[27] Exceptional slaves were able to acquire money via their specialized skills – drawing, rat-catching, fishing, storytelling, music-making – in short, any skill or talent that was in demand and could command a price. All these transactions reveal the many ways slaves were involved in the local cash economy.

Slaves spent money on a range of pleasures and material objects: tobacco and food, household items and drink, imported objects, finery and jewellery. They also spent their money on games of chance. Many of the artefacts bought by slaves were locally made, but others were imported (from Europe and North America to the Caribbean, from the Caribbean to North America). Most of these purchases seem to have been made at markets. Moreover, the markets themselves provided slaves with the opportunity (along with high days and holidays) to dress for the occasion. The gaggles and processions of slaves to and from the markets were characterized by elaborate dress, as slaves made the most of their free time to enjoy themselves as well as to profit and trade. Slave owners frequently complained about the pleasures which slaves found for themselves in and around the local marketplace.

Outsiders were especially puzzled by how slaves managed to acquire their lavish displays of clothing and how costly items found their way into slave homes. Of course, many slaves chose to deny themselves for much of the time, preferring to live and work in rags in order to appear in some eye-catching splendour at the appropriate moment, especially when attending church on the Sabbath.[28] Slaves also acquired goods by pilfering. Indeed slave owners throughout the Americas complained that slaves were natural thieves, always likely to steal from the whites. For their part, slaves did not regard such theft as stealing. Of course in *assuming* that slaves were thieves, each and every missing item was imputed to the slaves. Try as they might, slave owners could not prevent pilfering, especially the stealing of food and drink. If it was serious, organized – and discovered – slaves could expect serious punishments. Of the group of Salt River slaves caught stealing goods from the Jamaican estate store in 1753, one was hanged, another had 'both ears cropped, both nostrils slit, and marked on both cheeks; Cheddar's right ear cropped, right nostril slit, and marked on the left cheek'.[29]

Slave economic freedom was just as striking in North America. There, too, slaves controlled land, produced foodstuffs, raised livestock, made a range of marketable artefacts, and accepted money for a host of activities. In general, they engaged in a thriving market which was partly their own and partly linked to the broader local economy. Like their Caribbean counterparts, they worked at their independent tasks in the free time afforded them by their owners. Free time was not always free from work, but it allowed American slaves to accumulate material goods and money. Slaves in Louisiana – also dominated by a sugar industry – were often paid more, and for more tasks, than West Indian slaves.[30] But they were as one in enjoying the opportunities afforded by local markets, selling, buying and bartering. Like Caribbean slaves, Americans were keen to use the markets as a way of displaying themselves – and their best clothing – to an admiring world. In the remoter regions of the US, where markets were too distant from slave settlements, slaves sold their goods to travelling pedlars for onward sale to the markets. The patterns varied from place to place, and the cycle of slave independent economic activities revolved around the nature of the local crop. But the overall patterns were repeated time and again.

The importance of this independent slave economy transcended the simple material benefits which accrued to the slaves. Slaves developed a sense of their own independence and worth, and that awareness owed little to their owners or the social system to which they were assigned. They were able to control and modulate key areas of their social and economic lives, more or less without interference from those who claimed dominion over them. In the process, there emerged a clear drive to material accumulation; a personal and communal desire to acquire those

149

material artefacts which, in however small a fashion, made life more comfortable and pleasant. The slaves were, in effect, another example of that more broadly based pattern of material consumption which transformed the Western world in the eighteenth and nineteenth centuries.[31] It was not surprising, when slave owners sought to improve themselves materially and flaunted their prosperity, that slaves should imitate them when they could.

The significance of this independent slave economic activity, however, was not simply a matter of material accumulation. It was in essence the most striking aspect in a diversity of slave independent activities. Independent economic life allowed slaves to enjoy an enhanced independent social life and a greater diversity in the private world of slave sociability. The domestic slave environment – the homes and communities – were materially improved thanks to the slaves' own efforts. Of course it is very easy to exaggerate such improvements, and we need to recall that most slaves, throughout most of the history of black slavery in the Americas, lived out their lives in a poor, mean environment. But it is surely significant that what we know of slave purchasing power shows that it was directed towards improving the material quality of their lives – their food, their clothing, their homes. These improvements were on a modest scale, but they were part of the slave determination to improve themselves. When we look into the slave huts and cabins, when we see slaves dressed for church or for market, when we catch sight of slaves gathering for high days and holidays, we are looking at people *dramatically* removed from the wretchedness of their new-landed African forebears. Africans who landed in the New World naked or near-naked would have looked with some amazement on the levels to which their descendants had been able to raise themselves. And it needs to be stressed that such levels of improvement are to be measured largely by the efforts of the slaves themselves. The evolution of a distinct material culture among black slaves was, to repeat, the fruits of their own efforts. And those efforts were but one aspect of a varied pattern of slave independence which might, at first glance, seem out of place within so intrusive and total a system as slavery. What is clearer by the year, as more data comes to light, is the remarkable diversity of slave life, and the flexibility they were able to tease out of slavery.

150

The slave systems of North America and the Caribbean differed greatly, not least in their demographic fundamentals. And the facts of demographic life intruded even in the world of slave independence. North American slave owners rarely faced those massive armies of slaves, living at a distance, that were so common in the West Indies. In colonial North America, slaves were owned in relatively small numbers and lived close to the master/mistress, rapidly socializing to a number of white norms (most notably, of course, linguistic). The expansion of cotton slavery in the nineteenth century changed that balance between black and white, and the cotton plantations were larger than the older slave-holdings in the Old South. But, by then, as we have seen, the slaves were local, American-born; born into local society and knowing no other, save for the memories and folklore of older Africans.

At the centre of slave independence was the family. Slaves lived out their lives in the bosom of their families, loved ones and neighbours, enjoying a community which was at once local, yet in time spread to cover a wide geographic area (a process hastened, of course, by the forceful removal of slaves away from their immediate families). Wise slave owners appreciated the value of the slave family. At its crudest, it made economic sense. But, since all (or at least most) slaves had a monetary value, owners occasionally decreed that slaves had to be sold or removed. Nonetheless, it was the slave family which formed the nub of slave life and around which key areas of social and economic independence flowed. The slave family – the subject of revisionary and revealing research over the past generation – tended to be 'nuclear', with mother, father and children. Again, the attachment to family can be measured in the pained outcry when family members were removed by the slave traders and cast beyond the reach and even the ken of their relatives. It was here, within the family, that slaves learned those lessons of life which were particular to black slavery.

Slave families were both dependent and yet autonomous. They grew and thrived despite the pressures of slavery. But they were always under threat. Slave husbands lacked the legal authority over wives who were allowed white husbands, and slavery often demanded that many of them should be absent from the home (though this was hardly unique to slavery). Even the children, though reared and educated by parents and older relatives, were soon inculcated into the labouring routines of local slavery. They quickly learned that they belonged not just to their parents but also to their owners. Though this made for a set of conflicting loyalties, slave parents were eager to teach their children how to cope with these demands; to teach them the rules and conventions of dual loyalties and to acquire those knacks of dissembling which were features of slave society everywhere. In the relationships between slave parents and children, we can see a form of this distinctive dualism among the slaves. Loyalty was split between two apparently conflicting centres of power and obedience: owners and parents. From their earliest days, slaves came to appreciate that their independence was fissured by the cross-currents of slavery itself.

For all that, in and around the slave communities (which themselves varied from place to place) slaves sought to lead personal and communal lives which were removed from (if not utterly uninfluenced by) white people. The further they were removed, geographically, from white housing, the more autonomous slave social and cultural life (as had been true in the Caribbean for a long while). Here, slaves passed through those mundane routines of daily, weekly, seasonal life which were, at once, utterly ordinary and yet important because they were the crucible for slave independence. It was in the village, in the community, that slaves grew their own food, tended their beasts, made their clothing and furnishings, entertained themselves and celebrated the festivals of family and local slave life (itself increasingly Christian). However hard-pressed they might be as slaves, free time was enjoyed to the full. In the West Indies and North America, slaves invested their pleasures with an energetic enthusiasm which contrasted sharply with the listlessness of the work day. Slave owners everywhere were puzzled by the contrast: bored, lazy slaves came alive at nighttime, at weekends and on holidays. As ever, more slaves turned to Christianity, free time meant worship and all the associated activities spawned by chapel and church. Here, again, devout slaves invested their worship with an enthusiasm which was so missing in their labouring lives.[32]

Here, then, especially at high days and holidays, was a world turned upside down; pleasurable exuberance tolerated under specific terms, on condition that slaves returned to their labouring life at first light the following day. It was in the set-piece celebrations of the slaves' social lives that we can best see the cultural mix that became slave life. In slave religion and in slave pleasures, Africa was rarely far away. Though the slave trade had long ceased to play an important role in North America, memories of Africa survived, surfacing in particular forms during slave enjoyments and worship. African songs and stories, words and images – all and more floated in and out of slave culture, from the Sea Islands of Georgia to the swampy regions of Louisiana. But intermingled, especially for slaves in the new cotton regions, were the particular, distinctive experiences of America itself. And none were more painful, more haunting, than those in the nineteenth-century slave trade *within* the USA which saw the enforced westward surge of a million slaves across the face of North America.

It was perhaps in the world of religion that black independence seemed most striking. Yet it should also remind us of the inextricable links to the world of the slave owners. Though a number of African forms survived and mingled with black Christianity, the religion of US slaves was Christian. And Christianity was acquired from the whites. True, it was shaped and moulded to slaves' particular needs and requirements. But here was an alien, white religion, transformed by the slaves to their own ends. How much was autonomous and how much dependent? The rise of black Christianity throughout the English-speaking Americas provides evidence which historians can use in a host of ways. It ought to remind us as much of the limitations of slave independence as its achievements. For a start, slave owners in North America (and here they differed from West Indians) were generally keen to convert slaves – especially Africans – to Christianity, in part to wrench them free from those African habits which whites universally disliked and feared. Slaves were also assailed by various crusading sects, keen to win them over to their side. The end result was that slaves across nineteenth-century America were basically Christian. But theirs was a distinctive form of Christianity which seemed to owe as much to the social tone and needs of the slave quarters as it did to the strict theology of the dominant local sect. Black preachers – speaking to the condition, the needs, the experiences, of their enslaved congregation – were

153

normally more successful than white preachers. Moreover, the language and imagery of many Old Testament stories spoke directly to the slaves' condition, offering future redemption, escape from a land of bondage and an end to a lifetime of suffering. The pain of the cross would be followed by salvation in the hereafter.

Slaves both in the West Indies and North America shared similar cultural experiences. In the islands, slaves were converted late – from the 1780s onwards – partly a result of the planters' resistance to the idea, partly due to the slowness of the Christian churches themselves to tackle the Caribbean slave quarters. But the slave enthusiasm for Christianity, especially for non-conformity, produced worship of an entirely different kind. Loud and declamatory, sometimes convulsive, black Christianity was like nothing the whites had seen before. They did not intend, when they allowed or encouraged the rise of black Christianity, to have it shaped into a medium of independent black expression and identity. But that is precisely what it became. Their black congregations – often physically independent of the plantations, and beyond the control of white people – provided an opportunity for slaves to meet communally, distant from the place of work and away from the prying curiosity of white folks. Their chosen preachers were black – often enslaved – and their favourite texts (and hymns) spoke of freedom and oppression. They turned to the Bible and many inevitably began to master the art of reading. Literacy and the Bible went together to shape a potent force for change.

Literate, Christian slaves, bound together by the strong ties of congregation, addressed by powerful black preachers who spoke elevating words of freedom and promise: the world of slave Christianity was quite different from anything experienced by their masters and owners. In places, slaves even refused to stand or to make way for whites in church. In the brotherhood of a Christian church, slaves – in the West Indies and in North America – had created a tool for their own collective expression as much as for their own private thought and worship. Yet, to repeat, it had ultimately derived from the whites themselves. It was, at one and the same time, a sign of slave independence, yet no less an indication of the cultural interdependence between black and white.

Black Christianity could become a force which slave owners

found difficult to contain. In the West Indies, where plantocratic resistance remained steadfast throughout, black preachers and their volatile slave congregations were at the forefront of the major slave rebellions in the early nineteenth century. Enraged congregations of slaves, inspirational black preachers, the spread of a radical biblical vernacular – all and more fanned the embers of slave unrest with the draft from slave churches. In Barbados (1816), Demerara (1823) and, most stunning of all, Jamaica (1831–1832), Christianity and slavery blended in a volatile brew, spilling over into major slave insurrections. It was no accident that the massive slave upheaval of 1831–1832 was known as the 'Baptist War'.[33] Though North American slaves did not revolt on the West Indian scale, they too were played upon by rebellious Christian slaves. Sunday was the obvious day for seditious gatherings (no one would suspect slaves moving around freely on the Sabbath). Denmark Vesey, leader of the Charleston upheaval in 1822, used biblical language to appeal to his followers. When Vesey and others were caught and tried, they went to their deaths, with biblical quotes ringing in their ears, chosen to illustrate their wickedness. Less than a decade later, Nat Turner planned a similar uprising in Virginia, again using the Christian vernacular to make the point: 'I was ordained for some great purpose in the hands of the Almighty.' The outcome, however, was much the same.[34]

Christianity among the slaves did not *necessarily* become the cutting edge of independence or violent resistance. Throughout North America, black and white met together in the act of worship, notably where paternal owners sought to encourage piety among their slaves. Yet many whites remained uneasy at the nature and expression of black Christianity. It was altogether too distinctive – too black, sometimes too 'African' – for their liking. Black Christians did not always behave the way their masters and mistresses liked or approved of. At times their expression of Christian belief seemed less than civilized. Once more we are faced with that ambivalence which suffused white dealings with black Christianity. And once again we need to recognize the limits to black independence.

Slave autonomy emerged and thrived mainly because the slaves themselves needed and wanted it. It was an essential aspect of slave life. But it was tolerated by slave owners because they too benefited from it. Most obvious in economic terms (whites throughout the slave societies consumed goods produced and sold by slaves in their free time), the slave owners' acceptance of slave independence existed at many levels. Slave owners accepted that theirs was a system which thrived best when slaves were accorded a degree of independence – an element of freedom. They were granted days free from work, times of the year free for pleasures of their own making. They were allowed independence to create and maintain family ties and communal structures. Their social lives – including their religious practices (at least, if they were Christian) – were their own; theirs to shape and enjoy as they saw fit. Yet it would be foolish to overstate these areas of independent slave life and to suggest that they remained immune to their owners' scrutiny and intrusions.

When we examine the ways in which these various freedoms were *violated*, we can sense that most ubiquitous and persistent of slave fears: the sudden, capricious and sometimes irrational assaults on their lives and against their rights by slave owners. Despite slave independent activity throughout the slave societies of the Americas, despite the widespread acceptance of slaves' conventional rights (sometimes confirmed by local laws), here were rights which were readily denied, infringed or transgressed. Slave property could simply be removed. Slave housing could be shifted (if land were needed for other purposes). Slave families (or, worse still, individuals within the family) could be dispatched over the horizon. Wives, lovers, daughters or sisters might simply fall irresistible victim to predatory white sexuality. And, for all the recollections which slaves harboured about good masters and mistresses, they were normally weighed in the balance with others whose harshness or cruelties were the stuff of slave memory and legend.[35]

Slaves made their own lives more tolerable, more comfortable, more humane. But their efforts to shape an independence which ensured these qualities all took place within a system which was oppressive, violent and one-sided. It was more violent in the Caribbean than in North America. But the brutality of slave systems cannot simply be calibrated or distinguished by statistical differences (of revolts, executions, whippings and other violations). Slaves everywhere in the English-speaking world believed that they lived under unjust conditions. Though the most obvious of injustices took the form of physical violations, slave grievances went much deeper than complaints about brutality. This deep-rooted and universal antipathy to the world they lived in forms the backcloth against which we need to judge most aspects of slave behaviour. Areas of slave independent activity could scarcely begin to moderate the more deep-rooted slave antagonisms to the world they were obliged to tolerate.

9

ENDING SLAVERY

There are few more perplexing questions in the history of slavery than the manner of its ending. The British were the pioneers of the campaign; first against the slave trade, then against slavery in their own colonies and finally against slavery worldwide. This simple fact itself has prompted historical debate. Why should the nation which had perfected (if not pioneered) those systems which took most Africans into the Americas, and made most profitable use of them when they were there, renounce its past and become so instrumental in ending them? It was as if the international slave-poacher quickly and effectively turned international slave gamekeeper. The British became the world's pre-eminent abolitionist force.[1] In the process the British developed a political identity as *the* global power for good, safeguarding the down-trodden and defending the wronged. Yet this image, so persistently repeated throughout the nineteenth and twentieth centuries, has to be set in the balance against the history of British slavery (indeed of British imperialism in a wider setting). When slavery had ended, British commentators preferred to revel in British abolition – not British slavery.

The rise of the Atlantic slaving empire had quickly silenced the few voices raised against slavery in the early days. In the period of Spanish settlement in the Americas, the objections to European advancement in the Americas tended to be most voluble in support of the native Indian peoples. In demanding protection for those peoples, critics of New World policy tended to lose sight of the violation of Africa. Indeed, Africans came to be seen as a relatively easy way of *solving* the Indian problem. African imports would serve two functions: they protected Indians from the damage caused by entanglement with

158

Europeans, and they provided the kind of malleable and re-placeable labour which Indians seemed incapable of undertaking. African slaves were in effect the shield behind which the Indian peoples might be afforded some protection. In the event this is not what happened, and the history of the Indian peoples in the years of European contact was a series of disasters to parallel the miseries of the imported Africans.[2]

By the time the British settled their own colonies in the Americas in the seventeenth century, African slaves had already proved their value in the course of European expansion. The British simply adopted what others had pioneered but they, more than any other Europeans, proved how lucrative this system could be. It is true that during the late seventeenth century, when the British shipped ever more Africans into their Caribbean and North American settlements, some voices were raised in complaint. Quakers, themselves émigré victims of persecution, spoke out against slavery, but they were an isolated minority, scorned for their social style and theology alike, operating on the margins of 'respectable' society. In time, of course, they came to exercise enormous influence. But they failed to arrest the advance of the British slave system.

Until the period of the American Revolution, slavery generally went unchallenged. There were periodic debates about the *specifics* of slavery, and both colonial and metropolitan politics had occasionally been troubled by some of the more draconian laws and punishments slave owners felt to be necessary. London sometimes rejected or modified colonial laws when they were thought too severe. But these were quibbles about details, not principles. However, the debate shifted to a different plain from the 1760s, not least because of the ideological issues that lay at the heart of growing American independence. In their turn, those arguments were partly shaped by ideas and writings which flowed from Enlightenment thinkers, a number of whom were specifically critical of slavery. More corrosive of slavery, however, was the Enlightenment-sponsored debate about political and social rights in a much broader setting. If equality was to be the preserve of all men (and women?), both before the law and in social practice, how could slavery be justified?[3]

But slaves were only one (if perhaps the most striking) of a number of groups whose fate were considered by writers and critics in the wake of the Enlightenment. The treatment of

159

children, women, prisoners, the mad – even animals – was now exposed to critical scrutiny. One consequence of the Enlightenment was that, henceforth, all forms of social organization were exposed to scrutiny and criticism; no institution or individual could hope to escape examination simply because they had remained unchallenged in the past. Human institutions needed to be explained and justified, and few attracted more obvious and fundamental examinations than slavery itself.

This was most obviously the case in the newly created USA, for the nation and its Constitution had been forged through a debate about the basic principles of rights, and about the nature of governance. To compound that debate, a new economic philosophy emerged – enunciated most specifically in Adam Smith's *The Wealth of Nations* (1776) – which demanded the removal of restraints for the better functioning of economic life. This seriously threatened the British slave empire, which had thrived for a century past on a highly protected, mercantilist system (against which the Americans had rebelled). After 1776, however, new voices demanded freedom where once there had been restrictions and controls; freedom of capital and freedom of labour. Slavery was the very antithesis of free labour. The logic of the demands for a more open, freer conduct of economic affairs was to replace slavery by free labour.

At first, such claims were mere speculation; the preserve, by and large, of a small band of intellectuals. But the post-1776 debate about free trade was congruent with the much more broadly based debate about freedoms which flowed from the Enlightenment. It seemed likely that the debate might make its greatest impact in North America, where old colonial slavery seemed at odds with the new Constitution, and where political debate had to make frequent compromises in order to blend slavery with human and political rights. There was, from the moment of American Independence, a tension between American freedom and American slavery.[4] This tension was to survive as long as slavery itself survived in the USA. For the best part of a century, between the Declaration of American Independence in 1776 and the final abolition of American slavery by the Thirteenth Amendment in 1865, slavery posed a series of problems for the USA.

North American slavery did *not* fade away (as seemed likely in the last years of the eighteenth century), but revived and blossomed. It was yet another curiosity of slavery that, just when it seemed likely to fall into disuse, just when the old colonial slave systems seemed irrelevant to the new American order, it was given the kiss of economic life by cotton. Slavery, which seemed a dubious and morally questionable institution by 1776 had, within a generation, once more become essential. The figures alone give some indication. The 697,897 slaves of 1790 had grown to 3,953,760 seventy years later. By then, slavery thrived in nine new states.[5] Ironically the British – who in 1776 seemed more firmly wedded to their own slave system than the Americans – had, by then, learned to manage without slavery and had embarked on a global campaign against slavery.

The British campaign against slavery shared, naturally enough, many of the same intellectual origins as the American. But the British campaign grew in strength and effectiveness as the American cause waned in front of an increasingly powerful investment in cotton slavery. Again, Quakers were at the fore, founding a small London committee in 1787 to seek an end to the slave trade. Even that seemed a remote and impossibly ambitious aim. Among men of sensibility, the knowledge which had slowly accumulated about the nature of the slave trade pointed to an outrage which needed correction. Here (to a small band of the religious-minded) was a sin which shamed the entire nation. And the whole murderous business was to sustain an economic system in the Americas based on dubious economics. At first, and for many years afterwards, the campaign against the slave trade focused on its irreligion and inhumanity.

Evidence about the brutality of the slave trade was readily available. Shocking details from British court cases, dock-side folklore and the mortality of white sailors on slave ships, all confirmed by ex-slaves living in Britain, gave abolitionists the data they needed for a public campaign.[6] They faced powerful opposition, however. The absentee plantocracy, enjoying the fruits of their slaves' labours in the nation's most fashionable watering holes, allied themselves with metropolitan and maritime interests (banking, business and insurance) to promote the case for slavery and the slave trade. The slave lobby's case seemed overwhelming. There were few areas of Britain where local well-being remained unaffected by the slave empire. Dozens of ports sustained the slave trade, vast rural and urban hinterlands filled the ships with foodstuffs and manufactured goods, and most

British consumers had become addicted to the fruits of slave labours, most notably sugar.[7]

There were, then, very good reasons why the British should have maintained their Atlantic slave trade. It represented a large slice of British maritime trade and seemed vital to the continuing prosperity of the Caribbean islands. In 1787, the abolitionist call for an end to the trade seemed hopelessly unrealistic, for their demands seemed to be little less than a plea for the British to end one of their most entrenched and all-pervasive habits. Traders and planters were as one in claiming that abolition of the trade would bring ruin. Yet within twenty years abolition had been achieved. Nor was this simply a question, as many have claimed, of declining slave-based fortunes (of the British abandoning what had become unprofitable), for it is abundantly clear that the slave system continued, throughout the last years of the eighteenth century, to bring profit and material well-being to most of those actively involved.[8] How, then, can we explain what happened?

The London-based Abolition Society quickly found friends across the face of Britain, thanks initially to the network of Quaker sympathizers already in place. This network provided the framework of a national movement which was able to recruit local signatures (to abolitionist petitions), launch local initiatives and keep in touch with the London centre. From the first, women were at the forefront of British (and American) abolition, operating independently of male organization and leadership, creating influential female networks and distinctive styles of political campaigning. Their efforts reached into British domestic life, galvanizing legions of British women, providing new and unimagined scope for female activists. Forced by contemporary conventions to operate in 'separate spheres', female abolitionists (naturally enough) focused on the plight of slave women, broadcasting, denouncing and generally publicizing the outrages committed against slave women and slave families. Female abolitionists were as keen to see the establishment of 'normal' gender relations among the slaves as they were to see black freedom. They aimed to elevate slave women to their own role as guardians of hearth and family. It was not a campaign designed to upset the social order. Rather, it sought to encourage the cultivation of domestic harmony among the slaves of a kind to be found in the privileged homes of female abolitionists. It was, at once, an argument about gender, about class – and about freedom.[9]

These were also the years which saw a proliferation of non-conformist sects and their chapels, rooted generally in the 'new' Britain which was slowly emerging from the complex process of industrial and urban change. Slavery was a monument to everything that the 'new' men of this changing Britain disliked. The debate about liberty – spawned by the American break in 1776 and then, more seismically, by the Revolution in France in 1789 – encompassed belief in freedom of labour and economics. So there was a broad, secular attachment to ideals of freedom, which flourished most dramatically after 1791 in Britain through the emergence of a new brand of popular radical societies, all of which were abolitionist. But, again, it was religion which galvanized most people. This was especially true in non-conformist British chapels (from sects which were also thriving among slaves in the 1780s), who saw in the ill-treatment of non-conformist West Indian slaves an outrageous persecution of their co-religionists.

Slavery managed, then, to become an object of distaste among all sorts and conditions of British people in the last years of the eighteenth century. To working people, it represented an oppression far worse than their own. To their employers and economic theorists, slavery involved a denial of the basic freedom of labour which they cherished. To the devout, notably the non-conformists, slavery entailed a denial of religious freedom. To thousands of women (whose domestic pleasures were measured out by tea-drinking rituals made possible by slave-grown sugar), slavery was a violation of womanhood and of family itself. Here, then, was an issue on which master and man, men and women, could unite. It is surely also significant that the British could wax indignant about slavery because it was so distant. Unlike the Americans, the British did not have to live cheek by jowl with slavery or with the direct consequences of black freedom. They could demand full humanity for slaves apparently at little or no cost to themselves – an early case of that 'telescopic philanthropy' which was to become a feature of British life throughout the nineteenth century.

Abolitionist tactics were remarkably successful. Able to muster huge crowds, to garner tens of thousands of names to abolitionist petitions and to lobby MPs as never before, the abolitionist public campaigns were remarkable. The female-led sugar boycott, aimed at the sociability of female tea-drinking, was an attempt to hurt the West India lobby's income. Abolitionist Parliamentary tactics were less successful, in part because William Wilberforce was a poor Parliamentary tactician but mainly because Parliament was deterred by the shadow of the French Revolution and by the bloody upheavals in Haiti. It was easy for opponents of abolition to point to the bloodshed in France, but especially in Haiti, and to suggest that such turmoil would inevitably follow any tampering with the British slave system. All this (and the House of Lords) served to delay the ending of the slave trade. Yet it was a mere fluke that abolition did not squeeze through. When it did, finally, the British banned the slave trade in 1807.[10] But that still left 600,000 slaves labouring in the British islands.

The purpose in ending the slave trade was to deny planters access to the supplies of fresh Africans they regarded as essential. But no one really knew what the effects of ending the Atlantic trade would be. While the results were awaited, it was hoped that improvement – 'amelioration' to use the vernacular – would transform slavery. The evidence from the registration of slaves (a population census) illustrated what strenuous efforts slave owners made to make good the absence of fresh Africans. The increased slave discontent in the West Indies after 1807 was partly a result of the reorganization of slave-holdings. News about this discontent was fed back to Britain by British missionaries now active in the islands. It became ever clearer that slavery would *not* die a natural death, but rather its owners would persist with human bondage as long as they were permitted.

At times, it appeared that the slaves might take matters into their own hands. The great slave upheavals of 1816 (Barbados), 1823 (Demerara) and 1831–1832 (Jamaica) not only shook the plantocracy to its foundations but, as we have seen, entailed black suffering on an epic scale. More and more people in Britain were horrified by what they learned of slavery. For all the slave lobby's arguments about economic well-being, the system they defended involved suffering on a massive scale. By the mid-1820s, British abolitionists relaunched their political campaign, this time to secure full black freedom. And women were at the forefront of the new demands for immediate freedom.[11] The changed circumstances within Britain helped the campaign, most

164

notably the rising demand for reform on a broad front; emancipation fitted perfectly in a reforming climate. The slave revolts, with their tales of persecution, reasonable slave claims and savage plantocratic revenge, was grist to the abolitionist mill. The old slave lobby was in retreat, partly because its old political power-base in Britain was itself being corroded by demands for the reform of Parliament. Finally, the persecution of emergent, black Christianity persuaded more and more people of the need to end slavery. When Parliament was reformed in 1832, it was merely a matter of time before slavery was abolished.

That was partially effected on 1 August 1834 (though with a massive £20,000,000 compensation for the planters) and finally, and completely, on the same date in 1838. It was surely revealing that, despite rumours and fears that the freed slaves would revenge themselves on their former owners, slaves rejoiced peacefully. Many packed into their nearest churches, which were bedecked in flowers and palm fronds. They gave thanks for deliverance to the God only recently introduced in their midst. There was lavish praise for British abolitionists and politicians, for the Queen and for the British Parliament.[12] Everyone seemed to have forgotten the role that same Parliament had played in the creation and perfection of the slave system over the past two centuries.

The British, having freed 750,000 slaves, henceforth embarked on that global crusade against slavery which was itself to be part of their cultural imperial instincts throughout the rest of the century. Slave emancipation was a defining moment in the shaping of Britain's dealings with the wider world for the rest of the century. The British came to believe that they, above all other peoples, were blessed by an attachment to freedom. They, the lovers of freedom, found themselves pitched against evil forces the world over. It was a view, of course, which ignored Britain's slaving history, and also ignored the sound economic reasons for British attachment to global freedom. Others, notably the French and the Americans, disliked and distrusted the British posturing. But, for their part, the British felt secure in their identity as the world's crusader for freedom.

The most obvious and immediate target for abolitionists was the USA. There, the rise of cotton production had seen the revival of American slavery, pushing slave production westwards in a string of new states and creating that internal slave trade which saw armies of American slaves moving onwards, from their home regions, to relocation and work on the cotton frontier. It was a slave trade which lacked the physical horrors of the old Atlantic crossing, but it had its own traumas, not least the widespread pattern of family breakups.

Like the British, American abolitionists, mainly in the North, had long assumed that slavery would simply fade away. Cotton ensured that it did not. There were efforts (like the British Sierra Leone scheme of 1787) to ship American slaves back to Liberia, but this and other forms of anti-slavery simply failed in the teeth of cotton-based prosperity. Despite the rise of reforming sentiment across the USA – again paralleling the British reforming spirit – slavery remained intact. The slave-holding states turned their back on the idea of reform for obvious reasons: any attempt to change social relations might undermine the very foundations of slavery itself. In a world where outsiders were critical (and Northerners and British abolitionists became ever more critical) the South turned in on itself, developing into that separate world which was to become the stuff of caricature, then and since. Southerners came to pride themselves on their conservative difference, and the key to that difference was slavery. Social and political life in the North, transformed by dramatic industrial, population and urban changes, swept by reforming movements, diverged ever more sharply from Southern society. Southerners came to think of abolition as just another fashion spawned by a Northern society which had few points of contact with the South.

The South rooted itself in an identity which, if not anti-democratic, was traditional and conservative. It was a way of life, an ideology, which seemed in a time warp. Unable to contemplate a modernizing state based on the democratic ideals of 1789 (or 1776) and unwilling to embrace, even to contemplate, the transforming power of industrial change, the South and its spokesmen faced the early nineteenth century resistant to the lure of progress, appealing instead to a world which had collapsed elsewhere throughout the Western world. The centre of the Southern world was, of course, slavery.[13]

The ending of the British slave system in 1838 left the South exposed. Slave systems survived elsewhere (notably in Cuba and Brazil), but British emancipation left the South as the exception in an English-speaking world which was shaped and directed by an attachment to freedom in its broadest sense. The freedom to associate for political change, the freedom to invest, the freedom of labour, the freedom of expression and religion – all these and more had, cumulatively, produced a distinct tone of freedom on both sides of the Atlantic.[14] It is easy, of course, to forget the exceptions and there was no greater exception than Southern slavery, based as it undoubtedly was on the polar opposite of all the freedoms admired and advanced in the industrializing regions of the West. In an age when progress had unleashed boundless material well-being, when the material benefits of economic freedom were to be seen on all hands, slavery stuck out as an offensive reminder of an outdated way of conducting economic and social affairs.

To many contemporaries, in the North and in Britain, American slavery (indeed slavery everywhere) seemed a religious and moral outrage. The days had long gone when slavery was ethically neutral. The rise of new forms of religion, more especially crusading and evangelical non-conformity, had been instrumental in transforming slavery into a universal emblem of ungodly evil. This trend, first noticeable in the British abolitionist campaign in the 1820s, became ever more pronounced in the attacks on American slavery from the 1830s. Thereafter, abolition in the North was shaped by a crusade – a holy war against slavery and all its sins and a crusade demanding immediate emancipation.[15] In this, American abolitionists were greatly influenced by the tactics, the style – and the success – of British abolitionists. In their turn, the British now turned their evangelical attentions to North America, for the momentum and strength of British abolition was too powerful simply to stop in its tracks in 1838. Female abolitionists on both sides of the Atlantic came together in a remarkable (and effective) reprise of the tactics first tried in Britain before 1834. They formed what has been described as a 'transatlantic sisterhood', to provide and coordinate the attack on Southern slavery.[16] British abolitionists were seized with God's work and were keen to press on with their task by attacking slavery wherever it existed. America offered them a rich hunting ground.

British abolitionists felt they had a great deal to offer Americans, or indeed anyone else confronted by local slavery. After all, British abolitionists could claim to have brought down two major slave 'empires' – the Atlantic slave trade and slavery in the Caribbean. They had perfected abolitionist tactics, had

167

created a universal sense of moral outrage, and had won over all sorts of individuals and organizations. In its turn, abolitionist Britain offered a rich vein for American abolitionists to tap into. There developed, therefore, a flow of activists, men and women, black and white, criss-crossing the Atlantic, who lectured to sympathetic circuits in Britain and America and peppered the English reading public with abolitionist literature of the most varied and extensive kind.[17]

The real strength of American abolition was, of course, primarily indigenous. There were plenty of groups – religious, secular, progressive, industrial, utopian – keen to see an end to American slavery for their own particular reasons. Like the West Indian slave lobby before them, proponents of Southern slavery were forced to defend and justify Southern slavery as never before. The longer the debate went on, the more resistant the slave lobby became. When they glanced at the fate of the West Indian islands, especially at the sugar industry, the more confident they became that to end slavery would be to invite economic disaster. Black freedom had heralded anarchy in Haiti, in the British Caribbean it had ushered in a dramatic decline in the basic industry. Who could doubt that such a fate awaited the American South if denuded of its slaves?

Such claims were reinforced by other, overlapping pro-slavery arguments, most notably those advanced by Southern churchmen. To a white society well-versed in scriptural recitation and reading, biblical references to slavery provided religious grist to their secular mill. There thus evolved a theological singsong, as pro- and anti-slavery religious lobbies sounded their own particular religious descant back and forth across the divide between North and South.[18] To this there was added the bitterness of racial arguments, an element greatly assisted, as we have seen, by the early findings of social and natural sciences. Yet the strength of Southern racism derived not from the new sciences but from those populist instincts which had deep social roots throughout the English-speaking world (and which were articulated in mid-Victorian Britain as much as in the American South).

Southerners made the most out of the claims that slavery made better economic sense than free labour. Southern slaves, they claimed, were materially better off than many free labourers. It seemed ironic that, at a time when British factory reformers denounced 'factory slavery', proponents of slavery used the same point of departure; that there *were* labouring conditions worse than black slavery. This argument had a particular edge in the mid-1840s when the Irish famine exposed depths of labouring degradation and suffering not seen in the West for centuries. Ireland was, of course, utterly exceptional. But even the industrializing world, in the North and in Britain, yielded rich pickings for defenders of slavery. The abject conditions and blighted lives of industrial workers everywhere formed a sharp contrast to the cosy image of paternal care and material comfort portrayed by slavery's proponents. What the slaves felt about the matter was another issue (and one not generally addressed by slavery's Southern proponents).

There was, in fact, a confusion of pro-slavery arguments, each one advanced to counter critics in the North and from abroad. In response to the mounting attacks on slavery, its defenders responded in kind, turning the defence of slavery 'into a veritable pro-slavery crusade . . . ' The USA, however, was different. Unlike any other slave-owning society in the Americas, the slave owners of the South were prepared to fight rather than see their slave system destroyed.[19] It is impossible to disentangle the question of slavery from the South. It was not so much one issue, or even *the* issue, in the South, but rather Southern life itself. Unlike in the Caribbean, compensation was never an issue. The freeing of American slaves would involve not simply the termination of a system of labour, but the destruction of a way of life. In the siege mentality which had come to characterize the South by the 1850s, Southerners even threatened to leave the United States. The election of Lincoln in 1860, the secession of the South the following year, and the consequent Civil War, together ensured that slavery would indeed be ended. In the words of Peter Kolchin, 'Ironically, by going to war for the preservation of slavery, they took the only action that could forseeably have led to its speedy and complete abolition.'[20]

The American Civil War was not, however, 'about' slavery. It was about Southern secession. Indeed, initially Lincoln made efforts to keep the South in the Union by offering *not* to end slavery. But, as the war dragged on into a protracted blood-letting, slavery offered the North the cause and occasion to rally support and recruits, and to claim the high moral ground. Slavery thus became the issue which seemed to divide the two sides. Despite the Southerners' fear, the slaves did not revolt – though plenty

169

fled, to join the Northern armies or simply to free themselves – and slaves' refusal to rally to the Southern cause posed a grave weakness at the heart of the Confederacy.

What we can see among Southern slaves in the war was a sharpening of that culture of resistance which had characterized slavery across the Americas: foot-dragging, sabotage, indolence, truculence and refusal to abide by the old, accepted codes of discipline. As the war progressed, relations between black and white changed dramatically – in the main to the disadvantage of the whites. It was a ritual which West Indian planters a century before would have instantly recognized. But it was *not* another Haiti, not surprisingly perhaps because the Haitian slaves were overwhelmingly African, whereas Southern slaves were predominantly American and acculturated to local conditions. As victorious Union armies came close, local slavery simply collapsed, the slaves crossing the lines to freedom or simply downing tools, abandoning their white owners (who had claimed, to the last, that they knew them like no others). In truth, they scarcely imagined what passed through their slaves' minds. Many of the waverers in the North (those who sometimes doubted the slaves' claims to freedom) were won over by the thousands of slaves who joined the Union armies or who otherwise seized their freedom. In that process of self-emancipation, the slaves revealed the very personal qualities – of energy, initiative and enterprise – which their former owners claimed they did not possess. The slaves thus helped to undermine a central pillar of the slave owners' arguments.

As the slaves became more and more disaffected, Northern opinion became ever more radical, demanding not merely an end to slavery, but a demolition of the very society – the South – which had kept slavery and its mental outlook in place for so long. In January 1863, Lincoln issued the Emancipation Proclamation for all American slaves. Two years later, the Thirteenth Amendment confirmed black freedom throughout the USA.[21]

The fate and future of America's former slaves – the central issue at the heart of the 'Reconstruction' debate after 1865 – is not part of this story. But it is true to say that in the USA, as in the Caribbean earlier, the heady optimism which had fuelled the abolition campaign quickly grounded on the harsh economic realities of post-emancipation life. In both cases, ex-slaves faced cruel economic circumstances (as sharecroppers or peasants) in a world in which new variants of racism became part of the hostile social environment. Freedom did not of necessity produce enhanced material well-being. The heady ideals of freedom and equality, so basic to the war and the drive for emancipation, soon evaporated before a resistant and damaging racism which seeped across the English-speaking world.

It was a racism which had its intellectual roots in earlier experience and debates. Indeed the *racialization* of mankind – the invention of racial categories which formed so crucial a justification for New World slavery – provided the very divisions of mankind used by subsequent proponents of racist philosophy. Moreover, many of those nineteenth-century thinkers whose advocacy of freedom was basic to the advance of contemporary liberalism felt the need to justify the history of slavery as a means of human and economic advancement.[22] Ex-slaves thus emerged into Western cultures which were thoroughly steeped in a racist vernacular. Moreover, for all the high-flown rhetoric of transatlantic abolition, freed slaves found their freedom chastened by economic hardship. Freedom to labour was paralleled by the freedom of capital and management to employ on the most minimal of wages and conditions. The expression of abolitionist ideas had taken the loftiest of ideals – in America and Britain. But black freedom was bestowed by societies committed to an ideology of free-labour, ' . . . and convinced that free labour was essential to the dramatic growth and transformation of the capitalist world'.[23] The British anti-slavery crusade was not content, however, to rest on its laurels with the demise of American slavery. The closer they looked at the wider world, the clearer it seemed that forms of slavery could be detected in many other quarters.

10

FREEDOM AND VARIETIES OF SLAVERY

The course of nineteenth-century imperial expansion and the development of global trade and commerce brought European powers into direct contact with a multitude of social systems which seemed rooted in slavery. For their part, the British evolved an aggressive abolitionism which was both an expression of their own cultural identity and a statement of their intent to encourage freedom round the world. To challenge slavery and other forms of bondage had become an instinctive British political response. A century earlier, the instinct had been to enslave. The urge to dislodge local slavery and to encourage the development of indigenous freedom became a key theme in the unfolding of British cultural imperialism. It was, however, no easy task, for slavery was too ubiquitous and too entrenched to be loosened merely by British abolitionist rhetoric. To add to the complexities, the British were not above encouraging forms of bondage (most notably indentured labour) when it suited their economic purpose. To their opponents, the British seemed to want the best of both worlds: the acclaim for abolitionism and the benefits from bonded labour.

There was a paradox at the heart of nineteenth-century British attitudes to slavery. While fiercely opposing it at a number of points, they were keen to develop or use forms of bonded labour elsewhere. This was most striking in the Caribbean, where the flight of ex-slaves from the plantations prompted schemes of imported indentured Indians. Agents in India recruited some half a million by 1914, all shipped round the world in conditions uncomfortably reminiscent of the slave trade. This Indian diaspora saw Indians scattered throughout British colonial possessions,

172

from East and South Africa to the South Pacific, to fill a labour vacuum.

Abolitionists complained about indentured labour, but economic demand overcame moral scruples and the system survived to 1919. The abolitionist sentiment seemed more secure – more persuasive – when confronting *obvious* forms of slavery. When slavery appeared in a form familiar to Western eyes (for example, when it approximated to slavery in the Americas), it could be guaranteed a hostile British reception.

Tackling international slavery was easier where the British could exercise direct control over supplies of slaves or over those client states who were in no position to resist British demands. Thus the Royal Navy cruised the Atlantic and Indian Oceans, cutting supplies of Africans to slave societies in the Americas (notably Cuba and Brazil) and to Arab slaving societies to the East. In the Atlantic alone, the Royal Navy seized some 1,600 ships and 150,000 Africans in fifty years – at a cost to the Treasury of about £40 million.[1]

East Africa posed its own peculiar set of problems for the abolitionists. In the course of the nineteenth century some 3,000,000 slaves were sold from East Africa to Islamic societies, and slaves were to be found working in industries and in domestic service throughout the Gulf and the Red Sea region. African slaves were regularly shipped from Ethiopia, the Sudan, Somalia and East Africa. Even more displeasing to many British minds was the knowledge that much of the female slave trade to Islamic societies was for sexual slavery.[2]

In truth, wherever British soldiers, missionaries and traders set foot in the mid- and late nineteenth-century Africa, there they saw slaves, slavery and slave trades. The British sought to bring local rulers to heel, via threats from local British officials, treaties imposed by the Foreign Office, or by the power of the Royal Navy. Yet it remained an uphill battle. We now know, for instance, that as late as the first years of the early twentieth century, there were 'twice as many slaves in Islamic West Africa as there had been in Brazil and Cuba in 1870'. At much the same time, almost a quarter of the population of French Western Sudan were slaves, and a similar ratio (some 2,500,000) in the Sokoto Caliphate.[3] Viewed from London – or at least from the Foreign Office – slaves were a ubiquitous feature of the world's

173

landscape and they posed a challenge to what had become an ingrained sense of British abolitionism.

From the first, foreign sceptics appreciated the irony (some claimed, the hypocrisy) of the British position. Here, after 1838, was the world's most powerful nation – its power rooted in an expansive industrial base – acting as abolitionist gamekeeper when, since time out of mind, it had been the Western world's leading slave poacher. The pre-eminent slave trader and slave master of the eighteenth century had become the single-minded, self-righteous abolitionist of the nineteenth century. Understandably, this Pauline conversion irritated many, especially those who continued to use slaves to good economic ends. There were, after all, major communities which continued to thrive on slavery – most obviously Brazil and Cuba – where new crops, notably coffee and tobacco, dragged slaves into newly developed regions. To feed this Cuban and Brazilian appetite for slaves, a flotilla of men and vessels, from Europe and the Americas, ran the gauntlet of the Royal Navy to provide slave owners with much-sought-after cargoes of Africans. Thus it was that the Atlantic slaving economy, shaped and perfected in the seventeenth and eighteenth centuries, thrived for a half-century after the ending of British slavery.

Abolitionists succeeded in keeping the question of slavery more or less permanently in the public eye from the late eighteenth to the late nineteenth century. Despite the inevitable ups and downs in anti-slavery agitation, there were few periods when slavery was absent from public awareness or political debate.[4] This was helped by the unfolding story of British imperialism. As Europeans, but notably the British, involved themselves ever more closely with a host of distant societies, they encountered people who seemed beset by slavery. Missionaries in particular found evidence of slavery wherever they worked. Part of the urge to convert and proselytize was the desire to root out slavery and replace it by the kind of freedoms which the British regarded as their own. To bestow freedom and Christianity was a divine mission, sponsored by a host of churches and missionary societies and personified in those well-known missionaries – most notably David Livingstone – who entered the pantheon of late Victorian fame. The battle to win over Africa, in particular, to British ways was often portrayed (in Britain) as a battle against an enslaved barbarism which was

174

thought to characterize much of the continent. British missionaries – if they survived – wrote back to their metropolitan churches, knowing that few things could be guaranteed to provoke their backers' ire more than images of slavery. Letters, articles and reports from missionaries in the field, lectures on their return – all fed that remarkable British curiosity about slavery, that 'culture of anti-slavery', which was so powerful a political influence for much of the nineteenth century. It was, moreover, an influence which embraced all sorts and conditions, even affecting the young through the proliferation of boys' and girls' comics and magazines which promoted British imperial themes in glorified, pictorial form. There were, of course, other motives at work, not least the determination to pre-empt other European rivals, to claim chunks of Africa for British domination and, above all else, to lay bare the chosen region to British economic interests. Africa beckoned, for raw materials, tropical staples, unimaginable wealth and as a market for British goods.

The more Europeans learned of the wider world, the more they appreciated the universality of bondage. Indeed, the very *ubiquity* of forms of slavery provided expansive Europeans with an added justification for confronting and subduing indigenous peoples. In Africa and the Americas, in Southeast Asia and India, forms of slavery beckoned the crusading attentions of abolitionist outsiders. There was, however, much self-interest masquerading as Christian virtue. But in focusing on the evils of slavery – in portraying native cultures as corrupted by the evils of slavery – it was easy to secure the moral high ground. Yet here was a curiosity, for the British were better known, in the non-too-distant past, for their slaving skills than for their abolitionist scruples.

The power of British anti-slavery culture and the persistence of abolitionism should not deceive us, however. Throughout the nineteenth century – when anti-slavery became a leitmotif in British life – the British continued to use and benefit from different forms of bonded labour. Indian indentured labour was the most obvious case in point. But India itself is instructive. Forms of bondage long predated the arrival of the Europeans, but European economic interest sometimes unconsciously encouraged the spread of slavery. Existing forms of dependency (the labour dues paid to landowners, for example) suited European interests as much as the Indian landowners. It was, however, the

European encouragement of cash crops and of 'market relation-ships' which sponsored the spread of 'debt bondage'. People found themselves as enslaved to their debts as if they had been legally sold into slavery. To pay those debts, they often resorted to the sale of children.[5] The British were perhaps more confused by what they found – and by what they unleashed – in India than in any other region.

Initially, the British in India had been untroubled by Indian slavery, but as they sought to codify Indian law, and to bring local custom more in line with metropolitan sensibility, the sub-continent's 'staggering variety of forms of servitude' became clearer, all made more troublesome by linguistic problems which confused British observers.[6] Slaves were bought and sold openly, many wealthy Indians flaunted their array of domestic slaves, and economic change across India reduced more and more peo-ple to bondage. Nor was this simply a matter of Indian practice, for the policies of the East India Company and, later, the colonial government, made extensive use of unfree labour on major pro-jects across the continent. More difficult, however, was that servi-tude exercised by private employers which survived into the twentieth century.[7] Abolitionist pressures produced a number of anti-slavery laws in India, though local customs proved remark-ably flexible in avoiding the law. The challenge which India posed to abolitionists went far beyond the subcontinent itself. India, like Africa earlier, became a major exporter of unfree labour to all corners of the world. It was a sign of the abject con-ditions in India that millions volunteered to be shipped tens of thousands of miles from their homes, for work which seemed lit-tle more than slavery in another guise. In the period 1846–1932, about 28,000,000 unfree Indians migrated in this way. In all this, the British were instrumental and central. It is a comment on the flexibility of their attachment to freedom that they were able, when necessary, to embrace forms of bonded labour for their wider economic interests while proclaiming their attachment to freedom everywhere.

In places, Europeans *expected* to find slavery. Islam, with its theological and legal sanctioning of forms of bondage, had planted slavery from North Africa and Turkey to Southeast Asia. The Ottoman Empire, for example, was infamous for its use and importation of slaves, acquiring slaves (mainly for the harems) from Central Africa, the Nile and the Red Sea.[8] Slaves were also ubiquitous in the vast tracts of land controlled by the Dutch East India Company, from Malaya, through Sumatra, Java, Borneo and into New Guinea. Debt bondage was common, manual labour generally involved servility, and domestic slavery was widespread (and was frequently used by resident Europeans).[9]

European abolitionist forces sought to undermine slavery in Southeast Asia, but the real change came via indigenous pressures, notably the rise of powerful local states. These strong, new colonial states began to prevent the sale and shipment of slaves from their territories. Indeed, the Dutch used abolitionist arguments to move and act against small states and rulers who continued to trade in slaves.[10] Dutch abolitionism in Indonesia, like its British variant in Africa and India, could be used to advance the European imperial frontiers and expand areas of European control. Once again, however, the imperial power was not above using unfree labour – providing it could avoid appearing to treat labourers like slaves. Unpaid labour was used extensively by the Dutch in Indonesia for much of the nineteenth century to fight local conflicts, to produce export crops and to undertake building projects. More draconian still was the Dutch use of the convict gang. Convicts in the Indonesian gold- and coalmines in the last years of the nineteenth century endured abject conditions on a par with anything found among black slaves in the Americas; yet the former, technically at least, were not slaves.[11] By the mid-nineteenth century, the number of labourers employed in this way actually outnumbered the slaves owned by the East India Company in the previous century. The Hague's effort to bring freedom to local peoples throughout Southeast Asia were often defeated by powerful local groups. When new tobacco and rubber plantations were opened in the region after 1870, armies of indentured labourers poured in from distant countries: 'coolies' who 'suffered many of the horrors that had marked slavery in its cruellest form . . .'[12] And this was a system which survived until 1929. Thus, though slavery itself had been abolished in Indonesia in 1860, in practice, slave ownership lingered for much longer. Where the Dutch government's edict was only faint – in remote islands and regions – locals paid scant attention to orders from Holland.

It was clear enough that indigenous Asian slaveries thrived, as they had done for centuries, throughout the nineteenth century. Slavery in Thailand, for example, had long been fundamental to the country's social system. Slaves for debt, slaves as 'the traditional booty of war in mainland Southeast Asia', were commonplace. Thai slaves had an important role in economic practice and in legal theory, and they worked in a range of skilled and labouring occupations. But the development of an increasingly powerful state, deeply influenced by the West and intent on 'modernizing' local life, inevitably led to attacks on slavery (and on forced labour). But Thai legislation against slavery was not enacted fully until the years 1890–1915, though earlier efforts had been made to render local slavery more humane.[13] In this, Thai governments were pressured by Europeans. The threats – as with the Dutch in Indonesia – were simple enough: unless abolitionist (and other progressive) steps were taken, outside powers would intervene and impose their own solutions. Missionaries and soldiers insisted that slavery had no part in a civilized nation. If it was not removed, they would act to destroy it. Time and again throughout the nineteenth century Europeans demanded that local people, in widely different societies, should abandon local customs and should adhere to outside practices and associated philosophies. In Africa and Asia, Europeans were insistent that slavery should go, and freedom should reign. Naturally enough, it was not so simple, and local practice repeatedly proved more flexible than outside abolitionists liked. What needs to be stressed, however, is that European abolitionists found plenty to occupy their minds long after the collapse of their own slave systems. There was ample evidence that slavery thrived around the world.

But not all the pressures brought to bear on the wider world were abolitionist. In the late nineteenth century, new crops – tropical staples for export – were developed which seemed ideally suited to unfree labour. Parts of Africa, for example, were turned over to new forms of plantation production which functioned on slave labour. The clove plantations of Zanzibar and the cocoa plantations in the Gulf of Guinea all thrived on unfree labour. In the generation before World War I, the Western world devoured cocoa, in chocolates and drinking chocolate, as never before (hence the emergence of the British chocolate giants of Fry, Cadbury and Rowntree). European interests hurried to satisfy demand by converting new regions to cocoa production and, in the Gulf of Guinea, by reviving an old-established industry.

That region, though remarkably fertile, was hostile to human habitation. Though all kinds of labour were tried – from free to enslaved – local cocoa planters found slavery best suited to their needs. Despite pressure (notably from the British) these Portuguese cocoa planters still employed slaves on the eve of World War I. It was often disguised, however (with workers forced to sign contracts, to provide a veneer of free labour). But they were slaves in all but name. These cocoa slaves came from the African interior (and supplies were plentiful), they received small wages – but they rarely went home. This new slave system, though better than the systems of the eighteenth century, was nonetheless the occasion of appalling human tragedies. Disease was rampant and death rates high, and all who observed the cocoa plantations were horrified by the levels of workers' sufferings. Naturally enough, this cocoa slavery attracted abolitionist hostility, but these abolitionist pressures, notably to staunch the import of new slaves, did not fully succeed until the 1920s.[14] Time and again, the British urged other Europeans – the Portuguese, Spanish and Germans (whose plantations thrived in the region) – to force their planters to move from slave labour to free. Yet throughout the region the alternatives used were, on closer inspection, little more than slavery. Penal gangs, prisoners of war, indentured labour – all and more could be found toiling in cocoa in the early twentieth century. They were not slaves, but they were less than free.

So often slavery proper gave way, under pressure, to coerced labour, which seemed scarcely different. An end to slavery often ushered in not freedom, but bondage in its various, adaptable guises. One central problem was the massive expansion of plantation economies around the world. The plantation – best remembered for its association with American slave systems – confirmed its value in the second half of the nineteenth century as an agent of colonial consolidation and metropolitan profit. The Western consumer devoured products made possible by plantations (and plantation labour). Tea, sugar, coffee, cocoa, soap, bananas, fruit, coconuts, spices and cloves: all and more poured from nineteenth-century plantations. Then, as before, they used labour that was less than free. Wherever it thrived, the plantation was the agency for winning over land and converting it to fruitful and profitable labour. But all would have been impossible without the unfree labour which was so characteristic of plantation life.

179

There was, for years after the formal ending of black slavery in the Americas, a curious paradox. Powerful metropolitan voices and institutions were wedded to the promotion of freedom everywhere around the world. Yet, at the same time, the forces of international capital sought out new opportunities, many of which needed cheap, malleable, durable or replaceable labour. Tropical staples, grown on plantations, were especially prone to unfree labour. Time and again metropolitan/imperial powers were compliant in helping the recruitment of plantation labour, even when (as was the case with the British) they also struck an abolitionist posture. The indentured Indian labour schemes were government-sponsored and regulated. In colonial Africa, government officials used a host of stratagems (head and hut taxes, for example) to drive Africans to work on Lever's palm-oil plantations at the end of the nineteenth century (all for the production of British soap). Throughout the French, Portuguese and Belgian regions of Africa, similar devices were used to secure 'voluntary' labour for local plantations.[15] Yet, over and over again, servile unfree labour passed the test of freedom only by the thinnest of linguistic or legal deceptions. By the end of the nineteenth century, the major European colonial powers, led by the British, could have the best of both worlds. They could be aggressively and boastfully abolitionist, and point to their triumphs in winning over tracts of the globe to the side of freedom. Yet they were also active in converting other huge regions to tropical production, usually via plantations, courtesy of labour which was less than free. The forces of imperial expansion – the agents and administrators on the edges of imperial advancement and consolidation – might have insisted on local abolitionist measures, but they also sometimes connived at economic developments which lured untold millions into a life of labour which was less than free. In retrospect, it may seem contradictory. To many contemporaries, it seemed consistent. As the world was being won over to imperial domination, the formal vestiges of slavery were consigned to history. But the forces of economic progress – the intrusion of new crops, new land-management systems, new forms of production – demanded cheap, pliant and manageable labour from local (or immigrant) peoples. Though apparently blessed with the formal trappings of freedom, such labour was, often as not, ensnared in unfree systems which were every bit as restrictive as other forms of slavery. Imperialists frequently

180

congratulated themselves on their triumphs in liberating indigenous peoples from the primitive legacies of their past. Often,
however, they merely transmuted their problems into a modern
form (and one, moreover, which served outside rather than local
interests).

The campaign against slavery world-wide was an uphill
struggle. For a start, it was not always immediately clear who
was a slave. Sometimes slaves even *resisted* emancipation (dou-
bly confusing for Europeans, who assumed freedom to be among
mankind's most natural instincts). Worse still, in some places
colonial economic interests sometimes gave a fillip to local
bondage. The European – primarily British – anti-slavery campaigns had to persuade native peoples *and* exiled Europeans of
the need to end slavery. The fact that the abolition campaign was
active in many parts of the world – in Africa, India, Southeast
Asia, the Middle East – well into the twentieth century is the best
indication of the ubiquity and durability of slavery. Even today,
officers of the Anti Slavery Society will readily recite examples of
slavery surviving in a host of contemporary societies.

The British campaigns against slavery, in the years after emancipation in the Caribbean, involved much more than a single-
minded drive for freedom. It was at one level an expression of a
new-found British cultural identity projected on to the wider
world. Abolitionism was part of that remarkable British sense of
superiority. Was it not the British who pioneered an end to slavery and who stood in the vanguard of anti-slavery everywhere?
In retrospect, the obvious answer was that here was British
penance for past wrongdoings. What the British seemed anxious
to overlook (and, in many cases, clearly forgot) was their own
seminal role in shaping and perfecting that most extraordinary of
slave systems: black slavery in the Americas.

Nor was British history after 1838 an unblemished commitment to freedom everywhere. The British reinvented forms of
bondage to suit their economic interests. And even in the West
Indies, black freedom did not herald the anticipated success. A
poor black peasantry and a bonded Indian labour force were
faced by a new and aggressive racism which took the region's
economic decline as proof of the old racist assumptions against
black humanity. Even the humanitarians were disappointed with
the failure of the ex-slaves to become the kind of industrious
labour force they hoped for. By the time of the Morant Bay

rebellion in Jamaica in 1865, a major shift had taken place in attitudes towards the former slaves and their descendants.[16] The initial sense of equality – that black and white were the same – was swept aside by the emergence of a racist vernacular most virulently expressed, perhaps, by Thomas Carlyle. The sense of equality of the earlier period had, however, hinged on a denial of the culture of the slaves and the ex-slaves; a feeling that what mattered – what made them equal – was their membership of the superior civilization of white society. But this particular view of equality was an imagined world, swept aside by the rise of more powerful black cultural forms.[17]

Freedom – in the West Indies and North America – involved a marginalized existence on the fringes of a white society, itself beset by an intrusive and all-pervasive racism. Indeed, in the subsequent rise of Western material consumption, with its attendant widespread popular literacy, this racism found new forms of expression. In print (newspapers, books, comics, magazines and school texts), in graphic portrayal, in advertisements – in every form of visual material – the imagery of racism became basic to Western life. Grotesque and threatening, barbaric and pagan, sensual and uncivilized – the images of blacks in Western culture could match, step by step, the worst iconography of the old plantocracy. The line of descent, from Edward Long's plantocratic accounts in the eighteenth century to the 'nigger minstrels' of the twentieth century, was direct and unbroken.[18] This racist legacy of black slavery was to prove durable and resistant long after slavery itself had faded from Western thought and memory. The memory of slavery did not fade, however, among those millions of descendants of the slave system on both sides of the Atlantic. To that extent, the history of Atlantic slavery lives on.

NOTES

PREFACE

1 See B. L. Solow and S. L. Engerman (eds), *British Capitalism and Caribbean Slavery*, Cambridge, 1987. See also G. V. Scammell, *The First Imperial Age: European Overseas Expansion c. 1400–1715*, London, 1992.

2 Paul Gilroy, *The Black Atlantic: Modernity and Double Consciousnessness*, London, 1993; Michael L. Coniff and Thomas J. Davis, *Africans in the Americas: A History of the Black Diaspora*, New York, 1994.

3 S. B. Schwartz, *Sugar Plantations in the Formation of Brazilian Society, Bahia, 1550–1835*, Cambridge, 1985; Mary C. Karasch, *Slave Life in Rio de Janeiro, 1808–1850*, Princeton, 1987.

4 Gad Heuman and James Walvin (eds), *Slavery and Abolition*, Cass Books, London.

5 R. W. Fogel, *Without Consent or Contract*, London, 1989; Peter Kolchin, *American Slavery, 1619–1877*, New York, 1993; James Walvin, *Black Ivory: A History of British Slavery*, London, 1992.

6 Orlando Patterson, *Slavery and Social Death*, Cambridge, MA, 1982.

7 D. B. Davis, *The Problem of Slavery in Western Culture*, Ithaca, 1966; *The Problem of Slavery in the Age of Revolution*, New York, 1975; *Slavery and Human Progress*, New York, 1984.

8 For confirmation, see the annual bibliography compiled by J. Miller, published in *Slavery and Abolition*. The latest edition is 14(3), December 1993.

1 FORGING THE LINK: EUROPE, AFRICA AND THE AMERICAS

1 For the latest estimates see Paul Stannard, part IV, in K. F. Kiple (ed.), *The Cambridge World History of Human Disease*, Cambridge, 1993.

2 A. W. Crosby, *The Columbian Exchange*, Westport, CN, 1972, p. 36.

3 R. Wright, *Stolen Continents*, New York, 1992, p. 14.
4 Crosby, *Exchange*, p. 37.
5 P. D. Curtin, *The Rise and Fall of the Plantation Complex*, Cambridge, 1990, p. 24.
6 Ibid., p. 26.
7 Ibid., p. 38.
8 S. B. Schwartz, *Sugar Plantations in the Formation of Brazilian Society, Bahia, 1550–1835*, Cambridge, 1985, p. 70.
9 J. M. Postma, *The Dutch in the Atlantic Slave Trade*, Cambridge, 1990. pp. 14–17.
10 Ibid., pp. 17–18.
11 Hilary McD. Beckles, *A History of Barbados*, Cambridge, 1990, p. 13.
12 Ibid., pp. 16–18.
13 R. S. Dunn, *Sugar and Slaves*, London, 1973, p. 227.
14 McD. Beckles, *Barbados*, p. 21.
15 Ibid., pp. 22–23.
16 Dunn, *Sugar and Slaves*, p. 32.
17 P. D. Curtin, *The Atlantic Slave Trade: A Census*, Madison, 1969, pp. 52–64, 119.
18 The story of the relations between Europeans and Indians is best approached via the elegant essays in James Axtell, *Beyond 1492: Encounters in Colonial North America*, New York, 1992.
19 Bernard Bailyn and Philip D. Morgan (eds), *Strangers Within the Realm: Cultural Margins of the First British Empire*, Chapel Hill, 1991.
20 Alan Kulikoff, *Tobacco and Slaves*, Chapel Hill, 1986, p. 32.
21 Ibid., p. 40.
22 Ibid., p. 324.
23 Ibid., pp. 37–44.
24 'Letter of July 12 1736' in M. Tinling (ed.), *The Correspondence of the Three William Byrds of Westover, Virginia, 1684–1776*, 2 vols, Charlottesville, 1977, II, p. 487.
25 Jack Green, *Pursuits of Happiness*, Chapel Hill, 1988, p. 144.
26 For the story of slavery in this region, see Peter H. Wood, *Black Majority*, New York 1974; D. C. Littlefield, *Rice and Slaves*, Baton Rouge, 1981, C. Joyner, *Down by the Riverside*, Urbana, 1984; Betty Wood, *Slavery in Colonial Georgia, 1730–1775*, Athens, GA, 1985.
27 P. D. Morgan, 'Work and Culture: The Task System of the World of Low Country Slaves', *William and Mary Quarterly*, 1982, 39.
28 For example, see Vincent Harlow, *A History of Barbados*, Oxford, 1926, pp. 292–293.
29 This complex theme is still best approached through Winthrop D. Jordan, *White Over Black: American Attitudes Towards the Negro, 1550–1915*, Chapel Hill, 1968. But see also the important book, by Anthony Barker, *The African Link*, London, 1978.
30 P. D. Morgan, 'British Encounters with Africans and African-Americans, circa 1600–1780', in Bailyn and Morgan, *Strangers in the Realm*, p. 163.

NOTES

2 BUT WHY SLAVERY?

1 John Peter Demarin, *A Treatise Upon the Trade from Great Britain to Africa, by an African Merchant*, London, 1772, pp. 4–5.
2 John Hippisley, *Essay on the Population of Africa*, London, 1764, p. 1.
3 Ibid., p. 4.
4 Ibid., p. 17.
5 David Eltis, *Economic Growth and the Ending of the Transatlantic Slave Trade*, Oxford, 1987.
6 R. Austen, 'From the Atlantic to the Indian Ocean: European Abolition, the African Slave Trade, and Asian Economic Structures', in David Eltis and James Walvin (eds), *The Abolition of the Atlantic Slave Trade*, Madison, WI, 1981, ch. 7.
7 Philip D. Morgan, 'British Encounters with Africans and African-Americans, circa 1600–1780', in Bernard Bailyn and Philip D. Morgan (eds), *Strangers Within the Realm: Cultural Margins of the First British Empire*, Chapel Hill, 1991, p. 162, table 1.
8 Patrick Manning, *Slavery and African Life*, Cambridge, 1990.
9 P. D. Curtin, *Economic Change in Precolonial Africa: Senegambia in the Era of the Slave Trade*, 2 vols, Madison, 1975.
10 John Hancock, 'Black Africans in the Mediterranean World: Introduction to a Neglected Aspect of the African Diaspora', in Elizabeth Savage (ed.), *The Human Commodity. Perspectives on the Trans-Saharan Slave Trade*, London, 1992.
11 *The Laws of Jamaica*, London, 1684, p. 140.
12 *The Laws of Jamaica*, 2 vols, St Jago, 1792, II, p. 88.
13 Edward Long, *Candid Reflections*, London, 1772 ; Gary Nash, *Forging Freedom: The Formation of Philadelphia's Free Black Community, 1720–1840*, Cambridge, MA, 1988, p. 247.
14 For the latest contribution to this debate, see Jan Nederveen Pieterse, *White on Black: Images of Africa and Blacks in Western Popular Culture*, London, 1992, Chs. 1–2.
15 Robert Bisset, *The History of the Negro Slave Trade . . .* , London, 1808, pp. 9–13.
16 W. Jordan, *White Over Black: American Attitudes Towards the Negro, 1550–1915*, Chapel Hill, 1968, p. 104. .
17 Bisset, *History of the Negro*, I, p. 38.
18 Ibid., p. 46.
19 Ibid., p. 58.
20 Ibid., pp. 156, 229.
21 See Richard Nisbet, *The Capacity of Negroes for the Religions and Moral Improvements Considered*, London, 1789, pp. 20–21.
22 Demarin, *Treatise*, pp. 4–5.
23 L. E. Tise, *Proslavery. A History of the Defense of Slavery in America, 1701–1840*, Athens, GA, 1987, ch. 4.

3 VARIETIES OF LABOUR

1 P. D. Morgan, 'British Encounters with Africans and African-Americans, circa 1600–1780', in Bernard Bailyn and Philip D. Morgan (eds), *Strangers Within the Realm: Cultural Margins of the First British Empire*, Chapel Hill, 1991, p. 162.

2 For a good contemporary account of indentured whites in the West Indies see Richard Ligon, *A True and Exact History of the Island of Barbados*, London, 1657, pp. 44–46.

3 Orlando Patterson, *Slavery and Social Death*, Cambridge, MA, 1982.

4 'Letter of William Byrd, July 12 1736' in M. Tinling (ed.), *The Correspondence of the Three William Byrds of Westover, Virginia, 1684–1776*, 2 vols, Charlottesville, 1977, II, pp. 487–488.

5 The phrase is from Anthony J. Barker, *The African Link*, London, 1978, p. 62.

6 Ibid., pp. 60.

7 Ligon, *Barbados*, p. 46.

8 Alexander Falconbridge, *An Account of the Slave Trade on the Coast of Africa*, London, 1787, pp. 33–36; 'Voyage of the *James*, 1675–1676', in Elizabeth Donnan, *Documents Illustrative of the Slave Trade to Americas*, 4 vols, Washington, DC, 1930–1935, I, p. 205.

9 James Walvin, *Black Ivory: A History of British Slavery*, London, 1992, pp. 75–76.

10 T. H. Breen, *Tobacco Culture*, Princeton, 1985, pp. 46–53.

11 Alan Kulikoff, *Tobacco and Slaves*, Chapel Hill, 1986, p. 324.

12 Elizabeth Fox-Genovese, *Within the Plantation Household*, Chapel Hill, 1988, pp. 135–136.

13 Catherine Clinton, *The Plantation Mistress*, New York, 1982.

14 Peter Kolchin, *American Slavery, 1619–1877*, New York, 1993, p. 52.

15 B. W. Higman, *Slave Populations of the British Caribbean, 1807–1834*, Baltimore, 1984, p. 94, table 4.4.

16 D. G. Hall (ed.), *In Miserable Slavery: Thomas Thistlewood in Jamaica, 1750–1786*, London, 1989, pp. 202–203.

17 Kolchin, *American Slavery*, p. 93.

18 For the details of this debate see Michael Tadman, *Speculators and Slaves: Masters, Traders and Slaves in the Old South*, Madison, WI, 1989.

19 Kolchin, *American Slavery*, pp. 99–105.

20 R. W. Fogel and S. L. Engerman, *Time on the Cross*, 2 vols, London, 1974, I, pp. 144–147.

21 See the discussion about slave leisure in *Slavery and Abolition* 16(1), April 1995.

22 Kolchin, *American Slavery*, p. 111.

4 DOMINATION AND CONTROL

1 For a discussion of these ships and their armaments, see M. K. Stammers, '"Guineamen": Some technical aspects of slave ships', in

Anthony Tibbles (ed.), *Transatlantic Slavery: Against Human Dignity*, London, 1994.

2 B. Martin and M. Spurrell (eds), *Journal of a Slave Trader* (1788), London, 1962 edn., pp. 69–70.

3 See the description of slave sales in Alexander Falconbridge, *An Account of the Slave Trade on the Coast of Africa*, London, 1787, pp. 33–36.

4 The best introduction to this remains the classic essay by P. D. Curtin, 'The Epidemiology of the Slave Trade', *Political Science Quarterly*, 83, 1968. But see also Kenneth F. Kiple and Brian T. Higgins, 'Mortality Caused by Dehydration During the Middle Passage', in Joseph E. Inikori and Stanley L. Engerman (eds), *The Atlantic Slave Trade*, Durham, 1992.

5 See the graphic case of Job Ben Solomon in, P. D. Curtin, *Africa Remembered*, Madison, WI, 1967, p. 41.

6 Evidence of Dr James Chisholme, Report of Privy Council Committee on the Slave Trade, part III, Jamaica no. 6, *Accounts and Papers*, XXVI, 646a.

7 M. Craton and J. Walvin, *A Jamaican Plantation. Worthy Park 1670–1970*, London, 1970, p. 131.

8 B. W. Higman, *Slave Populations of the British Caribbean, 1807–1834*, Baltimore, 1984, p. 169.

9 Ibid., p. 200.

10 William Beckford, *A Descriptive Account of the Island of Jamaica*, 2 vols, London, 1790, II, p. 50.

11 Edward Long, *Candid Reflections*, London, 1772, p. 117.

12 Quoted in E. D. Genovese, *Roll, Jordan, Roll*, London, 1975, p. 299.

13 Genovese, *Roll, Jordan, Roll*, p. 65.

14 Peter Kolchin, *American Slavery, 1619–1877*, New York, 1993, p. 120.

15 R. Fogel and S. L. Engerman, *Time on the Cross*, 2 vols, London, 1974, I, pp. 145–147, 240.

16 Quoted in C. Joyner, *Down by the Riverside*, Urbana, 1984, pp. 54–55.

17 Quotes from C. T. Davis and H. L. Gates Jnr (eds), *The Slave's Narrative*, New York, 1985, p. 106.

18 R. B. Sheridan, *Doctors and Slaves*, Cambridge, 1985, p. 182.

19 Thomas Roughley, *Jamaica Planter's Guide*, London, 1823.

20 D. G. Hall (ed.), *In Miserable Slavery: Thomas Thistlewood in Jamaica, 1750–1786*, London, 1989, p. 72.

21 'Letter of July 12 1736', in M. Tinling (ed.), *The Correspondence of the Three William Byrds of Westover, Virginia, 1684–1776*, 2 vols, Charlottesville, 1977, II, p. 488.

22 John Reeves, 'A Statement of the Laws that at Present Subsist in the West India Islands . . . ', *British Sessional Papers*, 1789, XXVI.

23 Mary Turner, *Slaves and Missionaries*, Urbana, 1982, p. 134.

24 J. R. Ward, *British West Indian Slavery, 1750–1834*, Oxford, 1988, p. 203.

25 Higman, *Slave Populations*, pp. 199–200.

26 For details, see Willie Lee Rose (ed.), *A Documentary History of Slavery in North America*, New York, 1976, ch. 5.

27 Kolchin, *American Slavery*, p. 127.
28 Fogel and Engerman, *Time on the Cross*, I, pp. 36–37.
29 R. W. Fogel, *Without Consent or Contract: The Rise and Fall of American Slavery*, New York, 1989, pp. 137–147.
30 Ibid., pp. 111–118.
31 The phrase is taken from the title of Fogel's book cited in note 29.

5 COLOUR, RACE AND SUBJUGATION

1 P. D. Morgan, 'British Encounters with Africans and African-Americans, circa 1600–1780', in B. Bailyn and P. D. Morgan (eds), *Strangers Within the Realm: Cultural Margins of the First British Empire*, Chapel Hill, 1991, pp. 163–164.
2 For a discussion on this theme see Orlando Patterson, *Slavery and Social Death*, Cambridge, MA, 1982, pp. 176–179.
3 Ibid., p. 178.
4 Hilary McD. Beckles, *A History of Barbados*, Cambridge, 1990, pp. 15–18.
5 Alan Kulikoff, *Tobacco and Slaves*, Chapel Hill, 1986, p. 36.
6 James Walvin, *Black Ivory*, London, 1992, pp. 7–8.
7 This argument is most fully explored in Winthrop Jordan's classic book, *White Over Black: American Attitudes to the Negro, 1550–1915*, Chapel Hill, 1968.
8 'Licensing Casper van Senden to Deport Negroes' (1601?), in P. L. Hughes and J. F. Larkin (eds), *Tudor Royal Proclamations*, New Haven, 1964, III, pp. 221–222.
9 Elizabeth Donnan, *Documents Illustrative of the Slave Trade to America*, 4 vols, Washington, DC, 1930–1935, I, pp. 129–130.
10 'Second Voyage to Guinea' (1554), in R. Hakluyt, *Principal Navigations*, 8 vols, London, 1907 edn, IV, p. 57.
11 Quoted in Jordan, *White Over Black*, p. 11.
12 *Baxter's Directions to Slaveholders, Revived* (1673), Philadelphia, 1785 edn, p. 5.
13 Morgan Godwyn, *The Negro and Indian Advocate*, London, 1680, p. 20.
14 James Walvin, *Fruits of Empire: Exotic Produce and British Taste*, London, 1996.
15 Godwyn, *Negro and Indian Advocate*, p. 36.
16 Quoted in Peter Fryer, *Staying Power*, London, 1984, p. 148.
17 In James Walvin, *England, Slaves and Freedom, 1776–1838*, London, 1986, p. 32.
18 David Hume, *Essays, Moral, Political and Literary*, ed. T. H. Green and T. H. Grose, 2 vols, London, 1875, I, p. 252.
19 For a discussion about recent books on this theme, see James Walvin, 'In Black and White: Recent Publications on British Black Writings', *Slavery and Abolition*, 16(3), December 1995. See also Gretchen Gerzina, *Black England: Life Before Emancipation*, London, 1995.

20 For an interesting commentary on this topic see Gary B. Nash, *Race and Revolution*, Madison, WI, 1990.
21 Peter H. Wood, *Black Majority*, New York, 1974, p. 96.
22 Samuel Estwick, *Considerations on the Negroe Cause*, London, 1773 edn, p. 95.
23 Edward Long, *History of Jamaica*, 3 vols, London, 1774, II, pp. 352–383.
24 Ibid., pp. 370–371.
25 Estwick, *Considerations*, p. 95.
26 Long, *Jamaica*, II, p. 328.
27 Among the latest contributions to the debate about abolition are Clare Midgley, *Women Against Slavery: The British Campaigns, 1780–1870*, London, 1992; David Turley, *The Culture of English Antislavery, 1780–1860*, London, 1991.
28 There is a stimulating discussion in David Theo Goldberg, *Racist Culture: Philosophy and the Politics of Meaning*, London, 1993, especially ch. 4.
29 There was a growing awareness among educated Americans – and a host of political leaders – of the incompatibility between slavery and the natural rights claimed by growing numbers of Americans. See Nash, *Race and Revolution*, pp. 7–8.
30 This is well summarized in Peter Kolchin, *American Slavery, 1619–1877*, New York, 1993, pp. 63–68.
31 Nash, *Race and Revolution*, p. 19.
32 D. B. Davis, *The Problem of Slavery in the Age of Revolution*, Ithaca, NY, 1975, pp. 299–303.
33 Kolchin, *American Slavery*, p. 93.
34 For a discussion about the industrialization of the South, see Robert W. Fogel, *Without Consent or Contract: The Rise and Fall of American Slavery*, New York, 1989, ch. 4.
35 Ibid., p. 191.
36 These issues are discussed most specifically in R. W. Fogel and S. L. Engerman, *Time on the Cross*, Boston, 2 vols, London, 1974, I.
37 Peter Kolchin, *American Slavery*, pp. 179–180.
38 The broader story of British racial feelings towards the wider world can be approached via Edward Said's book, *Culture and Imperialism*, London, 1993.

6 MEN AND WOMEN

1 P. Lovejoy, 'The Impact of the Atlantic Slave Trade on Africa . . . ', *Journal of African History* XXX, 1989, pp. 385–386.
2 For a discussion of these issues see Patrick Manning, *Slavery and African Life*, Cambridge, 1990, pp. 22–23. See also Robin Law, *The Slave Coast of West Africa*, Oxford, 1991.
3 Manning, *Slavery and African Life*, pp. 49–50.
4 Ibid., p. 115.
5 Ibid., p. 132.

6 Marietta Morrissey, *Slave Women in the New World*, Kansas, 1989, ch. 7.
7 This evidence is usefully summarized in Robert W. Fogel, *Without Consent or Contract: The Rise and Fall of American Slavery*, New York, 1989, ch. 5.
8 Hilary McD. Beckles, *Natural Rebels: A Social History of Enslaved Women in Barbados*, London, 1987, p. 110.
9 J. Richard B. Sheridan, *Doctors and Slaves*, Cambridge, 1985, Ch. 8; Fogel, *Without Consent or Contract*, pp. 119–120, 151–152.
10 Hilary McD. Beckles, *A History of Barbados*, Cambridge, 1990, pp. 51–52.
11 McD. Beckles, *Natural Rebels*, London, 1989, p. 8.
12 Details to be found in Michael Craton, *Searching for the Invisible Man*, Ithaca, 1978.
13 R. W. Fogel and S. L. Engerman, *Time on the Cross*, 2 vols, Boston, 1974, I, pp. 78–86.
14 Ibid., pp. 152–153.
15 Barbara Bush, *Slave Women in the Caribbean, 1650–1838*, London, 1990, ch. 1.
16 The phrase comes from the volume, *Engendering History: Caribbean Women in Historical Perspective*, ed. Verene Shepherd, Bridget Brereton and Barbara Bailey, London, 1995.
17 Elizabeth Fox-Genovese, *Within the Plantation Household*, Chapel Hill, 1988, pp. 153–154.
18 Bush, *Slave Women*, p. 61.
19 These questions are discussed in Mechal Sobel, *The World They Made Together*, Princeton, 1987.
20 See the myriad accounts in Thomas Thistlewood's Jamaican diaries, in D. G. Hall (ed.), *In Miserable Slavery: Thomas Thistlewood in Jamaica, 1750–1786*, London, 1989.
21 P. Wright (ed.), *Lady Nugent's Journal, 1801–1805*, Kingston, 1966, p. 29.
22 Clare Midgley, *Women Against Slavery: The British Campaigns, 1780–1870*, London, 1992, pp. 20, 182–183.
23 Moira Ferguson, *Subject to Others: British Women Writers and Colonial Slavery, 1670–1834*, London, 1992; J. Fagan Yellin and J. C. Van Horne (eds), *The Abolitionist Sisterhood*, Ithaca, 1994, pp. 5–9.
24 Peter Kolchin, *American Slavery, 1619–1877*, New York, 1993, p. 108.
25 Bush, *Slave Women*, p. 61.
26 McD. Beckles, *Natural Rebels*, p. 15.
27 Fox-Genovese, *Plantation Household*, p. 39.
28 Modern students would not, of course, accept this as an adequate definition of race. The question of race will be dealt with elsewhere in this book.
29 The details on slave families can be found in Morrissey, *Slave Women*, ch. 6; B. W. Higman, *Slave Populations of the British Caribbean, 1807–1834*, Baltimore, 1984, pp. 364–373. For the USA, the classic study remains Herbert Gutman's *The Black Family in Slavery and Freedom, 1750–1925*, New York, 1977.
30 Orlando Patterson, *The Sociology of Slavery*, London, 1967, pp. 167–168.

31 Morrissey, *Slave Women*, ch. 4.
32 Quoted in Kolchin, *American Slavery*, p. 127.
33 Quoted in P. D. Morgan, 'Three Planters . . . ', in W. D. Jordan and S. L. Skempt (eds), *Race and Family in the Colonial South*, London, 1987, p. 57.

7 THE CULTURE OF RESISTANCE

1 See the comments of Martin Klein in 'Slavery, the International Labour Market and the Emancipation of Slaves in the Nineteenth Century', in Paul E. Lovejoy and Nicholas Rogers (eds), *Unfree Labour in the Development of the Atlantic World*, London, 1994.
2 James Rawley, *The Transatlantic Slave Trade*, New York, 1981, p. 142.
3 David Geggus, *Slavery, War and Revolution*, Oxford, 1982; Robin Blackburn, *The Overthrow of Colonial Slavery*, London, 1988.
4 Michael Craton, *Testing the Chains: Resistance to Slavery in the British West Indies*, Ithaca, 1982, chs 5–7.
5 George Cruickshank, *The Comic Almanac, 1834–1843*, London, n.d., p. 185.
6 The process known as 'amelioration' forms the basis for J. R. Ward's book, *British West Indian Slavery, 1750–1834*, Oxford, 1988.
7 Michael Craton, *Searching for the Invisible Man*, Ithaca, 1978, pp. 250–253.
8 B. W. Higman, *Slave Populations of the British Caribbean, 1807–1834*, Baltimore, 1984, p. 393.
9 H. McD. Beckles, 'From Land to Sea . . . ', *Slavery and Abolition*, 6(3), 1985, p. 82.
10 Runaway data is put to good effect in Billy G. Smith and Richard Wojtowicz's *Blacks who Stole Themselves*, Philadelphia, 1989.
11 Gad Heuman, 'Runaway Slaves in Barbados', in *Slavery and Abolition* 6(3), 1985, pp. 101–104.
12 Ibid., pp. 107–109.
13 P. D. Morgan, 'Colonial South Carolina Runaways . . . ', ibid., p. 75, n. 3.
14 Ibid., p. 69.
15 Peter Kolchin, *American Slavery 1619–1877*, New York, 1993, pp. 157–158.
16 Rhys Isaac, *The Transformation of Virginia*, Chapel Hill, 1985, pp. 329–332.
17 Alan Kulikoff, *Tobacco and Slaves*, Chapel Hill, 1986, p. 340.
18 Peter Fryer, *Staying Power*, London, 1984, pp. 127–128.
19 Craton, *Testing*, p. 241.
20 Quoted in Orlando Patterson, *Slavery and Social Death*, Cambridge, MA, 1982, p. 4.

8 CULTIVATING INDEPENDENCE

1 Alan Kulikoff, *Tobacco and Slaves*, Chapel Hill, 1986, p. 334.

2 Mary Beth Norton, Herbert G. Gutman and Ira Berlin, 'The Afro-American Family in the Age of Revolution', in Ira Berlin and Ronald Hoffman (eds), *Slavery and Freedom in the Age of the American Revolution*, Charlottesville, 1983, p. 178.
3 William Beckford, *A Descriptive Account of the Island of Jamaica*, 2 vols, London, 1790, I, p. 20; B. W. Higman, *Slave Populations of the British Caribbean, 1807–1834*, Baltimore, 1984, pp. 218–223.
4 D. G. Wright, *African Americans in the Colonial Era*, Arlington Heights, IL, 1990, pp. 109–110; R. A. McDonald, *The Economy and Material Culture of Slaves*, Baton Rouge, 1993, pp. 129–137.
5 See the aricles by Michael Craton, Howard Johnson and James Walvin in *Slavery and Abolition*, 16(1), April 1995.
6 Ira Berlin and Philip D. Morgan (eds), 'The Slave Economy', special issue of *Slavery and Abolition* 12(1), May 1991.
7 'Slave Trials', St Ann, Jamaica, 29 August 1788, National Library of Jamaica, MS 273.
8 Bryan Edwards, *The History, Civil and Commercial, of the British Colonies in the West Indies*, 3 vols, 3rd edn, London, 1801, II, p. 165.
9 Ibid., III, p. 283.
10 Ibid., p. 250.
11 J. R. Ward, *British West Indian Slavery, 1750–1834*, Oxford, 1988, pp. 112–114.
12 Ibid., p. 114.
13 B. W. Higman, *Slave Populations*, p. 210.
14 *Narrative of the Life of Frederick Douglass, an American Slave*, Boston, 1845 edn, p. 75.
15 Ibid., p. 76.
16 D. G. Hall (ed.), *In Miserable Slavery: Thomas Thistlewood in Jamaica, 1750–1786*, London, 1989, p. 94.
17 Ibid., pp. 94, 79, 80.
18 Ibid., p. 83.
19 McDonald, *Economy and Material Culture*, p. 21.
20 Hall, *In Miserable Slavery*, p. 60.
21 McDonald, *Economy and Material Culture*, pp. 27–29.
22 Ibid., pp. 31–32.
23 Hall, *In Miserable Slavery*, pp. 32, 62, 83, 86.
24 Barry Higman (ed.), *Characteristic Traits of the Creolian and African Negroes in Jamaica* (1797), Mona, 1976 edn, pp. 12–13.
25 M. Craton and J. Walvin, *A Jamaican Plantation: Worthy Park 1670–1970*, London, 1970, pp. 140–141.
26 'Slave Trials', op cit.
27 McDonald, *Economy and Material Culture*, p. 42.
28 Betty Wood, 'Never on a Sunday? Slavery and the Sabbath in Low-Country Georgia, 1750–1830', in Mary Turner (ed.), *From Chattel Slaves to Wage Slaves*, London, 1995.
29 Hall, *In Miserable Slavery*, pp. 59–60.
30 McDonald, *Economy and Material Culture*, pp. 60–63.
31 James Walvin, *Fruits of Empire: Exotic Produce and British Taste*, London, 1996.

32 See the comments of Frederick Douglass, *Narrative*, pp. 80–82.
33 Mary Turner, *Missionaries and Slaves*, Urbana, 1982; Michael Craton, *Testing the Chains: Resistance to Slavery in the British West Indies*, Ithaca, 1982, part IV.
34 Nat Turner's confession is in Willie Lee Rose (ed.), *A Documentary History of Slavery in North America*, New York, 1976, pp. 123–133.
35 P. Kolchin, *American Slavery, 1619–1877*, New York, 1993, pp. 167–168.

9 ENDING SLAVERY

1 The words 'abolition' and 'abolitionism' are used here to describe the broader campaign against both the slave trade and slavery.
2 For a graphic account of the story of the Indian people see Ronald Wright, *Stolen Continents*, Toronto, 1992.
3 For the relationship between the Enlightenment and anti-slavery, see D. B. Davis, *The Problem of Slavery in Western Culture*, Ithaca, 1966.
4 This issue is best approached via Edmund S. Morgan, *American Slavery, American Freedom*, New York, 1975.
5 Peter Kolchin, *American Slavery, 1619–1877*, New York, 1993, p. 93.
6 James Walvin, *England, Slaves and Freedom, 1776–1838*, London, 1986.
7 James Walvin, *Fruits of Empire: Exotic Produce and British Taste*, London, 1996, ch. 11.
8 The most trenchant statement of this case, see Seymour Drescher, *Capitalism and Antislavery*, London, 1986. For a recent account which places abolition in its broader setting, see Martin A. Klein, 'Slavery, the International Labour Market and the Emancipation of Slaves in the Nineteenth Century', in Paul E. Lovejoy and Nicholas Rogers (eds), *Unfree Labour in the Development of the Atlantic World*, London, 1994.
9 Clare Midgley, *Women Against Slavery: The British Campaign, 1780–1870*, London, 1992.
10 On the parliamentary course of abolition, see J. R. Oldfield, *Popular Politics and British Anti-Slavery*, Manchester, 1995; Jack Hayward (ed.), *Out of Slavery: Abolition and After*, London, 1985.
11 Clare Midgley, *Women Against Slavery*, p. 116.
12 For the most recent piece on abolition, see Seymour Drescher, 'Whose Abolition?', *Past and Present* 143, May 1994.
13 R. W. Fogel, *Without Consent or Contract: The Rise and Fall of American Slavery*, New York, 1989, chs 8–10.
14 These issues are addressed in S. Drescher and F. McGlynn, *The Meaning of Freedom*, University of Pittsburgh Press, 1993.
15 R. W. Fogel, *Without Consent or Contract*, pp. 264–265.
16 Clare Midgley, *Women Against Slavery*, ch. 6.
17 Ibid.

18 Larry E. Tise, *Proslavery: A History of the Defense of Slavery in America, 1701–1840*, Athens, GA, 1987.
19 Kolchin, *American Slavery*, p. 197.
20 Ibid., p. 199.
21 For a good summary, see ibid., ch. 7.
22 David Theo Goldberg, *Racist Culture: Philosophy and the Politics of Meaning*, London, 1993, ch. 2.
23 Martin Klein, 'Slavery', in Lovejoy and Rogers, *Unfree Labour*, p. 213.

10 FREEDOM AND VARIETIES OF SLAVERY

1 R. W. Fogel, *Without Consent or Contract: The Rise and Fall of American Slavery*, New York, 1989, pp. 217–218.
2 See essays in William Gervase Clarence-Smith (ed.), *The Economics of the Indian Ocean Slave Trade in the Nineteenth Century*, London, 1989.
3 Paul Lovejoy, 'The Impact of the Atlantic Slave Trade on Africa . . .', *Journal of African History* XXX, 1989. For the latest data, see Paul E. Lovejoy and Jan S. Hogendorn, *Slow Death for Slavery: The Course of Abolition in Northern Nigeria, 1897–1936*, Cambridge, 1993.
4 David Turley, *The Culture of English Antislavery, 1780–1860*, London, 1991.
5 M. Klein (ed.), *Breaking the Chains*, Madison, 1993, p. 13.
6 D. Kumar, 'Colonialism, Bondage and Caste in British India', in ibid., p. 116.
7 Ibid., p. 119.
8 E. R. Toledano, 'Ottoman Concepts of Slavery', in Klein, *Breaking the Chains*, ch. 1.
9 A. Reid, 'The Decline of Slavery in Nineteenth-Century Indonesia', in Klein, *Breaking the Chains*, ch. 2, p. 68.
10 Klein, *Breaking the Chains*, pp. 71–72.
11 Ibid., p. 73.
12 Ibid., p. 75–77.
13 David Feeny, 'The Demise of Corvée and Slavery in Thailand, 1782–1913', in Klein, *Breaking the Chains*, ch. 3.
14 W. G. Clarence-Smith, 'Cocoa Plantations and Coerced Labour . . .', in Klein, *Breaking the Chains*, ch. 7.
15 R. Oliver and G. N. Sanderson (eds), *The Cambridge History of Africa*, Cambridge 1985, VI, pp. 15, 78, 517–518, 534–536, 550, 752–753.
16 Thomas Holt, *The Problem of Freedom: Race, Labor, and the Politics of Freedom in Jamaica and Britain, 1832–1938*, Baltimore, 1992. On the rebellion, see Gad Heuman, *'The Killing Time': The Morant Bay Rebellion in Jamaica*, London, 1994.
17 Catherine Hall, 'Gender Politics and Imperial Politics', in Verene Shepherd, Bridget Brereton and Barbara Bailey (eds), *Engendering History: Caribbean Women in Historical Perspective*, Kingston, 1995.
18 Jan Nederveen Pieterse, *White and Black: Images of Africa and Blacks in Western Popular Culture*, London, 1992.

INDEX

195